W9-BUS-867

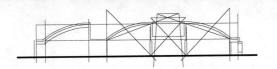

Donated to the
Leonard E. Shore Memorial Library
in memory of
Dr. James F. Murray
1920-2003
Leafs Team Doctor 1948-1964

Team Canada Doctor in 1972

MAPLE LEAF LEGENDS

75 YEARS OF TORONTO'S HOCKEY HEROES

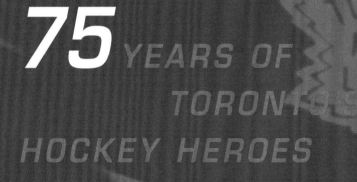

MIKE LEONETTI

FOREWORD BY DARRYL SITTLER

WITH PHOTOGRAPHY FROM THE HOCKEY HALL OF FAME, DENNIS MILES AND THE LEGENDARY HAROLD BARKLEY ARCHIVES

ADDITIONAL ESSAYS BY KERRY BANKS, JOHN IABONI, JIM KERNAGHAN, GARE JOYCE, MICHAEL MCKINLEY, JIM O'LEARY, AND HALL OF FAME WRITER FRANK ORR

RAINCOAST BOOKS

Vancouver

This book is dedicated to all the Maple Leaf players who played on all the Stanley Cup-winning teams, who were named NHL all-stars or award-winners or were elected to the Hockey Hall of Fame.

Page 1: *Charlie Conacher, an NHL all-star for five straight seasons from 1932 to1936.* (HHOF)

Page 5: *Action shots of the great 1930s trio known as the "Kid Line": (left to right) Charlie Conacher, Joe Primeau and Harvey Jackson.* (HHOF)

Text copyright © 2002 Mike Leonetti
Photographs credits follow captions; see details of sources page 252

Edited by Scott Steedman
Design by Val Speidel

All rights reserved. No part of this publication may be reproduced or transmitted in any form or by any means, electronic or mechanical, including photocopying, recording or by any information storage and retrieval system now known or to be invented, without permission in writing from the publisher.

Raincoast Books
9050 Shaughnessy Street
Vancouver, British Columbia
Canada   v6p 6e5
www.raincoast.com

In the United States:
Publishers Group West
1700 Fourth Street
Berkeley, California
94710

Raincoast Books is a member of CANCOPY (Canadian Copyright Licensing Agency). No part of this publication may be reproduced, stored in a retrieval system or transmitted in any form or by any means without prior written permission from the publisher, or, in case of photocopying or other reprographic copying, a license from CANCOPY, One Yonge Street, Toronto, Ontario, M5E IE5.

Raincoast Books acknowledges the ongoing financial support of the Government of Canada through The Canada Council for the Arts and the Book Publishing Industry Development Program (BPIDP); and the Government of British Columbia through the BC Arts Council.

National Library of Canada Cataloguing in Publication Data

Leonetti, Mike, 1958–
Maple Leaf legends

ISBN 1-55192-553-2

1. Toronto Maple Leafs (Hockey team)—Biography. 2. Hockey players—Ontario—Toronto—Biography. I. Title.
GV848.5.A1L465 2002   796.962'092'2713541   C2002-910551-X

Library of Congress Catalogue Number: 2002091844

Printed and bound in Canada at Friesens

1 2 3 4 5 6 7 8 9 10

RECEIVED
MAY 1 5 2003

Contents

Foreword by Darryl Sittler

Introduction *The Toronto Maple Leafs: A Canadian Success Story* 8

The '20s and '30s

Introduction 16

Irvine 'Ace' Bailey 20 • Andy Blair 20 • Lorne Chabot 23 • Francis 'King' Clancy 24 • Charlie Conacher 28 • Harold Cotton 30 • Clarence 'Hap' Day 31 • Reginald 'Red' Horner 33 • Dick Irvin 35 • Harvey Jackson 36 • Joe Primeau 37 • Frank Selke 39 • Conn Smythe 40

The Father of the Leafs: Conn Smythe, 1895–1980 by Michael McKinley 44

The '40s

Introduction 46

Syl Apps 52 • Max Bentley 56 • Gus Bodnar 57 • Walter 'Turk' Broda 58 • Lorne Carr 62 • Bob Davidson 63 • Bill Ezinicki 65 • The Metz Brothers 67 • Walter 'Babe' Pratt 69 • David 'Sweeney' Schriner 71

Hockey Night in Canada: Radio and TV, 1927–2002 by Frank Orr 72

The '50s

Introduction 74

Bill Barilko 78 • Foster Hewitt 80 • Ted Kennedy 82 • Howie Meeker 86 • Gus Mortson 88 • Tod Sloan 89 • Sid Smith 90 • Stafford Smythe 91 • Jim Thomson 93 • Harry Watson 95

Bill Barilko's Final Trip by Kerry Banks 96

The '60s

Introduction 98

George Armstrong 104 • Bob Baun 108 • Johnny Bower 110 • Carl Brewer 114 • Dick Duff 116 • Ron Ellis 118 • Tim Horton 120 • George 'Punch' Imlach 124 • Leonard 'Red' Kelly 126 • Dave Keon 130 • Frank Mahovlich 134 • Bob Pulford 138 • Terry Sawchuk 140 • Eddie Shack 142 • Allan Stanley 144

Behind the Bench: 75 Years of Leafs Management by Jim Kernaghan 146

property of
L. E. SHORE
MEMORIAL LIBRARY
THORNBURY, ONTARIO, N0H 2P0

The '70s

Introduction 148

Paul Henderson 152 • Lanny McDonald 154 • Jim McKenny 158 • Mike Palmateer 159 • Bernie Parent 161 • Jacques Plante 162 • Borje Salming 164 • Darryl Sittler 168 • Ian Turnbull 172 • Norm Ullman 174 • Dave 'Tiger' Williams 176

Salming and the European Invasion by Jim O'Leary 178

The '80s

Introduction 180

Harold Ballard 184 • Vincent Damphousse 186 • Todd Gill 187 • Al Iafrate 188 • Gary Leeman 189 • Ed Olczyk 190 • Mark Osborne 191 • Rick Vaive 192

A Leaf for Life by Gare Joyce 196

The '90s

Introduction 198

Glenn Anderson 202 • Dave Andreychuk 204 • Wendel Clark 206 • Dave Ellett 210 • Doug Gilmour 212 • Sylvain Lefebvre 216 • Jamie Macoun 217 • Felix Potvin 218 • Bob Rouse 220 • Peter Zezel 221

Two Homes: The Gardens and the Air Canada Centre by Frank Orr 222

The New Century

Introduction 224

Shayne Corson 228 • Ken Dryden 229 • Curtis Joseph 230 • Tomas Kaberle 232 • Bryan McCabe 233 • Alex Mogilny 234 • Pat Quinn 235 • Gary Roberts 236 • Mats Sundin 238 • Darcy Tucker 240 • Dmitry Yushkevich 241

The Rebirth of Playoff Mania: '78, '93, '99 and 2002 by John Iaboni 242

Conclusion *The Future of the Maple Leafs* 244

Index 250

Acknowledgements 252

Foreword

My National Hockey League career began in June 1970, when the Toronto Maple Leafs selected me in the first round of the entry draft. The draft was not that big a deal in those days, and I found out they had selected me eighth overall while working at my summer job in London, Ontario, installing swimming pools. We had the radio on when the news came. The Leafs never interviewed me, and I had no idea that they were going to take me, but I was very happy. Although I had grown up a fan of the Montreal Canadiens, Toronto was close to home and I was aware of the great tradition the team had forged over its long history.

Like most young players, I went to my first training camp with high hopes of making the team. I was just 20 years old, but I think the Leaf management was impressed with my determination and work ethic. I often stayed out after practice with captain Dave Keon, polishing my skills. When general manager Jim Gregory showed me my stall in the dressing room, I saw sweater number 27 hanging there. It was a special feeling to get that number because I knew it once belonged to Frank Mahovlich, one of the greatest Leafs of all time. It made me want to live up to expectations.

Luckily, I made the team to start the 1970–71 season and never spent a day in the minors. I scored my first goal against the Detroit Red Wings on November 28, 1970, in a 9–4 win at Maple Leaf Gardens. They played me on left wing that year, but my rookie season was cut short when I broke my wrist. I made it back for the playoffs, but we were knocked out by the New York Rangers.

When centre Jim Harrison jumped to the World Hockey Association a couple of years later, I had the opportunity to play my natural position. I was much more comfortable in the middle than on the wing. I started to score goals and points, and in 1975 the team named me captain. It was a big honour, and I knew the role had tremendous prestige and responsibility. I was following in the footsteps of great Leafs like George Armstrong and Keon, and fortunately I had support from the other players.

My approach was to lead by example. Under coach Red Kelly, the Leafs were an exciting young team that grew together. Although we were lacking in depth, we were always a hard team to beat.

I had a very memorable game on February 7, 1976 at Maple Leaf Gardens. I recorded 10 points — six goals and four assists — that night against Boston. I probably played better in other games, but that night everything I touched seemed to end up as a goal.

By 1978, the Maple Leafs were ready to challenge in the playoffs under new coach Roger Neilson, and we upset the favoured New York Islanders. We had added some good checkers to our team and were an aggressive club. The Leafs were very physical against the Islanders and we beat them in seven games. But then we had to face the Montreal Canadiens. From goalie Ken Dryden on out, they had too much for us or any other team in the NHL.

I left Toronto in 1982. It was a good move for me because I needed a change at the time, but I came back to work for the Maple Leafs in 1991 in a front office capacity. I'm very pleased to be working for the team, helping to restore the pride and lore that have been a part of Toronto's history in the NHL. It's phenomenal how the alumni are being treated now, which wasn't always true. There is a strong appreciation of the past. Leaf management wants to make former players feel part of the organization.

The Leafs have treated me very well. It was very special to be told that my sweater number 27 will be honoured. It makes me very happy that my wife, Wendy, knew about this before she died. It was also nice that the club recognized the 25th anniversary of my ten-point game.

Players want to come to Toronto because they know it's an honour. I know how they feel. In the early '70s I was approached by the Toronto Toros of the WHA to sign a contract with the rival league for more money than the Leafs were offering. I had to listen to what they were proposing but it was my dream to play in the NHL. Most of all, it always felt right to be a Maple Leaf.

I dare say that all of the players profiled in this book would express the same sentiments. Enjoy this look back at 75 years of Maple Leaf history.

Darryl Sittler
Toronto, July 1, 2002

(Dennis Miles)

Introduction

The Toronto Maple Leafs:
A Canadian Success Story

The best thing that ever happened to Constantine "Conn" Falkland Kerrys Smythe was getting fired as general manager of the New York Rangers. Determined to succeed in professional hockey, he returned to his hometown, Toronto, and went about achieving his dream.

Knowing that the green-shirted Toronto St. Patrick's (previously known as the Toronto Arenas) of the National Hockey League were in financial trouble and were about to be sold to American interests based in Philadelphia, Smythe and a couple of partners gathered together $160,000 to buy the franchise but were still about $40,000 short of the asking price. To make up the shortfall Smythe persuaded one of the owners, mining executive John Paris Bickell, to retain his interest in the St. Patrick's club and the deal to keep the team in Toronto was completed. The ownership change became official on February 14, 1927, and a hockey dynasty was born.

Facing page: *After an 11-year drought, the Maple Leafs won the Stanley Cup on April 22, 1962, when Punch Imlach's crew won a 2–1 contest in Chicago.* (AP)

Above: *Lanny McDonald celebrates his overtime game-winning goal as the Maple Leafs defeat the New York Islanders in seven games with a 2–1 victory during the 1978 playoff series.* (AP)

Conn Smythe set the tone for the Maple Leafs teams under his direction when he said, "If you can't beat them in the alley, you can't beat them on the ice." The great Leafs teams never lost the challenging spirit of this axiom. (HHOF)

white uniforms (it has been said Smythe selected those colours to represent Canada's blue sky and white snow) and playing in the best hockey arena in North America. With those changes in place, Smythe went about the task of creating a winning team.

The Gashouse Gang

Smythe understood that people needed to identify with their local hockey heroes, and that a spiffy new uniform and a beautiful arena were not enough. He sought out the most colourful character he could find and landed all-star defenceman Francis "King" Clancy. It cost Smythe two players and a great deal of money, but Clancy had just the right mix of skill and flair to make him a fan favourite.

This was the first of many clever moves by Smythe to acquire the best talent available. Clancy joined the likes of Reginald "Red" Horner, Clarence "Hap" Day, Charlie Conacher, Harvey "Busher" Jackson, Joe Primeau and Lorne Chabot to form a flamboyant group that became known as "the Gashouse Gang." They were well managed by Smythe and his extremely capable assistant, Frank

As good as Smythe was at putting together hockey teams — the Ranger's club he assembled won the Stanley Cup in 1928 — he was even better at marketing his product. Sensing that the team name "St. Patrick's" appealed only to a narrow segment of the Toronto population, he changed it to "Maple Leafs" to honour what he felt was a national symbol in Canada; he had worn maple leaf badges on his Canadian army uniform during World War I.

Smythe also realized his team would need a new building if it were to become an attraction in a cosmopolitan city, so he established Maple Leaf Gardens Limited and set to work erecting an arena. Canada was in the middle of the Depression, but he somehow had Maple Leaf Gardens built in six months after overcoming financial problems by planning to pay workers partly with Gardens stock. On November 12, 1931, the dream became reality when the Maple Leafs played their first game in the new hockey shrine they would call home for the next 68 years.

The city of Toronto now had a team decked out in blue-and-

The Leafs' first Stanley Cup-winning team. The 1932 squad beat the New York Rangers by scores of 6–4, 6–2 and 6–4 to sweep the best-of-five series. (HHOF)

Selke, and coached by Dick Irvin. They won the Stanley Cup in 1932 and would dominate the NHL for the rest of the decade.

The late 1920s and early '30s were a first "golden age" of sports in North America. The New York Yankees of baseball had George "Babe" Ruth selling out wherever he and the "Murderers Row" New York Yankees played. Running back Red Grange was the darling of college football, a very popular game at the time, and boxing was dominated by another great showman, champion Jack Dempsey. Bravado brought out fans who would pay well to watch the best athletes perform. For men like Smythe, pride demanded that the team he ran didn't just have to win, it had to win with panache.

Hockey Night in Canada

The early Maple Leafs heroes were known not just to Torontonians but to an entire nation thanks to the radio broadcasts of Foster Hewitt. Hewitt began his career in 1923 by covering a game between Toronto Parkdale and Kitchener. He was soon the voice of professional hockey in Canada and the United States and Smythe came to realize that having Hewitt broadcast Leafs games could swell interest in the club. The two men struck up a business arrangement and Hewitt's Saturday night hockey broadcasts on coast-to-coast radio in the 1930s and '40s became the most listened-to events in Canadian history.

At its peak, the Imperial Oil-sponsored hockey broadcast starring Hewitt and the Maple Leafs was carried by some 39 Canadian radio stations in various cities and towns. A 1942 survey found that 74 per cent of those polled declared themselves at least occasional fans of the broadcasts. Families gathered around the radio to listen to Hewitt describe the Leafs exploits and he soon became as popular as the players he described.

During World War II, Hewitt's broadcasts provided a feeling of normalcy in a troubled time. The Leafs' amazing 1942 Stanley Cup triumph after a 3–0 deficit in a seven-game series against the Detroit Red Wings was heard all over Canada and in Newfoundland on the night of April 18; thousands of Canadian soldiers stationed overseas tuned in for the dramatic win at Maple Leaf Gardens.

Foster Hewitt was the voice of hockey and the Toronto Maple Leafs. His radio broadcasts helped to make the Leafs a legendary team. (HHOF)

Interest in the Leafs during the war years remained high, and the team went on to its greatest successes by winning the Cup in 1945, 1947, 1948 and 1949. The radio broadcasts made recruiting easy because every young hockey fan wanted to play for the champions in Maple Leaf Gardens (that was still somewhat true in 2002, though there were by then 30 NHL teams and no broadcaster of Hewitt's stature).

As good as radio was for the Maple Leafs, Smythe was not one to sit still as technology changed. When television broadcasts began in 1952 he was intrigued by the possibilities, if not sure how the new medium would affect his hockey empire. Although the Leafs were at the forefront (with the Montreal Canadiens) in allowing games to be televised, Smythe protected season-ticket holders by not letting the camera roll live before 9 p.m. — the games started at 8 p.m.; an entire Leafs game was not broadcast on TV until the late '60s.

Radio and television rights garnered the team more than $300,000 a year by 1957 and by 2002 that figure was in the millions. Such revenue helped make Maple Leaf Gardens Limited debt free by 1957. Smythe watched the company books closely to make sure that his interests and those of the team were well-protected.

Foster Hewitt began as the television play-by-play man, in what was actually a simulcast with radio, but turned the TV duties over to his son Bill by 1958 and returned to the radio booth. The television broadcasts on CBC Television were dubbed *Hockey Night in Canada,* by Hewitt, and became a great success. The family gathered around the TV set on a snowy Saturday night became a Canadian tableau. In 2002, 50 years after the first broadcast, *Hockey Night in Canada* was still a thriving national institution and its stars were still the Toronto Maple Leafs.

The Second Golden Age

After winning the Stanley Cup in 1951, the Leafs began a steep decline that would last for seven years. It was probably no coincidence that Smythe was less attentive to team affairs during this dark period in their history. His son Stafford soon took over, removing the extremely successful Hap Day from any active role in management and rebuilding the Leafs by recruiting good prospects from the club's junior teams. By the late '50s the Maple Leafs were ready to roll again just as television was becoming more prominent.

The baby-boom generation grew up watching the Leafs win the Stanley Cup in 1962, 1963, 1964 and once again in 1967. Those championships made heroes of a new group of Maple Leaf players who were now instantly recognizable because of television. Interest in the Leafs was never higher and, by the 1963–64 campaign, the waiting list for season tickets contained 10,000 names. The team was so popular that road games were shown at movie theatres, selling out as well; prices at the theatres ranged from $1.25 to $2.50 and the Leafs even tried a pay-per-view experiment for some games. The club was a well-oiled machine in the '60s, winning both on and off the ice.

In 1961 Stafford Smythe and his two partners, Harold Ballard

and John Bassett, bought out Conn's shares in the team and Maple Leaf Gardens for $2 million. They moved to reinvent the arena to pay off their loans as soon as possible, adding seats and hosting wrestling, basketball, ice shows, rodeos, political rallies and rock concerts as well as hockey games. Advertising signs became more prominent and eventually were placed along the boards and even on the ice. The debt was quickly paid and the Gardens' coffers overflowed with profits.

The '50s and '60s saw the development of hockey memorabilia and collectibles as strong marketing tools. The NHL and the Leafs in particular saw the opportunity to exploit the images of hockey's heroes by flogging calendars, colouring books, trading cards, ministicks, drinking glasses, photos (like the "Beehives"), coins, media guides, team pennants and recordings. A Leafs sweater could be purchased at Eaton's and bobble-head figurines were first seen in the early '60s.

Leafs players helped to sell cars, peanut butter, shaving cream, glue and homes. The players did not make much (if anything) on these promotions, as the club controlled the rights; coach and general manager George "Punch" Imlach wanted all the players to share in the financial rewards, though it was usually the star players who were most prominent in selling products or services.

A Long Drought

Just when the Leafs juggernaut looked unstoppable, the 1967–68 season brought expansion for the NHL. The team was never as successful afterward. As well, the death of Stafford Smythe brought to the fore Harold Ballard, a man largely incapable of running a hockey team but excellent at making money and keeping control of the business. As the '70s began, the Leafs could no longer claim to be Stanley Cup champions but they would never lose money, even with the incompetent Ballard in command.

New playing heroes emerged, but the Leafs were only a breakeven proposition on the ice. Ballard kept raising ticket prices (installing gold-coloured seats up front) and fans kept paying in the hope that the team might one day recapture glory. By the '80s, even

The 1992–93 Maple Leafs came to within one game of the Stanley Cup finals by dismissing the Detroit Red Wings and St. Louis Blues in the playoffs before losing another seven-game series to the Los Angeles Kings. (Dennis Miles)

the most ardent follower had to admit all was lost. The Leafs experienced their worst decade and were no longer the darlings of *Hockey Night in Canada*. The once-proud franchise was now the NHL doormat. However, the proud fans did not abandon the team and their fierce loyalty meant the Leafs were still a moneymaker.

The Big-Money Era

Ballard's death in 1990 gave the Maple Leafs a chance to become revitalized. Cliff Fletcher was hired from the Calgary Flames and finally the Leafs again had a well-qualified man running the team. He modernized the entire operation and acquired star players such as Doug Gilmour and a top-flight coach in Pat Burns. By the 1992–93 season the Leafs were once again the main attraction on *Hockey Night in Canada* and nearly made it to the Stanley Cup finals for the first time since 1967, falling just one game short.

Fletcher also upgraded the Leafs operation off the ice, not least by giving fans more opportunity to buy high-quality team merchandise. As the team improved, souvenir sales soared and the decrepit concession stands at the Gardens were upgraded and began to sell alcohol and decent food. The improvements were expensive, but Fletcher realized Toronto would accept higher ticket prices if the team was winning. Where Ballard used to raise ticket prices $1 at a time, Fletcher put them up by several dollars every season, with few complaints. The Leafs had entered the big-money era.

A New Home

The Leafs' grand old home was showing its age by the '90s and the modern game had outgrown Maple Leaf Gardens, especially as space was needed for lucrative corporate boxes. Like Conn Smythe 70 years earlier, the Leafs new owner, grocery-store magnate Steve Stavro, set out to build a new arena. The search for an appropriate site was controversial, but the issue was finally resolved when the club bought the Toronto Raptors team of the National Basketball Association and took over construction of the arena the Raptors were building for themselves. The state-of-the-art stadium, with its price tag of $265 million (the Gardens was built for $1.5 million), would have two tenants; a new, private company, Maple Leaf Sports and Entertainment (MLSE), was born out of the merger.

The Leafs marketed their last season at the Gardens as "Memories and Dreams" and staged a year of nostalgic events that came to a climax on February 13, 1999, when the team played its final game in the venerable old building. A week later, on February 20, the Leafs made a seamless transition to their new home, the Air Canada Centre, named after a sponsor. The first game in the beautiful ACC building, its seats no farther from the ice than those at the Gardens, was a 3–2 win over old foes the Montreal Canadiens. A new generation of Leaf fans had a new place to call home and nobody seemed to mind that the Gardens had been vacated. The Leafs installed a modern large-screen scoreboard, upgraded their game presentation to be more of an "entertainment package" and opened a store that sold designer clothing in addition to all the usual souvenirs.

The Leafs Today and Tomorrow

The Leafs were once again pioneers in new technology, establishing their own website (www.leafs.com) and spending millions of dollars on a digital television station (Leafs TV) devoted entirely to the team, the first of its kind in North America. By 2002 the Maple Leaf organization had evolved into a modern corporation with a hierarchical structure. Unlike Maple Leaf Gardens Limited, which had to answer to shareholders, the new private company doesn't have to disclose its revenues, but it is safe to say that profit is in the millions of dollars each year. Staying in the black is assured as long as the team makes the playoffs; the Leafs have not missed the postseason

Doug Gilmour (#93) would do anything to help the Leafs win a game, including dropping his gloves when pressed. (Dennis Miles)

since moving to the Air Canada Centre and have made it to the Eastern Conference final twice.

The Leafs are demanding more money than ever from their fans: according to *Sports Illustrated* magazine, Toronto had the highest-priced ticket in the NHL in the 2002 playoffs, at US$583. The green seats at the Gardens or the ACC have always been considered a good buy, but in 2001–2 they were $64 each. Greens did not increase in price from 1931 to 1957 when they rose from $1 to $2; by the 1968–69 season they were going for $4; in 1979–80 they were still a reasonable $7. The 1985–86 season brought a hike to $11; by 1990–91 they were

$19. The trend continued: $26 in 1992–93, $38 in 1995–96 and so to $70 for the 2002–03 season. It's a good bet season ticket prices will continue to rise in the years to come.

The team has also reached out to the community more than ever. The Maple Leafs have always been prominent in helping charities and now its community relations department organizes outreach programs for the team, which supports various children's charities, educational initiatives and minor-hockey development.

The team asked fans to write stories and submit photos about their experiences as Leaf fans and printed those memories on season tickets: that initiative came from Leafs president Ken Dryden and was one of the best-received promotions since "Young Canada Night," in which youngsters were given free tickets for Leaf games around the Christmas holidays. The team also started "Buds Club" to promote the team to youngsters, but it was evident that the love of the Leafs was already passing from generation to generation. Few professional athletic teams have such a devoted following, and that fan loyalty made the franchise one of the most valuable in sports.

How did the Maple Leafs retain so many fans without winning a championship since 1967? Supporters put up with bad management, poor coaches, broken promises, huge ticket-price increases, awful draft choices, some terrible players and one cantankerous owner who never showed he cared about them. Yet they never stayed away in any great numbers and tickets were still strongly sought-after on most nights. The myth that the Leafs have not had an unsold seat since 1946 is untrue — it was perpetuated by the team at one time — but the club has never really suffered at the gate. Having a large number of corporations buying season's tickets obviously helps, and the owners were smart to keep the seating capacity at the ACC at around 19,000 so that demand for tickets would never wane too much.

The Leafs still had a special relationship with their fans in 2002. Like any love affair it has had many ups and downs, but it was as strong as ever. While the team held a special place in the hearts and minds of Torontonians, a recent Canadian Press survey found that 30.4 percent of those polled across Canada listed the Leafs as their favourite team (Montreal was next at 21.6 percent, followed by Vancouver, Edmonton, Ottawa and Calgary). There is no doubt that *Hockey Night in Canada* helps keep the Leafs mystique alive, but the extraordinary relationship between the team and the public is best understood by looking at the men who have worn the Leafs jersey over the past 75 years.

Maple Leaf Legends

As soon as a player puts on a Maple Leaf sweater, he carries on a tradition. Leafs players are expected to do the right things on and off the ice and though some have failed, many have become heroes. Being a former Leaf is a badge of honour worn proudly, and most players love the recognition: NHL players who could make more money elsewhere sign with Toronto because they want to wear the Maple Leafs sweater.

Leaf fans love their hockey legends and will never forget the likes of Charlie Conacher, King Clancy, Red Horner, Hap Day, Syl Apps, Turk Broda, Ted Kennedy, Max Bentley, George Armstrong, Dave Keon, Johnny Bower, Frank Mahovlich, Tim Horton, Darryl Sittler, Lanny McDonald, Borje Salming, Wendel Clark, Doug Gilmour, Curtis Joseph and Mats Sundin. All of these players and many others brought something special to the team and the city. Although they were not perfect, they were for the most part good citizens and realized they represented something special.

People in Toronto demand a great deal of their hockey players but they never forget a warrior. If Canadian-born players have always understood what it is to be a Maple Leaf, by 2002 it was becoming common for non-Canadians to appreciate what it is to play in Toronto. The special bond the fans have with the Leaf players is the key to understanding how this team continues to thrive 75 years after its birth.

This book focuses primarily on players who have worn the Leafs sweater with distinction and on a few outstanding managers and coaches. It is a tribute to players who have won Stanley Cups, scored overtime winning goals, won major awards, been named all-stars, set NHL records, established club marks, been drafted with high

Wendel Clark (#17) was the Leafs' captain and inspirational leader during the 1993 and 1994 playoffs, when his play earned an outstanding 36 points in 39 games. (HHOF)

hopes and shown a willingness to carry on the Maple Leaf tradition that Conn Smythe began so many years ago. The decade-by-decade player profiles cover the 75 years of Leafs history, illustrated by photographs selected from a variety of sources but primarily from the archives of Harold Barkley, the Hockey Hall of Fame and Museum in Toronto and longtime Leafs photographer Dennis Miles.

Here is the history of a hockey franchise with a proud past and a secure future. The Maple Leafs are a Canadian success story.

When Conn Smythe and his partners bought the Toronto St. Patrick's NHL franchise on February 14, 1927, they vowed to make the team something all of Toronto would be proud of for years to come. Smythe's first move was to change the team nickname from "St. Pat's" to "Maple Leafs" (the team didn't change colours and become the famous "blue and white" until the following season). On February 17, 1927 the Leafs won their first ever game, 4–1 over the New York Americans. It was the beginning of something special, but Smythe knew there was plenty to be done if hockey was to become a major source of entertainment in Toronto. By the end of the '30s, he had fulfilled virtually all of his early aspirations for the franchise. Here is a quick look back at how that happened.

Facing page: *Hockey's greatest shrine: Maple Leaf Gardens in the '30s.* (HHOF)

Above: *Bill Carson led the Leafs in goals scored in the 1927–28 season, with 20. He played a total of 96 games as a Leaf, scoring 43 goals and adding 18 assists.* (HHOF)

Management and Coaching

During their growing years the Leafs were superbly managed and coached. Smythe maintained ultimate control but he was ably assisted by Frank Selke, a superior judge of young talent. Selke convinced Smythe that the Leafs needed a development system and the Toronto Marlboros became a production line for young-sters tabbed to be future NHL players. Smythe was no slouch him-self at spotting talent: he had built the New York Rangers into Stanley Cup winners and brought that keen eye with him to Toronto.

With the management team in place, Smythe started looking around for a coach. When Art Duncan faltered in 1931, Smythe went after the best available and landed Dick Irvin for the post. Irvin had been a great player in the early days of the NHL and had coached in Chicago for some time before the Black Hawks let him go. Irvin proved to be a wise choice as the Leafs won the Cup in his first season and Toronto consistently challenged for the cham-pionship under his guidance.

Best Trades and Acquisitions

With his hockey sense, Smythe decided which players to keep from the St. Patrick's club and who to bring in. The Leafs made many great moves in building their team. The most notable acquisition was defenceman Francis "King" Clancy from Ottawa. Colourful and talented, Clancy provided much of the fire the Leafs needed to become champions. Lorne Chabot was brought in to tend goal in a deal with the New York Rangers and was later traded for another quality netminder in George Hainsworth. Harold Cotton, who was acquired from Pittsburgh, and free agents such as Irvine "Ace" Bailey and Andy Blair all contributed to the Leafs' first Cup win. Bill Thoms was brought in from Syracuse in 1933 to give the Leafs some scoring punch and the smallish Ken Doraty arrived in 1935.

As the Leafs started to make changes toward the end of the decade, excellent deals brought in Dave "Sweeney" Schriner, Wally Stanowski and Walter "Turk" Broda. Syl Apps was signed, as was Gordie Drillon, in moves that set up the Leafs nicely for the '40s. Every-thing Smythe touched turned to gold during the Leafs' first decade.

The Leafs square up against the Chicago Black Hawks on opening night at Maple Leaf Gardens on November 12, 1931. The Hawks won, 2–1. (HHOF)

Notable Events

So many positive things happened to the Maple Leafs during their early years that it's difficult to pick just a few. Broadcaster Foster Hewitt began doing play-by-play of Leafs games on the radio and the team became popular right across the country. Listening to Leafs games on Saturday night became a family event over the long Canadian winters. The team had plenty of heroes like Charlie Conacher to root for and playing for the Leafs became the dream of many. Smythe's legendary feuds with managers such as Art Ross of Boston and Jack Adams of Detroit made him as quotable as anyone in the history of the game.

During the height of the Depression, Smythe managed to build Maple Leaf Gardens, with the assistance of Selke. Built in an incredible six months, the Gardens soon became the greatest hockey arena in the world. From November 12, 1931, opening night, until February 13, 1999, the night the doors were closed for the last time, this hockey shrine hosted 68 years of memories and dreams.

On the ice, the Leafs teams of the '20s and '30s were full of flamboyant characters who loved playing hockey. They have often been referred to as "the Gashouse Gang." In 1929, Leafs defenceman Clarence "Hap" Day scored four goals in one game, tying an NHL record that would not be surpassed until 1977. In 1931, the Leafs won the Stanley Cup in the Gardens, and on April 3, 1933, they won one of the longest games in NHL history, when they edged Boston 1–0 after 104 minutes of overtime during a playoff game. The Leafs also had the toughest player in the NHL in the person of defenceman Reginald "Red" Horner, who led the league in penalty time for eight straight years between the 1932–33 and 1939–40 seasons.

Worst of the Decade

The worst thing that happened to the Leafs in the '30s was the 1933 injury to Ace Bailey. A vicious hit by the Bruins' Eddie Shore ended Bailey's playing career (and nearly his life). The Leafs missed the spirited Bailey for the rest of the decade, losing in the finals six times, including a 1940 loss to the Rangers.

The Leafs should have won more Stanley Cups, as they were the better team in every losing matchup, but they seemed to lack something at the key moment. It's been speculated that they lost some of their discipline in the finals and relied too heavily on a few quality players, such as centre Joe Primeau. These performances would cost Irvin his coaching job in Toronto.

The worst loss was to Chicago in 1938 against a Black Hawk team that had won only 14 of its 48 regular-season games, while the Leafs had won 24. Chicago was even forced to pull goaltender Alf Moore from a Toronto drinking establishment to play one game as an injury replacement, but the Leafs still lost the series and the Cup three games to one in the best-of-five matchup.

Bottom-line Results

During the last four seasons of the '20s, the Leafs were under .500, with a record of 71–81–24 (including the 1926–27 season, when the team was still called the St. Patrick's for a good part of the year). Starting in 1930–31 and until the 1939–40 season, the Leafs posted a very impressive 238–168–70 record. They finished first in the Canadian Division of the NHL four times and won their first Stanley Cup. But their record was marred by losses in the finals to the Rangers (twice, in 1933 and 1940), the Montreal Maroons (1935), Detroit (1936), Chicago (1938) and Boston (1939). This lack of ultimate success keeps this Leafs era from being referred to as a dynasty, but in every other way the team certainly deserved that title.

Best Leafs of the Decade

IN GOAL: Lorne Chabot and George Hainsworth.

ON DEFENCE: Red Horner, Hap Day and King Clancy.

AT FORWARD: Joe Primeau, Andy Blair, Harvey Jackson, Ace Bailey, Harold Cotton and Charlie Conacher.

IRVINE 'ACE' BAILEY

IRVINE "ACE" BAILEY was not big in stature when he began his hockey career. As a result the native of Bracebridge, Ontario, started off by playing in goal but quickly abandoned the nets for a defensive position. Being a defender did not exactly suit him, either, and a junior coach named Mike Rodden suggested he try the wing. It was probably the best advice the youngster ever received, and he soon became a pretty good right-winger who was noticed for his play at both ends of the rink. Bailey won a scoring title with Peterborough, a senior hockey club, in 1924. When Rodden became coach of the Toronto St. Patrick's of the NHL, he remembered Bailey and signed him on November 3, 1926.

Bailey quickly showed he belonged in the big league by scoring 15 goals and 28 points in 42 games, a fair total in a low-scoring era. Along with Hap Day, he was one of the few players to survive when the St. Patrick's became the Maple Leafs during the 1926–27 season.

Bailey slumped a little the next year with only nine goals and 12 points in 43 games, but then he reeled off three straight years of 20 or more goals (22, 22, 23), taking the NHL scoring title in 1928–29 with 32 points in 44 games. While he was not afraid to be aggressive (he grew to 5'10", 160 pounds), Bailey was not much of a fighter and was on the wrong end of a few scraps in his rookie year. Lionel Conacher of Chicago, Sprague Cleghorn of Boston and Duke Keats of Detroit all got the better of him in punch-ups. These losses convinced Bailey to stick to hockey and he became known as a stylish winger. Two of his strengths were his ability to carry the puck and his penalty killing.

The last three years of Bailey's playing career with the Leafs were less productive, although he did score 10 goals in 1932–33, his last full season in hockey. A vicious hit by the Bruins' Eddie Shore during a game in Boston ended his playing days and he became a longtime employee at Maple Leaf Gardens, where he was best known for manning the penalty box gate.

When Bailey retired from playing, Conn Smythe announced that no Leafs player would wear sweater Number 6 again. This is still true, despite Bailey's personal request, made many years later, that it be given to Ron Ellis. Three decades later, Bailey was shabbily treated by Leafs owner Harold Ballard, who sent him a letter informing him his services were no longer required. This Hall of Fame member and early Leafs legend, who scored the team's first Stanley Cup-winning goal in 1932, surely deserved better treatment.

Tragically, Bailey did not live to see the Leafs formally honour his sweater retirement: a players' strike in 1992 scuttled a planned ceremony and he passed away before the rescheduled occasion on October 17, 1992.

Ace Bailey scored the first Stanley Cup-winning goal for the Maple Leafs in 1932. (HHOF)

Facing page: Ace Bailey is taken off on a stretcher by Toronto and Boston players on December 12, 1933. (AP)

Leaf file:

Ace Bailey's career came to a sudden end on the night of December 12, 1933 at the Boston Garden. Leafs defenceman Red Horner had decked Bruins hard-rock star Eddie Shore with a great hit in the second period of the game. Shore was knocked into the boards as he carried the puck and the other Leafs defenceman, King Clancy, picked up the loose disc and charged up the ice. Bailey dropped back to cover Clancy just as an enraged and somewhat dazed Shore was getting back on his feet. The Bruin was determined to run at the first Leaf he saw and that happened to be the unsuspecting Bailey. Shore hit Bailey from behind and the Leafs winger went down, and Bailey's head struck the ice with what was called a "sickening thud." A doctor was summoned, and Bailey was taken out on a stretcher and rushed to hospital. Doctors operated quickly and relieved pressure on his brain, but last rites were adminis-

tered and Leafs owner Conn Smythe made arrangements to ship the body home. Newspapers in Toronto were forced to install special phone lines to give and receive updates on Bailey's condition.

But after weeks of recovery the Leafs player was finally able to take the train back to Toronto. He would never play hockey again.

A couple of benefit games were held to help Bailey out. He had considered suing Shore but was told it might net him only $5,000, so he decided not to pursue the matter in court. He did better financially with the proceeds from the benefit games: the Bruins sent him $7,800 raised in a game between Boston and the Montreal Maroons, and the Leafs netted him a further $20,000 by playing a group of NHL all-stars — including Shore — on February 14, 1934. Bailey and Shore shook hands before the game and the Maple Leaf Gardens crowd roared its approval.

Maple Leaf stats:	GP	G	A	P	PIM
regular season	313	111	82	193	472
playoffs	21	3	4	7	12

ANDY BLAIR

TORONTO OWNER and manager Conn Smythe rarely forgot a good hockey player no matter what team he played for. Such was the case for lanky (6'1", 180 pounds) centreman Andy Blair, who impressed Smythe with his play for the University of Manitoba team when it won the Allan Cup in 1928. Smythe did a deal with the New York Rangers, who had been talking to Blair, and he joined the Leafs for the 1928–29 season.

The mustachioed native of Winnipeg had an excellent first season for the Leafs, with 12 goals and 27 points in 44 games. In 1930–31, the Leafs' first Cup-winning season, he was teamed with Bob Gracie and Frank Finnigan to create what became known as "the Pepper Boys line." The Leafs' third line (going with three lines was the idea of new coach Dick Irvin) earned its nickname from the players' "peppery" style of play. Blair's biggest contribution came in the Stanley Cup finals against the New York Rangers (a best-of-five affair that the Leafs won in three). He scored the first two goals in the third and Cup-clinching game at Maple Leaf Gardens which saw the Leafs win 6–4.

In the 1933 playoffs, Blair had a big hand in ending one of the longest games in NHL history. On April 3, the Leafs faced the Boston Bruins in the fifth and final game of the semifinals. The winner would advance to the finals against the New York Rangers, due to begin the following night in New York. The Leafs and Bruins simply could not score and the 0–0 deadlock dragged on into the early hours of the morning. The teams even debated different ways of ending the marathon — pulling the goalies was discussed — but the game continued. Then, after 104 minutes of overtime, Blair intercepted a pass from the Bruins' Eddie Shore and got the puck over to Ken Doraty. The smallest Leaf made no mistake in firing the puck past goalie Cecil "Tiny" Thompson to give the Leafs a 1–0 win. The team scrambled to catch a train to New York, not arriving until 4:30 the next afternoon, just in time to lose the first game of the finals. The Rangers took the Cup and the series in four games.

In 1933–34 Blair scored 14 times, his highest season total. But by 1935–36 he was down to five goals and nine points in 45 games. The Leafs sold him to Chicago in May 1936 for $7,500 and he played only one season for the Black Hawks before retiring.

🍁

Andy Blair led the Leafs in assists with 15 in his first season, 1928–29. (HHOF)

Maple Leaf stats:

	GP	G	A	P	PIM
regular season	358	74	83	157	290
playoffs	38	6	6	12	32

LORNE CHABOT

WHEN CONN SMYTHE acquired Lorne Chabot in 1928, the young goalie had just won the Stanley Cup with the New York Rangers. The Montreal native had incurred a serious eye injury during the playoff run and while the Rangers were worried that he would not recover, Smythe, who was not enamoured with current Leafs goalie John Ross Roach, leaped at the chance to sign Chabot.

In an era of small goalies, the large Chabot, at 6'1" and 185 pounds, was an imposing figure in net. He moved well for a man of his size and had eagle eyes and a reputation as a clutch goalie with nerves of steel. Chabot was also known for wearing a hat to cut the glare of bright lights, and he was not afraid to let his temper show: he once belted a goal judge when he disagreed with a call. He won 20 or more games with the Leafs on four occasions and had his best year in Toronto the season they won their first Cup (1931–32), when he won 22 times and recorded four shutouts. He won five games in the playoffs alone and saved his best performance for the finals against his old club, the Rangers.

In the first game of the finals played at Madison Square Garden,

Chabot faced a barrage from the Rangers that nearly saw the Leafs blow a 5–1 lead. Even a series of terrific saves could not stop the Rangers from narrowing the gap to 5–4. Then Chabot discovered that one of his pad straps was loose. He managed to delay the game for little more than a minute, but it seemed to cool off the New Yorkers just enough. The Leafs added an insurance goal and won 6–4. Toronto won the second game in Boston and then came home to clinch the series. The Rangers' Frank Boucher got three past Chabot, who was nonetheless spectacular in helping the Leafs to a 6–4 win. It was sweet revenge for Chabot — and for the Leafs, who beat former teammate Roach in the New York net.

Chabot's final year in Toronto was 1932–33. He won 24 games, but the season ended in disappointment when the Rangers got even by beating the Leafs in the Stanley Cup finals. During the summer Smythe traded Chabot to Montreal; he would play for the Maroons, Black Hawks and Americans before retiring at the end of the 1936–37 season. A first team all-star (1935) and Vezina Trophy winner (1935), Chabot won 201 games and recorded 73 career shutouts. Amazingly, he is not in the Hall of Fame.

❦

Lorne Chabot wears a hat to counter the glare of the arena's bright lights. (HHOF)

Maple Leaf stats:	GP	Wins	Losses	Ties	Shutouts	GA
regular season	214	103	80	31	33	2.20
playoffs	21	11	10	–	2	1.57

FRANCIS 'KING' CLANCY

WHEN THE SMALL BUT spunky Francis Michael "King" Clancy showed up at the Ottawa Senators practice in 1921, he confidently told manager Tommy Gorman that he was ready to play in the NHL for the Senators. The Ottawa club just happened to be the defending Stanley Cup champions and, after one look at the 5'7", 155-pound Clancy, it was all Gorman could do to keep from laughing. But Clancy's father, Tom, best known as "King," was a well-known athlete in the Ottawa area, so out of respect for the senior Clancy, Gorman agreed to give the young man a tryout. As the other Senator players looked on, he showed he could be daring with the puck and was willing to take on all customers. Gorman signed Clancy to a substitute contract that paid $800 a year, and Clancy became a popular figure very quickly. It was the start of a long career in hockey for the little Irishman.

Clancy insisted he was a defenceman so that he could play more, but he soon showed that he could carry the puck up the ice too. He had lots of drive in his play and his offensive forays changed the game by showing that defencemen could also produce some points. He earned 15 goals in 78 games in his first three seasons in Ottawa, an unheard-of total for a defenceman in that era. The Senators won the Stanley Cup in 1923 and the 1924–25 season saw Clancy score 14 goals and 21 points in 29 games. He won another Cup in 1927 and added seasons of 13 and 17 goals for the Ottawa club. In 1929–30 Clancy recorded 40 points in 44 games but it would be his last season in the nation's capital. The Senators were running into money troubles and looking for some quick cash when Conn Smythe of the Maple Leafs came calling.

The Toronto manager would be erecting a beautiful new building for his hockey club and knew he needed a strong team to fill it every night. He was also aware that his team was close to being a champion but needed help on the blue line. He liked the way Clancy played the game and he knew the Ottawa club was in dire need of cash. But cash was not readily available.

Smythe was not a drinker or smoker but didn't mind gambling a little. He was also a racehorse owner and often found himself at the track. One day he was all set to place a bet on a horse called Frothblower when he was taunted by another patron (the former Leafs doctor Smythe had recently fired) because Smythe was not willing to back his own horse, the long shot Rare Jewel. The teasing by a former employee steamed Smythe, who changed his betting strategy to go with Rare Jewel across the board. As luck would have it the horse came home a winner and Smythe earned between $11,000 and $14,500. The next day he gave Ottawa $10,000 and would agree to pay a total of $35,000 and hand over players Art Smith and Eric Pettinger. The deal was completed on October 11, 1930.

Clancy agreed to go to Toronto and the Leafs had a major piece of the puzzle in place for their championship aspirations. In his second season with the team, Clancy scored 10 goals and added 19 points as the Leafs opened Maple Leaf Gardens and then took their first Stanley Cup in the spring of 1932. Clancy stayed active as a player with the Leafs until 1936–37; his only goal that year was scored on a penalty shot. He retired just six games into the season, but not before he'd earned "King" as his own nickname and had been twice named to the NHL's first all-star team (1931 and 1934) and second all-star squad (1932 and 1933). He also produced three straight seasons of 20 or more points while with the Leafs.

After spells coaching the Montreal Maroons and refereeing, he eventually returned to Toronto to work behind the bench when Hap Day offered him a position in the organization.

As the Leafs' head coach during the '50s, Clancy had only moderate success (he did win a championship in the minors), but it returned him to the team he loved. He became the Leafs' assistant general manager for life (although he did coach again in 1967 and 1972), and later was a vice president under the ownership of Harold Ballard. He was in charge of nothing in particular, but he was a great ambassador for the Leafs and the game of hockey and his storytelling was superb. His son, Terry, played for the Leafs from 1968 to 1973.

Facing page: *King Clancy was the first Leaf to be honoured with a special night, held on March 17, 1934. A crowd of 11,000 attended 'King Clancy Night.'* (HHOF)

Above: *The Leafs of the '20s and '30s were known to have a lot of fun and played many pranks on each other. Here Hap Day (left),* King Clancy *(centre) and Frank Finnigan appear to be planning some mayhem.* (HHOF)

King Clancy coached the Leafs between 1953 and 1956 and again in 1966–67 and 1972–73. His overall record is 80–81–45. (HB)

Leaf file:

King Clancy was not a large man but his spirit was always big enough to take on larger players. On the night of February 13, 1932 Clancy got into a scrap with Montreal defenceman Harold Starr, who was a burly 5'11" and 176 pounds. Starr tossed Clancy like a rag doll and knocked him all over the ice. Finally he sat on top of Clancy, who demanded to be let up. Starr complied but rubbed it in by telling Clancy he had taken care of him that night. Clancy quickly replied that he had never seen the day Starr could lay a hand on him and went at the bigger man again. The result was no better for Clancy, who was fined $25 for brawling.

On another occasion, in Boston, Clancy was ready to take on a heckling fan who just happened to be heavyweight boxing champion Jack Sharkey.

The Business of the Maple Leafs:

For the longest time all hockey players signed their contracts at training camp. This gave management the upper hand most of the time but players like King Clancy didn't seem to mind. Clancy would usually ask Smythe "Where do I sign?" without any regard for what he might actually be worth to the team. Naturally Smythe loved to hear this and would simple tell Clancy, "This is what I can pay you." Clancy believed Smythe was nothing but fair. One year he asked for $10,000, but Smythe got him to take $8,500 with the promise of a $1,500 bonus "if the team had a good year."

Maple Leaf stats:

	GP	G	A	P	PIM
regular season	286	52	78	130	383
playoffs	37	6	6	12	54

Yeah, I guess those few years I was planning to spend in Toronto got out of hand, didn't they? It wasn't a bad move (from Ottawa) really, because a guy couldn't have asked for a better life than I've had.

King Clancy, Leafs program, November 14, 1981

CHARLIE CONACHER

CHARLIE CONACHER WAS the first Toronto-born player to star with the Maple Leafs. He was born on December 20, 1910, and attended Jesse Ketchum Public School. His older brother Lionel was a natural at all sports and was later named Canada's greatest athlete of the first half of the 20th century. He set a great example for Charlie, who was 10 years his junior, but unlike Lionel Charlie decided he would excel at one sport and chose hockey.

He started out as an unsuccessful goalie and was a big, stumbling skater (he would fill out to be 6'1" and 195 pounds). He was determined to work at it though, and at the age of 16 he tried out for the North Toronto junior club and made the team.

Conacher joined the Toronto Marlboros of the Ontario Hockey Association where he practised his stickhandling and shooting. His shot improved until it was a feared weapon and his leadership skills became evident as well. He was named captain of the Marlboros and made it to the Memorial Cup in 1928 and again in 1929, when the Marlboros faced the Winnipeg-based Elmwood Millionaires. Conacher had a pair of goals in the game that clinched the championship for his team and coach Frank Selke. In all, Conacher had 28 goals in 15 playoff games in taking the Marlies all the way. His performance got him a contract with the Leafs and the right-winger signed on October 7, 1929, making the big team on his first try.

The first contract Conacher signed was quite lucrative for the era, a $20,000 deal for two years. He knew the Leafs needed his scoring touch and was able to get more out of Conn Smythe than many others. He quickly proved he was worth the money by twice leading the NHL in goals scored, in 1930–31 (when he scored 31 times) and 1931–32 (34). In his first game with the Leafs on November 14, 1929, Conacher ripped a shot past Chicago goaltender Charlie Gardiner breaking a 2–2 tie. A few nights later young Charlie went against his brother Lionel and the New York Rangers in Madison Square Garden. Lionel tried to nail him with a bodycheck, but missed. Charlie then put a big shot past Rangers goalie Roy Worters and added an assist in a 4–3 Leafs win. It hadn't taken long for Charlie to prove that he belonged in the NHL.

Teamed with Harvey "Busher" Jackson and Joe Primeau, the trio formed the legendary "Kid Line," an offensive force that dominated the NHL for several years. "Big Bomber" Conacher was the marksman on the line and chalked up three more seasons of leading the NHL in goals, with 32, 36 and 23. The strapping winger who wore sweater number 9 suffered many injuries as he was targeted by the opposition and he lost a kidney in 1930. By 1936–37 Conacher's injuries reduced him to playing just 15 games. The next year saw him named team captain, but he would play in only 19 games and score seven times. Still, he was the first Leafs hero and many youngsters pretended to be Conacher when they played. The future Hall of Famer was sold to Detroit for $16,000, then played two seasons with the New York Americans before retiring. Between 1948 and 1950 he also tried his hand at coaching in Chicago, with limited success.

Maple Leaf stats:	GP	G	A	P	PIM
regular season	326	200	124	324	411
playoffs	41	14	12	26	39

Facing page: *Charlie Conacher was an NHL all-star selection for five straight seasons from 1932 to 1936.* (HHOF)

Charlie Conacher (left) poses with linemates Syl Apps (centre) and Harvey Jackson. Conacher scored five goals in one game on January 19, 1932, against the New York Americans. (HHOF)

Leaf file:

The 1936 playoff series between the Maple Leafs and the Bruins was a two-game total-goal affair. The Bruins won the first game 3–0 at home with goalie Tiny Thompson earning the shutout. The next game was played at Maple Leaf Gardens on March 26 and the Bruins scored early to gain a 4–0 series lead. Then Charlie Conacher took matters into his own hands. First, he set up King Clancy for a power-play goal, then ripped one of his famous shots to make it 4–2. Red Horner scored to make it 4–3, and Conacher scored again to tie the series and then set up Harvey Jackson to give the Leafs a 5–4 lead. Buzz Boll added one more for Toronto and Conacher finished off a great night with another goal to help seal an 8–3 victory in game 2 and an 8–6 series win. The pelting rain didn't stop a crowd from gathering outside the Gardens on Carlton Street to cheer for their hero Conacher.

The Leafs went on to beat the New York Americans that year to make it to the finals, but lost the Stanley Cup to Detroit.

HAROLD COTTON

A NATIVE OF NANTICOKE, Ontario, Harold Cotton was toiling for the Pittsburgh Pirates when he heard that Conn Smythe was interested in acquiring his services for the Toronto Maple Leafs. The rumour perked up the homesick left-winger. The next time the Leafs played the Pirates, Cotton scored twice, impressing Smythe even more but driving up his price: to make the deal the Leafs manager had to give Pittsburgh $9,500 and the rights to Toronto left-winger Gerry Lowrey. Smythe willingly paid the high figure because he felt sure he was getting a gutsy player — just what his team needed in 1929.

Cotton had played four years of junior hockey in the Toronto area before going down to Pittsburgh to play for the Yellowjackets, who later joined the NHL as the Pirates in 1925–26. After four years and 24 goals with the Pirates he joined the Leafs, where he made a strong contribution as a persistent checker and quality penalty killer. He played well on a line with Ace Bailey, and although he stood 5'10" and weighed only 155 pounds, he was fearless and very willing to mix it up. He hurled his body around the ice and took plenty of spills as a result. On one occasion he got carried away and challenged referee Cooper Smeaton to a fight, but was talked out of it. Another time, when Cotton learned that a

Leafs-Bruins playoff game was going to be stopped because no one could score, he blurted out: "Nobody is going to call this game!" That was the spirit Smythe was looking for when he acquired the feisty Cotton.

Cotton enjoyed his best year as a Maple Leaf in 1929–30, scoring 21 times in 41 games and racking up 38 points. He never scored over 20 again, but had three more seasons of double-digit scoring. When the Leafs won the Stanley Cup in 1932, Cotton had two goals and two assists in seven playoff games. He was still with the Leafs in 1934–35 when he had 11 goals and 14 assists in 47 games, but was sent to the New York Americans to start the next season. He spent two years in New York before ending his playing days.

After retirement Cotton became a fixture in the early days of CBC Television's *Hockey Night in Canada* as a member of the Hot Stove League, a regular intermission feature on the Saturday night telecasts. He became known as a storyteller with a good sense of humour. He also forged a long career as a scout for the Boston Bruins. Cotton later became director of field operations for the Minnesota North Stars before retiring to Trent River, Ontario, after 53 years in hockey. He lost his hair in his later years and became known as "Baldy."

Left-winger Harold Cotton played with the Leafs from 1928 to 1935. He scored 21 goals in 41 games in the 1929–30 season. (HHOF)

Maple Leaf stats:	GP	G	A	P	PIM
regular season	285	68	88	156	252
playoffs	34	2	7	9	35

CLARENCE 'HAP' DAY

CLARENCE DAY was not thrilled with his given name and was pleased when his bright and cheerful disposition earned him the nickname "Happy," soon cut to "Hap." Born on June 14, 1901, in Owen Sound, Ontario, Day displayed a great enthusiasm and love for hockey from an early age. He would walk five miles to play a game as a boy and then trek all the way home in a wet uniform afterwards. He played junior hockey in towns like Midland and Collingwood and moved up to play senior hockey for the Hamilton Tigers between 1922 and 1924, scoring 10 goals in 21 games and getting 33 points. As a left-winger Day proved to be very alert and, although he was not heavy (175 pounds on a 5'11" frame), he showed he could take a physical beating and never back down.

Day was a smart player on the ice and a bright student in the classroom. He studied pharmacy at the University of Toronto and believed his future lay in that field. But Charlie Querrie had different ideas. Querrie was the coach and manager of the Toronto St. Patrick's of the NHL and was very impressed with Day's abilities on the ice. In fact, he thought Day was the best prospect he had ever seen and was determined to land him for his team. Querrie signed Day by assuring the recent graduate that he could open his pharmacy and still play hockey. The money wouldn't hurt, either. Day, convinced he could do both, gave pro hockey a chance. It would prove to be a life-altering decision.

In his first three seasons he scored 35 goals in 106 games, but when the St. Pat's became the Maple Leafs he was switched to defence by the new owner, Conn Smythe. Day was one of the few players kept on when the team was sold and he became the first ever captain of the Maple Leafs. His goal-scoring dropped off, but Day became quite adept at playing on the blue line. He was not a bruiser like teammate Red Horner and did know how to skate off an opponent, which earned him great respect. When all else failed, Day was not shy about using the clutch-and-grab techniques that would become a trademark of Leafs teams for years to come.

On occasion Day could provide some notable offence, such as the time he tied an NHL record (since broken) for defencemen by scoring four goals in one game on November 19, 1929 against the Pittsburgh Pirates. His point total each season was between 15 and 20, a more than respectable total for defencemen in this low-scoring era. He became quite popular (his wedding in July 1937 drew a crowd of 3,000 fans who waited outside the church), and his teammates would follow him anywhere. It was also no surprise that when Maple Leaf Gardens opened, Day had a pharmacy located just west of the main entrance.

Day stayed with the Leafs for 10 years, until the end of the 1936–37 season. On September 23, 1937, he was sold to the New York Americans in a cash deal, but he played only one year there before retiring. After becoming an associate of Conn Smythe in a sand and gravel business Smythe owned, Day went on to become the most successful coach in Leafs history by winning five Stanley Cups. He also managed the team for seven years before his relationship with Smythe was severed. Day was elected to the Hall of Fame as a player in 1961.

Hap Day was the Maple Leafs' first captain. He was also the first Leaf to score a hat trick, which he did on January 28, 1928 against the New York Rangers. (HHOF)

Maple Leaf stats:	GP	G	A	P	PIM
regular season	548	86	113	199	588
playoffs	47	4	7	11	56

Hap Day became the Leafs coach in 1940 and posted a 259–206–81 record, with five Stanley Cup wins to his credit. (HHOF)

Leaf file:

Toronto captains have always had a way of rising to the occasion and leading the team to victory. Hap Day started this tradition during the 1932 playoffs, when the Leafs were hoping to win their first Stanley Cup. Toronto had beaten Chicago but was down in the two-game total-goal series against the Montreal Maroons when Day took matters into his own hands. Trailing 2–1 at home on April 2, 1932, Day took the puck up the ice as the Gardens crowd urged him on. The defenceman battled his way through Montreal defenders Nels Stewart, Lionel Conacher and Andre Wilcox before rifling a 12-foot shot past goalie Flat Walsh to tie the game. The Leafs won it in overtime and went on to win the Cup against the New York Rangers. Day also scored the first ever Maple Leafs goal in a final series when he beat John Ross Roach in the Rangers net on April 5, 1932.

REGINALD 'RED' HORNER

DEFENCEMAN RED HORNER was born on May 28, 1909, on the family farm near Lyndon, Ontario. When he was 10 years old his family moved to Spadina Road in Toronto and the young Reginald began attending Huron Street Public School. Horner was a big, rangy youngster who weighed 160 pounds by age 16. He also had a strong interest in playing hockey, so one day he reported to the Mutual Street Arena and tried out for the Toronto Canoe Club junior team. He could not make an impression on the coaches but Horner was a determined young man. He developed a rapport with Frank Selke, to whom he delivered groceries. Selke managed a junior hockey team and eventually agreed to give the enthusiastic youngster a tryout.

Horner was a poor skater, but he was so determined that Selke decided to keep him around. The defenceman continued to work on his skating and very willingly took on all comers, becoming a physical blueliner who played the stay-at-home style. He made no apologies for playing it tough and was a natural leader who was elected team captain of the junior Toronto Marlboros in 1928. He played very well in the Memorial Cup playoffs that year, bagging 12 points in 11 games before the Ottawa Gunners knocked the Marlboros out of contention.

Horner played a couple of games for the senior Marlboros at the start of the 1928–29 season. Then, on December 22, 1928, Conn Smythe approached him after a Saturday afternoon contest at Varsity Arena and asked him if he would play for the Maple Leafs that very night. Horner readily agreed. In the game, he decked Frank Fredrickson of the Pittsburgh Pirates and was penalized. The Leafs lost 3–2 but Smythe was delighted with his find. He saw right away that Horner was going to bring to the Leafs blue line the elements he wanted, and Horner signed a contract that paid $2,500 for the rest of the season.

The red-haired Horner soon gained a reputation as an NHL bad boy and by the 1932–33 season he led all players with 144 penalty minutes. It would be the first of eight straight seasons in which the rugged Leaf lead the NHL in penalty time. Because of his size — an even six feet tall and a solid 190 pounds — Horner stood above most players in the game at the time and was a disliked and marked man. The great Nels Stewart slashed him in his rookie year, forcing Horner to miss five weeks with a broken hand. Another time he was told that gangsters were going to get him during a game at the Chicago Stadium: when a light bulb fell from the ceiling and shattered on the ice, Horner was sure that someone had taken a shot at him. Although he is sometimes called the first enforcer in hockey, he was generally a clean player and did not use his stick on the opposition. More than just a tough guy, Horner could also handle the puck and it is a tribute to his overall ability that he was elected to the Hall of Fame.

When Hap Day was traded away, Horner was named team captain, a position he held for two seasons before he retired after the 1939–40 season. When Doug Gilmour became Leafs captain in 1994, it was Horner who presented him with the sweater bearing the "C" at a press conference.

Horner was also present for the closing of Maple Leaf Gardens in 1999. In a touching moment, he told team captain Mats Sundin to take a special flag commemorating the Leafs' former home to the new location and reminded him: "Don't ever forget" those that played and triumphed at the grand old building.

Red Horner led the Leafs in penalty minutes 10 times between the 1929–30 and 1939–40 seasons. (HHOF)

We loved
body contact
and we played
better against
bruising teams
like the Rangers. Close-
checking, hard-hitting
styles were what Conn
Smythe and Dick Irvin
preached. Red Horner, Leafs program, October 14, 1978

Leaf file:

Red Horner played a major part in the incident that ended the career of teammate Ace Bailey in Boston on the night of December 12, 1933 (see page 21). He was the player who body-slammed Boston's Eddie Shore into the boards, and Shore was probably hunting for Horner when he got up and ran at Bailey. When Horner saw the damage Shore had inflicted on Bailey, he turned on the Bruins star and said: "What did you do that for, Eddie?" Horner promptly belted Shore with a mighty punch that knocked down the Boston player, causing a severe cut to his head when he hit the ice. Horner's defence of his teammate cost him a six-game suspension.

Red Horner was captain of the Leafs for two seasons in the late '30s. (HHOF)

Maple Leaf stats:	GP	G	A	P	PIM
regular season	490	42	110	152	1,264
playoffs	71	7	10	17	170

DICK IRVIN

DICK IRVIN WAS one of the first hockey stars whose fame was based on his goal-scoring prowess. He began his career with the Winnipeg Monarchs and the Portland Rosebuds of the Pacific Coast Hockey Association. After completing military service in 1918–19, Irvin played six seasons in Regina before returning to Portland for the 1925–26 season, when he scored 31 goals in 30 games. He joined the Chicago Black Hawks the next season and led the NHL in assists, with 18 in 43 games. When an injury brought his playing career to a sudden end, Irvin turned to coaching. He coached the Black Hawks for 126 games but was let go at the end of the 1930–31 season.

Toronto manager Conn Smythe was not happy with his team or its coach, Art Duncan, at the start of the 1931–32 season. Smythe sent Irvin a telegram in Regina, telling him to wait for a phone call; when Smythe called, he asked Irvin to come to Toronto to coach the Leafs and Irvin accepted. At his first game, on November 28, 1931, Irvin sat beside the team bench while Smythe handled the coaching duties. The Leafs were up 4–1, but the Boston Bruins came back to tie the score. Smythe then motioned to Irvin that he should take over and the Leafs won the game 6–5 on an overtime goal by Andy Blair.

When he took over the team, Irvin felt that the Leafs were talented but not in the best of condition. He stressed conditioning, discipline and work ethic. He graded each player after every game and saw that he had enough talent to form three lines, a luxury he could not afford in Chicago. It all came together that first season when the Leafs won their first Stanley Cup while playing in their beautiful new arena, Maple Leaf Gardens.

The most successful and glamorous team of the decade would not win another championship in the '30s. In 1933 the New York Rangers, whom the Leafs had beaten the previous year, won back the Cup in the finals, and Detroit knocked Toronto out in the semifinals in 1934. For five of the next six years the Leafs went to the finals but could not win the Cup, losing to the Maroons (1935), the Red Wings (1936), the Black Hawks (1938), the Bruins (1939) and once more to the Rangers (1940). The Leafs could have won every one of those finals had the star players come through when it mattered. Many commentators speculated that they relied too much on their centre, Joe Primeau. It was also whispered that Irvin was not tough enough on his charges and not adept at coaching in big games. He eventually agreed with Smythe that the 1939–40 season would be his last as coach. When Bryan Hextall scored in overtime to clinch the Cup for New York at Maple Leaf Gardens on April 13, 1940, Irvin's career with the Leafs was over.

Smythe then helped Irvin land the coaching job with the Montreal Canadiens, who were in dire straits in 1940 and on the verge of going out of business. Irvin went to Montreal and did an excellent job, winning three Stanley Cups. Smythe would later say that Irvin had saved hockey in Montreal.

🍁

Dick Irvin during the 1931–32 season. (HHOF)

Maple Leaf stats:	Games	Wins	Losses	Ties
regular season	427	216	152	59
playoffs	66	33	32	1

HARVEY JACKSON

MAPLE LEAFS assistant manager Frank Selke spotted 16-year-old Harvey Jackson practising on his own at the junior Marlboros hockey arena. Jackson worked at the rink as an ice scraper and cleaner, and when his duties were done he would practice skating and shooting at an empty net. Selke was impressed with his skills and signed him up. Jackson became part of the Leafs development system when he joined the Toronto Marlboros for four games in the 1927–28 season. The next season he scored 25 goals in 22 games, playoffs included. Clearly the Leafs had a young goal-scoring star on the horizon.

Jackson made the Leafs as an 18-year-old in 1929–30 and scored 12 goals in 31 games. When Harold Cotton was injured, Jackson was placed on a line with Joe Primeau (22 years old) and Charlie Conacher (20). On their debut night, December 29, 1929, the Leafs beat Chicago 4–3 with the so-called "Kid Line" scoring two goals, including one by Jackson. The young left wing showed plenty of natural talent and a skating stride that allowed him to shift and manoeuvre with the puck while going at full speed. Jackson was also a terrific stickhandler, with a laser of a backhand shot. His good size (5'11", 195 pounds) meant he was difficult to knock off the puck and his goal-scoring abilities and good looks made him a star. He scored 18 goals in his first full season and then led the NHL in points with 53 in 1931–32, when the Leafs won the Stanley Cup. In total Jackson scored 20 or more goals as a Leaf five times in his career and was a first-team all-star four times (and a second-team all-star once).

The "Kid Line" was eventually broken up — Primeau retired and Conacher was often injured — so Jackson played on a line with his brother Art and Pep Kelly. In 1936–37 he formed another effective line with newcomers Syl Apps and Gord Drillon. Jackson played three more years as a Leaf before he was dealt to the New York Americans in May 1939.

Jackson's career in Toronto was cut short by a drinking problem that did not sit well with Conn Smythe. After a couple of years with the Americans, he moved to the Boston Bruins before retiring from the NHL in 1944 with a total of 241 career goals.

Jackson had a difficult time after he retired. His drinking grew worse and he was often seen selling broken hockey sticks outside Maple Leaf Gardens. His two "Kid Line" mates entered the Hall of Fame but Jackson was denied his rightful place by Smythe, who thought he was weak in character and integrity. It was only after Smythe had removed himself from any active role in the selections for the Hall that the star left-winger was inducted in 1971. Sadly, he had passed away in 1965 at the young age of 55.

❦

Harvey Jackson was given the nickname 'Busher' by trainer Tim Daly because of Jackson's brash attitude. (HHOF)

Maple Leaf stats:	GP	G	A	P	PIM
regular season	434	186	165	351	342
playoffs	54	17	8	25	43

JOE PRIMEAU

AN OLD HOCKEY MAXIM says that the centreman is the most important player on any line. Joe Primeau served as the key man for the Leafs trio known as "the Kid Line" but many wondered if the smallish centre could survive the rigours of professional hockey. Primeau was only 5'11" and 153 pounds, and some of the NHL's most aggressive defencemen, such as Ching Johnson and Earl Seibert of the Rangers and Lionel Hitchman and Eddie Shore of the Bruins, showed him no mercy. But Primeau soon proved that he could take the checks they dished out and he did so in a gentlemanly fashion. His stylish play and good results helped him to thrive in the NHL and led to a place in the Hall of Fame.

Primeau had first thought about a career in baseball as a left-handed pitcher, but he was steered into hockey by Frank Selke, a superb judge of athletic talent. Primeau played junior hockey for four years with the Toronto St. Mary's and Toronto Marlboros in the Leafs development system and showed a good scoring touch, tallying 26 goals and 31 points over his final two seasons in just 17 games. It was rumoured that Conn Smythe had signed him for the New York Rangers, but when Smythe was let go by New York he took Primeau with him to Toronto. By the 1927–28 season many thought that Primeau was ready for the Leafs. But he suited up only twice for the big club, instead playing 41 games with the minor professional Toronto Ravinas where he racked up 26 goals and 13 assists. The Ravinas had such poor attendance that they could afford to dress only eight players in the second half of the season. This gave Primeau plenty of ice time to develop his skills.

In 1928–29 he played in six games for the Leafs. But in the last game he lost a key faceoff to Nels Stewart of the Maroons, costing Toronto a goal. Smythe decided that Primeau needed more time to develop and sent him to London, Ontario, to play for a team called the Panthers in the same minor pro league he had played in the year before. He produced 22 points in 35 games, and the following year, he made the Leafs for good. In his rookie year, Primeau had 26 points, 21 of them assists, and started to show a flair for setting up plays. In 1930–31 he led the NHL in assists with 32 and again in 1931–32 with 37. The "Kid Line" took three of the top four places in scoring that year, with Harvey Jackson winning the scoring title with 53 points, Primeau coming second with 50 and Charlie Conacher fourth with 48; only Montreal's Howie Morenz broke up a 1–2–3 finish by coming third with 49 points. Primeau topped off a great season by winning the Lady Byng Trophy, combining great play with sportsmanship.

He became the perfect centre between two star wingers as soon as he realized that he couldn't split the puck in two. Soon each winger was getting his share of goals. Conacher led the NHL in scoring in 1933–34 with 52 points, and Primeau once again led the league in assists with 32. However, by the 1935–36 season Primeau was reduced to four goals and 17 points in 45 games. His career was over.

He went on to become a very good coach with St. Michael's College School in the Leafs system, helping to bring along youngsters such as Tim Horton. He was named coach of the Leafs in 1950–51, and the team won a Stanley Cup for their rookie leader, making him the only man to have coached a Memorial Cup, Allan Cup and Stanley Cup winner. It looked like Primeau would have a long career as a big-league coach, but he worried far too much and had to give up the job by the 1953–54 season. He finished with a 97–71–42 record, good for the second-best winning percentage of .562 of all former Leafs coaches; only Dick Irvin is higher at .575.

Joe Primeau coached the Leafs to the 1951 Stanley Cup championship. His overall record as Toronto coach between 1950 and 1953 was 97–21–42. (HHOF)

Something
I really prize
is my gold coin
from that series
[the 1932 Stanley
Cup finals against
New York]. We
[the entire team]
were given gold

coins when we won and

they serve as a

lifetime pass

to Maple Leaf

Gardens.

Joe Primeau, Leafs program, October 14, 1978

Joe Primeau led the Leafs in assists for four straight years between 1929–30 and 1933–34. (HHOF)

Maple Leaf stats:	GP	G	A	P	PIM
regular season	310	66	177	243	105
playoffs	38	5	18	23	12

FRANK SELKE

BORN IN KITCHENER, ONTARIO, on May 7, 1893, Frank Selke Sr. trained to be an electrician but could not ignore the lure of hockey. By the age of 20 he was managing local hockey teams while working. Employment opportunities took him to Toronto and he kept moving up the hockey ladder by showing a keen eye for talent. Selke developed many youngsters in junior hockey, first with St. Mary's and then with the Marlboros.

While in Toronto he hooked up with Conn Smythe by convincing the Leafs manager of the value of a development system. He told Smythe that he had many players under wraps on his junior team that could help Toronto win. Smythe made Selke his right-hand man, effectively an assistant general manager. Selke joined the Leafs in 1929 and went to work making sure the team had a constant supply of quality prospects.

Selke was also instrumental in the building of Maple Leaf Gardens. It was the middle of the Great Depression and funds to complete construction of the new arena were drying up. Selke used his trade union background to help convince the workers to take 20 per cent of their pay in Maple Leaf Gardens stock. To show that he believed in the new building, Selke mortgaged his own home to buy $3,500 worth of stock. The Gardens was built on time. The building became a Maple Leafs "factory," as all the important developmental teams played games there under the careful eye of Selke and top scout Squib Walker.

Selke stayed with the Maple Leafs until 1946, when Smythe forced him out upon returning home at the end of World War II, because he believed Selke was disloyal and plotting to oust him as president of the Gardens. In fact, there was a coup attempt, and Selke had tried to steer clear of the politics involved, but that was not good enough for Smythe.

The Leafs owner was especially enraged when Selke dealt defenceman Frank Eddolls to Montreal for Ted Kennedy. It turned out to be a very astute move by Selke — one of many he made during his years in Toronto — but Smythe was livid that he was not consulted before the deal was made. Smythe later insisted that he wouldn't have blocked the trade, but maintained that he should have been told about it beforehand — not an easy task, considering that he was overseas fighting at the time. The Leafs won the Stanley Cup in 1945 but did not even qualify for the playoffs the following season. That sealed Selke's fate as Smythe held him responsible for the team's decline.

Selke left to become general manager of the Montreal Canadiens, where he built a powerhouse team that won six Stanley Cups, including five in a row between 1956 and 1960, a feat yet to be duplicated. He stayed with the Habs until 1964 and left the team in great shape: it went on to win four Cups between 1965 and 1969. Among other achievements, Selke started the tradition of hockey calendars and was a major contributor to the building of the Hockey Hall of Fame.

Leaf star Syl Apps discusses strategy with Frank Selke. (HHOF)

CONN SMYTHE

CONSTANTINE "CONN" Falkland Kerrys Smythe was born in Toronto on February 1, 1895, and grew up in a modest fashion. He attended the University of Toronto, where he studied engineering and played for the varsity hockey team. Although he was not a great player, Smythe was team captain and his club won the Ontario Hockey Association championship in 1915. He then enlisted in the Canadian Armed Forces and served his country with honour in the Great War; among other decorations for his heroics, he won the Military Cross in 1916. At age 24 he returned home not quite sure what to do with himself. But hockey was still firmly in his veins.

After finishing his studies at U of T Smythe became a manager of sorts for the varsity team. In addition to league play, he would take the team down to Boston, where its well-organized play impressed all who watched. Smythe also started to make a name for himself with his flair for quotable comment. For a time he also managed the U of T varsity graduates and had good results in taking them to the Allan Cup title once and the finals on another occasion. The grads also won an Olympic gold for Canada in St. Moritz, Switzerland, in 1928.

In 1926 the New York Rangers were about to enter the NHL and were looking for a competent manager. Smythe's name was passed on to their owner, Colonel John Hammond, who promptly hired the eager young man. Smythe put together a fine roster of players, including Frank Boucher, Bill and Bun Cook, Ching Johnson, Murray Murdoch and Lorne Chabot, that would win the Stanley Cup by 1928. But Colonel Hammond heard about a player named Cecil "Babe" Dye that Smythe had passed on. After consulting a trusted friend who suggested that anyone who ignored Dye was not much of a hockey man, Hammond acted rather hastily and fired Smythe in favour of Lester Patrick.

A settlement was reached on Smythe's contract, though he later had to complain to the president of Madison Square Garden to get all of the $10,000 he was owed, and he returned to Toronto deter-

mined to make it in pro hockey. To fulfill his dream, Smythe began pursuing the purchase of the Toronto St. Patrick's hockey club. Smythe appealed to the team's owners to not sell the team to Philadelphia interests that were willing to pay $200,000, though his own group of investors was $40,000 short of funds.

He was able to strike a deal with J.P. Bickell, agreeing to let Bickell stay on in the new ownership group providing he left his money in the team. The team name was changed to "Maple Leafs" (a national symbol in Smythe's view, since he had worn it on his army uniform) and the colours were changed to blue and white. It took Smythe one year to get everything together and on February 14, 1927, the Toronto Maple Leafs were officially born.

Just as he had for the Rangers, Smythe signed and traded for quality talent as he tried to make the Maple Leafs the talk of Toronto. A few players, such as Hap Day and Ace Bailey, were kept from the St. Patrick's team but Smythe and his chief aide, Frank Selke, also brought in many new recruits, including Charlie Conacher, Harvey Jackson, Joe Primeau, Andy Blair and Red Horner. Good trades brought Lorne Chabot, Harold Cotton and King Clancy into the fold. When Smythe removed himself from coaching — he readily acknowledged he was not at his best behind the bench — and hired Dick Irvin as bench boss, all the pieces were in place for the Leafs' first Stanley Cup victory, which duly came in 1932.

Another important development was the building of Maple Leaf Gardens. It was not an easy task to erect such a grand building during the Great Depression, but Smythe pulled it off with a little help from his friends. He was fortunate to have mining magnate Bickell still involved with the team: Bickell was very supportive of the Gardens project, and when Smythe secured the land at the corner of Church and Carlton Streets from the Eaton family, Bickell convinced many bankers (including the president of the Imperial Bank of Commerce, Sir John Aird), businessmen and associates to invest. He also provided the financial know-how in issuing Gardens stock, which would eventually be used to pay workers when funds

Conn Smythe addresses his players: (left to right) *King Clancy, Red Horner, William 'Flash' Hollett and George Hainsworth.* (HHOF)

Facing page: *Conn Smythe the hockey player.* (HHOF)

Conn Smythe (wearing the white hat) *was not afraid to mix it up on or off the ice.*
(HHOF)

were running short. Completed in just six months, the Gardens was by far the finest hockey arena in the world. Smythe vowed it would be clean and well-kept and was true to his word. He also promised it would be home to an exciting and winning hockey club and most of the time he was able to keep his word on that, as well.

The Leafs didn't win any more Stanley Cups in the '30s, but they took the championship five times in the '40s and again in 1951. Smythe was never afraid of wheeling and dealing for quality hockey players and often tried to purchase those he coveted most. He was also a hockey innovator who came up with such ideas as charting ice times, tracking plus/minus statistics, filming games, analyzing goals for importance (game winners, for instance) and whether they came against strong or weak teams.

Even though he was plainly the boss, Smythe hired talented people to work for him, such as trainer Tim Daly, coaches Dick Irvin, Hap Day and Joe Primeau, box office manager Harry Bolton, chief scout Squib Walker, publicist Ed Fitkin and his own assistant manager, Frank Selke. He did not scrimp and gave the fans many winners.

Smythe was a short, sturdy man, a mere 5'7" in his cotton socks, but he could instill fear in anybody, especially those in his employ. He did not hesitate to rant at the players, either, for he believed it would give them the incentive they needed to prove him wrong. For example, during the 1933 semifinal series against the Boston Bruins the Leafs were down 2–1 in games when Smythe decided to step in and "motivate" his team. After a quiet team dinner, he rose from his chair and verbally ripped into each and every player. Hap Day was too concerned about his upcoming wedding, Smythe fumed; King Clancy was more interested in entertaining his mother, in from out of town; Charlie Conacher was always complaining about injuries; Harvey Jackson was making plans to go to his summer cottage; and Harold Cotton was afraid to go into the corners. When he was done, he stomped out of the room. The players were angry — but they went out and beat Boston to advance to the finals.

There was no doubt Smythe could hold a grudge, and woe to anyone who directly disobeyed an order. When Leafs forward Johnny McCormack had the audacity to get married during the hockey season, a breach of a strict Smythe rule, he soon found himself in the minors. Smythe did not drink or smoke and expected the Leafs players to conduct themselves accordingly off the ice. When Harvey Jackson began an alcohol-induced descent, Smythe would not back his one-time star for a deserved place in the Hall of Fame. When Leafs captain Jim Thomson was involved in founding the players' association, Smythe called him a traitor and sent him off to the hockey sad sacks known as the Chicago Black Hawks. When he decided that his main lieutenant had been disloyal, Frank Selke had no choice but to resign. But Smythe was also a charitable man who donated large amounts to the Ontario Society for Crippled Children and made sure the team gave its time to many worthy causes, as it still does today. He was a well-known horse owner and breeder and also ran a very successful sand and gravel business, which he bought in the 1920s and which gave employment to many Leafs during the summer.

By the '50s, Smythe was more interested in horses and spending the winters in Florida to help recover from his war wounds than he was in managing the Maple Leafs. Eventually he ceded some power to a hockey committee known as the Silver Seven, while retaining the final say. But soon his son, Stafford, wanted to run the whole show and Conn finally agreed in 1961. He believed that Stafford alone was taking over and paying him $2 million for his shares of the Gardens and the team, but it turned out that Harold Ballard — whom Smythe considered something of a pirate — and John Bassett were also involved in the purchase. This did not sit well with Conn, but there was nothing he could do after the papers were signed. The Leafs' future was sealed and Conn Smythe would soon play no further role in running the franchise. He wanted his grandson Tommy, Stafford's son, to manage the team one day, but this was the one dream he would not see fulfilled during his remarkable life.

Leaf file:

Conn Smythe coined the well-worn hockey phrase, "If you can't beat them in the alley, you can't best them on the ice." He loved tough hockey players and was not above joining the fray himself. On the night Ace Bailey was badly injured in Boston (see page 21), Smythe attacked a Bruins fan that had the audacity to suggest Bailey was faking. Connecting with a wild swing and punch, Smythe was promptly arrested and was held in jail until 2 a.m., when Art Ross, the Bruins manager, helped to spring him once he realized how seriously Bailey was hurt. Smythe eventually reached a settlement with the fan. Another time, Ross accused Smythe of having no class, so the Leafs owner decided to prove him wrong. Before a game in the Boston Garden, Smythe dressed up in

a tuxedo and had one of his players deliver a bouquet of flowers to Ross near the Bruins bench. Attached was a card, written in Latin, which told Ross exactly where he should stick the flowers.

The Business of the Maple Leafs:

When Maple Leaf Gardens opened on the night of November 12, 1931, the total gate was $19,677.50, based on seat prices of $2.75, $1.85, $1.40 and 95 cents with an attendance of 13,233. By the Leafs' third season in the Gardens, 1933–34, total gate receipts were $253,000 for 24 home games. By the mid-60s the Leafs were pulling in some $2 million for 35 home games.

Maple Leaf stats:

		Games	Wins	Losses	Ties
AS COACH:	regular season	176	71	81	24
	playoffs	4	2	2	–
AS GENERAL MANAGER:	regular season	1,665	774	617	274

THE FATHER OF THE LEAFS: CONN SMYTHE, 1895–1980

by Michael McKinley

WHEN THE BOY was just 11 years old, his mother Mary died, broken from alcoholism and general despair. The boy's first name, Constantine, was his mother's maiden name, but he thought it too prim. So when someone pointed out that he had never been christened, the boy seized the chance: from now on he would just be Conn — a rugged, fearless name that he would try to live up to. And so, the child became the father of the man.

Conn Smythe literally was the father of the Leafs, and much of their lore. While photos suggest a spats-wearing free spirit who'd buy you a drink and tell you a joke, the truth is more interesting, and it begins with the hot gleam in his eye. Conn Smythe was a teetotalling warrior who could lead men into battle both on the ice and off it, inspiring them by example and by word to "never say die." He could also make those around him wish for a speedy death should they ever get on his wrong side. And figuring out just what side was the "wrong" or the "right" one of this complex prodigy is what makes Smythe such a compelling figure in the Leafs' pantheon, even now, nearly a quarter century after his death.

He was a patriot, and he was brave. The bantam-weight Smythe was always the smallest kid, anywhere, and had to fight harder for what he wanted: on the street, on the ice, and for his beloved country. He charged the enemy cannon in World War I and again in World War II, by which time he was 47 years old. He was so outraged at the poor training and equipment of Canadian army recruits late in WWII that, while he lay seriously wounded in his hospital bed, he took on the federal government and won better conditions for the grunts fighting the war. They say he saved thousands of lives.

He could spot talent, and often looked for it where no else thought to look. Charlie Conacher, Joe Primeau, Hap Day, Ace Bailey, Red Horner, Turk Broda, Max Bentley, Lorne Chabot, Busher Jackson, Teeder Kennedy, Syl Apps and King Clancy are some of hockey's greatest stars and just a few of Smythe's catches.

He was a forgiving bigot. The son of Belfast Protestants, Smythe publicly mistrusted both Catholics and francophones, whom he saw as being loyal to something other than King and Country. He once began an after-dinner speech with, "Ladies, Gentlemen, and Frenchmen," yet he briefly overlooked Rocket Richard's dodgy birthright when he tried — and failed — to woo the Canadiens star to Toronto. Yet he also paid the tuition of future Leafs studying at St. Michael's College high school in Toronto, a Roman Catholic hockey factory.

He was an unforgiving moralist. If a player crossed Smythe's concept of the team — or of how a Canadian "gentleman" should behave — he was gone. One such victim was Harvey "Busher" Jackson, a silky golden boy on the Leafs "Kid Line" in the 1930s. When Jackson later had problems with alcohol and was reduced to begging outside Maple Leaf Gardens, Smythe saw him no longer as a Leaf but as a degenerate to be shunned. Despite repeated calls for Jackson to be named to the Hall of Fame, Smythe blocked each initiative until the day he died.

He was a calculated gambler. Smythe had bet his New York Rangers severance pay on a hockey match to win money to buy the Leafs and he bet on his own winless nag Rare Jewel to buy Francis "King" Clancy and give his Leafs a marquee name. Still, he had star defenceman Walter "Babe" Pratt suspended for gambling, only coming to his senses when the Babe said he'd never bet on his own team.

Smythe was a devoted family man. A virgin despite being a war veteran when he married his beloved Irene, he became the proud father of five children. He hoped the Leafs would be a family dynasty, but his son Stafford went into disastrous partnership with Harold Ballard and died a ruin at age 50. It was the great sorrow of the elder Smythe's life.

In the end, Conn Smythe was a hockey man of unparalleled genius who built a dynasty on the back of his own romantic fearlessness. He vowed to create a team in Toronto worthy of the palace he would build for it, and he did, as the Depression felled titans around him. He said his team would win the Stanley Cup in its first season in Maple Leaf Gardens, and it did. Then he dared the others to come and take the glittering silver cup away from the boys in the blue and white, his University of Toronto colours — the boys wear-

Conn Smythe always believed his team had to best the opposition in the alley, so this 1970 brawl against Boston would have pleased him. (AP)

ing that maple leaf, the one worn by Smythe and his fellow soldiers in World War I, the one that became the emblem of his country.

When people speak of the Leafs as "Canada's Team" it is because the larger-than-life Smythe made them national heroes. And perhaps his greatest stroke of inspiration was to give them their own Homer, in the form of a radio announcer named Foster Hewitt, whom Smythe lodged in the fancifully named "Gondola" high above the ice at the Gardens. Hewitt's radio play-by-play cut through the howling winter nights from Newfoundland to BC, and the Leafs took root in the national imagination, becoming English Canada's last bastion against the perfidious Montreal Canadiens and the Yanks. The fact the Leafs won seven Stanley Cups under Smythe's tenure didn't hurt, either, and he even broke his no-booze

rule to sip champagne from "the Jug." It was pure Smythian symbolism: the triumph of Christian virtue mixed with the quenchless thirst of the poor, motherless kid who'd had to fight for everything and anything.

Smythe's complex character was the smithy that forged "Canada's Team," and that heroic and belligerent spirit still colours the franchise today. This can make some people wary of the Leafs, who carry Smythe's genes — thinking themselves a virtuous breed apart, fighting a just cause, suspicious that those who are not with them are unpatriotic or worse. But the Leafs won't give up on their doubters there: instead, they will happily fight you the hard way, in some dirty alley if they must, to win you over on the ice. It was Conn Smythe's motto. And they are still Conn Smythe's team.

The '40s was the most successful decade in Leafs history. Shrewd trading and

player development brought the team a wealth of talent that was the envy of the National

Hockey League. The decade was overshadowed by the horrors of World War II and Leafs

players and managers gave of themselves to defeat enemies in Europe.

This did not stop the team from winning five Stanley Cups, in 1942,

1945, 1947, 1948 and 1949. The success was built upon

strong management and coaching, with the same people

running the team for the entire decade. The one notable

departure was that of Frank Selke in 1946, but he had

put many pieces in place to keep the Leafs on top,

and Conn Smythe and Hap Day filled in any gaps.

Here is how the Leafs ruled the NHL for

this decade.

Facing page: The Maple Leafs have just won the 1947 Stanley Cup by beating the Montreal Canadiens and the celebration is about to start as (left to right) Garth Boesch, Harry Watson, Bill Ezinicki, Syl Apps and Joe Klukay get ready to leap onto the ice. (HHOF)

Goalie Frank "Ulcers" McCool recorded three consecutive shutouts (1–0, 2–0 and 1–0) in the 1945 finals against Detroit when the Leafs won the Stanley Cup in seven games. The native of Calgary, Alberta posted a 34–31–7 record in two seasons with the Leafs. (HHOF)

Leafs captain Syl Apps shared in three Stanley Cup wins with the Leafs while coach *Hap Day* (right) *took his club to the championship five times. In this photo, both men celebrate the 1942 miracle win over Detroit.* (HHOF)

Management and Coaching

The most important move the Leafs made was to bring in former Toronto player Hap Day to coach the team after Dick Irvin left for Montreal. The players respected Day. His "defence first" style wasn't always pretty, but Day believed that holding a team to two goals or less in every game was possible, and he was confident that he had just enough offence in players like Syl Apps, Walter "Babe" Pratt and Ted Kennedy. The Leafs were certainly aggressive and were not afraid to go to youth, as they did in 1947. Most of all, the Leafs were always prepared for the playoffs.

Smythe was officially the team's general manager but these duties often fell to Selke while the Leafs owner was away in Europe. It all worked pretty well until Smythe returned from the war and suspected a coup to remove him from the presidency of the Gardens might be brewing. He soon alienated Selke, who left for Montreal (reuniting with Irvin), but Smythe was confident he could do the job without his longtime assistant. The team flourished in the late '40s without Selke, but the next 10 years would be a different story.

Best Trades and Acquisitions

Smythe was on top of his game in the trading of players, picking up Babe Pratt, Harry Watson and Cal Gardner — all of whom scored Cup-winning goals — in terrific deals. Selke acquired Ted Kennedy — who also scored a Cup winner — in a deal with the Canadiens without consulting Smythe, much to Smythe's displeasure. Kennedy turned out to be perhaps the greatest Leaf of all time and eventually became team captain.

Lorne Carr came to the Leafs from New York and made his mark by scoring goals while winger Bill Ezinicki (picked up from the minors) and defenceman Bill Juzda (acquired from the Rangers) were a physical presence. Turk Broda, Gord Drillon, Sweeney Schriner and Wally Stanowski, all picked up in trades in the previous decade, also played a strong role on the championship teams of the '40s. Bill Barilko, Garth Boesch, Howie Meeker and Gus Bodnar were excellent free-agent signings, while the junior teams — which now included the St. Michael's College Majors — continued to produce high-quality players like Bob Davidson, Nick Metz, Gus Mortson, Jim Thomson and Gaye Stewart. The Leafs had so much depth that they could afford to trade five players to the needy Chicago Black Hawks for one star in Max Bentley.

Notable Events

Any look at the '40s has to start with the 1942 finals against Detroit. The Leafs were down 3–0 in games and had to win the fourth in Detroit. Inspired by player changes made by Day, they stormed back to tie the series and then won the seventh game 3–1 at the Gardens on a winning goal by Pete Langelle. This spectacular comeback — the greatest in Stanley Cup history — captured the hearts and

Leafs stars of the '40s (in uniform, left to right): Gus Bodnar, Bob Goldham, Harry Watson, Bud Poile and Gaye Stewart. (HHOF)

minds of Canadians and provided a welcome diversion in the middle of the war effort.

Smythe and his team should also be recognized for their off-ice contribution to Canada during World War II. A World War I veteran, Smythe was in his mid-forties at the time, but that did not stop him from going overseas once more. He also encouraged his players to enlist, and many did.

Back on the ice, other notable events included a five-goal game by rookie Meeker, a six-assist game by Pratt and a goal by Bodnar just 15 seconds into his first NHL game. The Leafs were the first NHL team to win the Cup for three straight seasons and showed the rest of the league how a quality organization should be run.

Worst of the Decade

There were some disappointing moments for the Leafs despite all the success. One low point occurred in the 1944 playoff semifinals, when Montreal star Maurice "Rocket" Richard set an NHL record by scoring five goals against the Leafs in one game. The Habs went on to knock out the Leafs with a resounding 11–0 victory. After winning the Stanley Cup in surprising fashion in 1945, the Leafs missed the playoffs in 1946; this was a big shock, but served as the impetus for change to start the run of three consecutive championships.

Another low point was Babe Pratt's suspension for gambling, although he was eventually reinstated. But the biggest blow was the retirement of centre Syl Apps. One of the greatest captains in Leafs history, Apps decided to go out on top after the 1948 Cup victory. After scoring 201 career goals, Apps was certainly missed, although the impact of his loss was not that bad since the Leafs had acquired another centre in Bentley.

The decade ended on a down note when the Leafs lost the 1950 finals in seven games to Detroit, which used an injury to Gordie Howe as inspiration to deny the hated Leafs a fourth straight Cup. Kennedy was unjustly blamed by some for Howe's injury (a serious hit to the head when he crashed into the boards), and the Leafs had to expend a great deal of energy fighting off the Red Wings' physical assault in retaliation.

Bottom-line Results

It would be difficult to call any decade in which five Stanley Cups are won anything but a resounding success. The Leafs' record from 1940–41 to 1949–50 (which also happens to be the exact time time frame that Day coached the team) was a highly respectable 259–206–81 and is even more impressive given that many players missed dozens of games (and entire seasons) because of the war. The Leafs nearly lost the Cup to Detroit in 1945 after leading the series 3–0 but came back to win the seventh game. They won the first of three straight Cups by beating rival Montreal in the 1947 finals. They finished first in 1947–48 with a 32–15–13 record and waltzed to the Cup in just nine games; Smythe always said this was the best team he ever managed. The Leafs also won the Cup after a fourth-place regular-season finish in 1948–49.

Best Leafs of the Decade

IN GOAL: Turk Broda, with honourable mention to Frank "Ulcers" McCool, who recorded three shutouts in the 1945 finals.

ON DEFENCE: Babe Pratt, Wally Stanowski and Bill Barilko.

AT FORWARD: Syl Apps, Max Bentley, Gaye Stewart, Gord Drillon, Bob Davidson, Lorne Carr, Sweeney Schriner, Nick Metz and Howie Meeker.

Max Bentley (left) enjoys a soft drink and a laugh with teammate Turk Broda. (HB)

SYL APPS

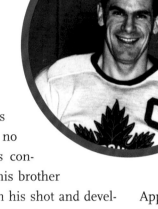

Like many Canadian boys, Syl Apps began playing hockey with the encouragement of his father, Ernest. In fact his father wanted him to excel at all sports and young Syl did become a local athletic legend in his hometown of Paris, Ontario, but there was no doubt that hockey was special. Ernest Apps constructed a rink in the backyard and Syl and his brother would practise there for hours. Syl worked on his shot and developed his smooth skating style with consistent hard work. Ernest Apps died when Syl was only 16 years old, but the son would more than fulfill his father's dreams.

Apps was such a good athlete that he was selected to compete for Canada at the 1936 Olympic Games in Berlin, Germany. He finished sixth in the pole vault there and went on to win the event at the British Empire Games. The six-foot, 173-pound Apps was also a very good baseball and football player, and it was while he was playing halfback at McMaster University in Hamilton, where he was studying political economy, that he came to the attention of Leafs manager Conn Smythe.

Smythe was watching a McMaster football game and was impressed with captain Apps, who displayed brawn, brains and personality in leading the team. The Toronto owner left his wife in the stands and went to find a phone so that he could add Apps to the Leafs' protected list. Smythe was a little concerned about Apps' lack of hockey experience, even though the young student also played hockey at McMaster. Apps joined the Hamilton Tigers of the senior Ontario Hockey Association and won a scoring title in 1935–36 when he had 38 points (22 goals, 16 assists) in just 19 games.

After signing with the Leafs on September 2, 1936, Apps began his NHL career by scoring 15 goals in his rookie season, 1936–37, adding 29 assists, the highest in the league. His 45-point total (in 46 games) placed him second in NHL scoring, behind Sweeney Schriner of the New York Americans, and earned him the Calder Trophy as rookie of the year. And Apps was just getting started. In 1937–38 he once again finished second (to teammate Gord

Drillon) in league scoring, with 50 points (21 goals, 29 assists) in 47 games.

The next three seasons were still pretty productive but injuries held him back. He fractured his collarbone in 1939–40 and played only 27 games, recording 30 points; a knee injury in 1940–41 kept him out of seven games, though he still managed 20 goals and 44 points in 41 appearances. Apps racked up 41 points in 38 games in 1941–42, despite being hampered by an ankle injury. In the playoffs he was outstanding as the Leafs won their second Stanley Cup, leading all post-season scorers with 14 points (five goals, nine assists). Apps showed great leadership as team captain when the club was down 3–0 to Detroit in the finals and led the Leafs to a remarkable comeback.

Great skating was the heart of Apps' game. He could glide up the ice with an effortless stride and his great shot got him many goals. He could not be riled very often during games, but opponents knew to look out if he got mad: he could be physical when challenged. Although linemates like Bob Davidson and Bill Ezinicki usually handled the rough stuff, Apps was not afraid to mix it up when the time came. He once took on Jimmy Orlando of the Red Wings twice in one brawl-filled playoff game and went after Joe Cooper, a big Chicago defenceman. But generally Apps played in a gentlemanly fashion, and comported himself in the same way off the ice. He did not drink or smoke and the worst language he is reported to have used when angry was "by hum." Smythe was proud to have Apps as team captain because he inspired the values the Leafs owner wanted to see in all his players.

Apps played 29 games for the Leafs in 1942–43 and then went off to help in the war effort for the next two years. When he returned to the club in 1945–46, he quickly shook off the rust and scored 24 times in 40 games. The next two seasons were Apps' best in a Leafs uniform in terms of goal scoring, with 25 in 1946–47 (earning 49 points) and 26 in 1947–48 (earning his best ever points total of 53) as the team took two straight Cups.

Then, at the height of his playing career, the Leafs captain

Syl Apps (second from left) captained the Leafs to three Stanley Cup wins, in 1942, 1947 and 1948. Here he poses with other Leafs captains: (left to right) Bob Davidson, Ted Kennedy and Hap Day. (HHOF)

decided to retire and pursue a life in public service. There is no doubt that Apps could have kept playing and the Leafs did everything they could to persuade him to remain, but his mind was made up. He was determined to go out on his terms and leave a winner.

In 1949 Apps was named Father of the Year (he gave the $100 prize to charity), and in 1963 he was elected for the first of three terms to represent the Conservative party in the Ontario legislature.

He was well-respected as corrections minister under Premier Bill Davis and later served as athletics commissioner for Ontario.

The last years of his life were difficult, as he contracted an incurable neurological illness that took away his speech and ability to walk. He remained very alert, however, and found ways to understand and communicate. When he died on December 24, 1998, Canadians mourned a true sports legend and hero.

Leaf file:

Syl Apps knew he was going to retire at the end of the 1947–48 season and, although he considered himself a team player, he liked the idea of finishing his career with 200 goals, quite an accomplishment in that era. On the last night of the season, March 21, 1948, Apps had 198 goals and the Leafs were in Detroit. He scored career goal 199 when the puck hit his skate and bounced into the net. Then Harry Watson and Bill Ezinicki set Apps up for his 200th. Watson was clear in front and could have scored himself, but he spotted the slick centre open near the Detroit net and wanted to help out his teammate: Apps obliged by making no mistake in beating Detroit goalie Harry Lumley. Apps later said that he blasted the puck as hard as he could for that goal. He retrieved the puck and was mobbed by his teammates while the Red Wings fans gave him a roaring ovation. To top off the evening, Apps scored another by taking the puck through two Detroit defenders and then shooting past Lumley into the far corner of the net. It was Apps' 201st and last goal as a Leaf.

Facing page: *Syl Apps (with captain's 'C' on sweater) has just set up teammate Sid Smith (standing beside net), who is about to put the puck into the New York Rangers net.* (HHOF)

Above: *Toronto's Syl Apps puts a shot past Frank Brimsek of the Boston Bruins.* (HHOF)

Inset: *Syl Apps tries to swat the puck past Montreal goaltender Bill Durnan.* (HHOF)

Maple Leaf stats:	GP	G	A	P	PIM
regular season	423	201	231	432	56
playoffs	69	25	29	54	8

MAX BENTLEY

CONN SMYTHE needed a replacement when star centre Syl Apps was planning to retire after the 1947–48 season. Knowing that the cellar-dwelling Chicago Black Hawks were in desperate need of players, he decided to journey to Chicago to try to acquire Max Bentley.

Smythe knew he would have to make Black Hawks manager Bill Tobin a great offer, so he tempted him with a whole Leafs line — the so-called "Flying Forts": Bud Poile, Gaye Stewart and Gus Bodnar — plus defenceman Ernie Dickens. When Tobin asked for defenceman Bob Goldham as well, Smythe resisted at first, then relented. Chicago threw in forward Cy Thomas to complete the five-for-two trade on November 2, 1947.

Bentley was scoring leader in Chicago, winning the Art Ross Trophy twice (with 61 points in 1945–46 and 72 in 1946–47). With his arrival the Leafs boasted the finest set of centremen in the NHL. Ted Kennedy, Apps and Bentley formed one of the greatest trios in NHL history and the Leafs took the 1947–48 Cup with all three playing a prominent role. Bentley recorded 48 points (23 goals, 25 assists) in 53 games and added 11 points in nine playoff games. With the retirement of Apps, Bentley and Kennedy were joined by Cal Gardner at centre and the Leafs won two more Cups (1949 and 1951) with the new triumvirate. Bentley never won another scoring title as a Leaf, but posted 23-, 19-, 23-, 21- and 24-goal seasons. In 1950–51 Bentley earned 62 points in 67 games, the third-best in the NHL and his best total in Toronto. He might have scored more with another team, but the Leafs always stressed defence first.

Bentley was lucky to be in the NHL at all after a tryout with the Montreal Canadiens detected a heart problem. At 5'10" and 155 pounds he was also considered too small and many teams shied away from the Delisle, Saskatchewan native. Bentley had developed his superb puck-handling skills playing on the frozen fields around his family farm. His strong wrists, built up by milking cows, allowed him to shoot the puck with speed and accuracy. He and his brother, Doug, were local legends. Their father did not want his sons to leave the farm, but the lure of big-league hockey was strong and Doug finally landed a job with the Chicago Black Hawks. He convinced management to give his brother a chance and Max quickly proved that he could handle himself in the NHL. He became known as "the Dipsy Doodle Dandy" (they said he could literally dance on his skates) and nobody questioned his heart any more.

Bentley was a worrier by nature and that probably shortened his career. He played well for Toronto in 1951–52 (24 goals and 41 points in 69 games), but in the next year he scored just 12 goals and took some time off because he felt he was playing poorly. The Leafs sold him to the New York Rangers in 1953 and he retired from the NHL soon after. Bentley returned to Saskatchewan, where he played hockey for three more seasons and tried coaching. He was elected to the Hall of Fame in 1966.

Max Bentley (with alternate captain's 'A' on sweater) tries to beat Detroit defenceman Leo Reise Jr. to a loose puck. (HHOF)

Maple Leaf stats:	GP	G	A	P	PIM
regular season	354	122	134	256	136
playoffs	40	14	24	38	8

GUS BODNAR

No player in Leafs history ever had as memorable a start to his career as centre Gus Bodnar did on the night of October 30, 1943. The Leafs were facing the New York Rangers to open the 1943–44 season at Maple Leaf Gardens and the native of Fort William, Ontario, went out to centre ice to take the opening faceoff. He took off right from the draw and carried the puck between the New York defencemen, then fired it past Rangers goalie Ken McAuley 15 seconds into the game. The goal set a speed record for players appearing in their first game that still stands today. It would be the start of a great season for Bodnar.

Bodnar was surprised to even make the team in his rookie year. He was a brash kid, who tried to impress everyone with his stick-handling at training camp until hard-rock Leafs blueliner Wilfred "Bucko" McDonald nailed the 5'10", 160-pound Bodnar with a bodycheck. He carried Bodnar to the bench and told the newcomer to stop trying to embarrass the veterans on the team — and to get a haircut. Bodnar followed the instructions. He also learned to keep his head up when he carried the puck. He ended his rookie year with 22 goals (his highest total with the Leafs) and 40 assists. His 62 points made him tenth in league scoring and he won the Calder Trophy as the best rookie in the NHL, the third Leaf to win the award. The next season Bodnar scored only eight times, but he had a very respectable 36 assists and added three goals in the playoffs on the way to winning the Stanley Cup.

Bodnar recorded 37 points in 49 games in 1945–46, when the Leafs missed the playoffs. A second Cup was in the offing in 1946–47, but he managed only four goals and 10 points in the regular season and played in just one playoff game. By this point the Leafs had eyes for Chicago centre Max Bentley, and Bodnar and his linemates Gaye Stewart and Bud Poile were deemed expendable. He played seven seasons in Chicago and saw why the Black Hawks were perennial basement dwellers, making the playoffs only once. He did have one memorable night with Chicago — on March 23, 1952 — when he assisted on all three goals that winger Bill Mosienko scored in 21 seconds to set an NHL record. Bodnar had softened up Ranger goalie Lorne Anderson earlier by scoring just 44 seconds into the game.

Bodnar was traded to Boston in 1954 and the 1954–55 season was his last in the NHL. He finished with a respectable 142 career goals and 396 points in 667 games played. Bodnar then tried his hand at coaching and was the mentor of the Toronto Marlboros when they won the Memorial Cup in 1967 with a team that included future Leafs Brian Glennie, Mike Pelyk, Gerry Meehan, Doug Acomb and Mike Byers. In 1978 he coached the Canadian entry at the world junior championships, a bronze-medal-winning team that featured a young man named Wayne Gretzky.

🍁

Gus Bodnar is presented with the Calder Trophy as the NHL's best rookie for his performance in the 1943–44 season. [HHOF]

Maple Leaf stats:	GP	G	A	P	PIM
regular season	187	48	105	153	60
playoffs	19	3	1	4	4

WALTER 'TURK' BRODA

BORN ON MAY 15, 1914, Walter Broda was a rather chubby kid who wanted nothing more than to play hockey in his hometown of Brandon, Manitoba. He was not selected for the school team because he was an awful skater, but they needed someone to play in net and Broda happily took the job. The kid they called "Turkey Egg" (later shortened to "Turk") because of the freckles on his face soon showed an excellent sense of timing when he had to make a save. He never left the nets again for the rest of his hockey career.

Broda won his first big test at a provincial playoff in Winnipeg for a local team in 1931. In 1932 his family moved to Winnipeg and Broda played in goal for the Winnipeg Monarchs of the Manitoba Junior Hockey League. His junior career caught the attention of Detroit scout Gene Houghton and he signed a form locking him into the Red Wings system. When he attended his first training camp with Detroit the Red Wings were stacked in goal, with veterans John Ross Roach and Normie Smith. There was no room for Broda so he was sent to play for the Detroit Olympics of the International Hockey League for the 1935–36 season. He did very well there, with a 28–18–3 record in 47 appearances. The team went on to win the championship in the playoffs with Broda allowing only eight goals in six games and posting a 1.32 goals-against average.

Watching the last playoff game was Maple Leafs manager Conn Smythe, who took note of Broda's performance, in which he let in only one goal. As it happened, the Leafs were thinking about bringing in some net competition for the declining George Hainsworth. The Red Wings were more than willing to move one of their extra goalies and tried to pawn off on Smythe a netminder named Earl Robertson. But the Leafs owner had watched Robertson let in eight goals in the same game, so he wisely asked for the rights to Broda instead, purchasing them for $8,000. The Leafs' goaltending concerns were taken care of for more than 14 years with the completion of that transaction. If Detroit manager and long-time arch-enemy of Smythe's, Jack Adams, had known how Broda would come back to haunt him in the years to come, he would never have sold him to the Maple Leafs.

Broda started his career with Toronto in 1936–37 and quickly won the number one goaltending job from Hainsworth: the veteran was released just three games into the season. Broda proved worthy of the vote of confidence by posting a 22–19–4 record, with three shutouts and a 2.30 goals-against average.

He had many strong points, not the least of which was his ability to bounce back from a bad goal or bad game. For example, his first game as a Maple Leaf was against the Detroit Red Wings at the Gardens on November 5, 1936. He gave up one goal to Syd Howe of the Red Wings, then Detroit's Larry Aurie took a shot from near centre ice that somehow trickled through Broda's pads and into the net. He had played well to that point, but the fluke goal hushed the Gardens crowd and made them question the new goalie. The game ended as a 3–1 loss for the Leafs. But a few days later, on November 14, Broda bounced back to win his first NHL game with a 6–2 victory over the Chicago Black Hawks at the Gardens.

Broda was known for his great playoff performances and took five Stanley Cups while with the Leafs. A "money" goaltender always rises to the occasion and Broda first did so against the Red Wings in 1942, when the Leafs were down 3–0 in games during the finals. He virtually shut the door in the last four games, ending with a 3–0 shutout in game 6 and allowing a single marker in game 7, a 3–1 Leafs victory. It was sweet revenge for Broda, who had lost in the finals in 1938, 1939 and 1940. From then on he never lost in the finals again and took the Cup in 1947, 1948 and 1949. He also had a hand in the Leafs' 1951 triumph. By the time his career was over Broda had played in 101 playoff games for the Leafs and won 59 of them.

Always a portly type (although his excess weight never seemed to hurt him), Broda became famous for his "battle of the bulge" during the 1949–50 season when Smythe ordered the netminder to lose some poundage — or else! His weight battle became front-page material: diet charts were produced and his wife was inter-

Turk Broda slides across his crease, hoping to stop Edgar Laparde (number 10) of the New York Rangers before he has a shot at an open net. (AP)

Leaf file:

In his career with the Leafs Turk Broda twice won the Vezina Trophy, given at that time to the goalie who allowed the fewest goals against his team. The second time he took the award came down to the final night of the 1947–48 season. The Leafs and Detroit had fought for first place all through the season, and the Leafs were leading by one game going into the last week, with Broda locked in a fierce battle with the Red Wings' Harry Lumley for the Vezina Trophy.

They were tied at 138 goals allowed, although the Leafs had played one more game. Then Lumley earned a shutout in the last week, maintaining the tie, so it all came down to the last weekend of the season and a home-and-home series between Toronto and Detroit. Ted Kennedy scored two as the Leafs won the first game 5–3 at the Gardens. Then Toronto took the second game 5–2, thanks to a career-ending hat trick by Syl Apps. The Leafs finished in first place and Broda secured his second Vezina Trophy.

No wonder Conn Smythe felt the 1947–48 Leafs were his greatest team.

Turk Broda looks behind him to see if he has stopped a shot by Montreal's 'Rocket' Richard. (HHOF)

viewed, and when he hit his target the headline in the *Toronto Star* read "Broda hits 190!" That number was interesting, considering Broda was listed at 5'9" and 180 pounds in his official NHL record. The new, svelte Broda went out and won his first game 1–0.

The Leafs honoured him with a new car and a special night after he retired in 1951. He became a respected junior coach, taking the Toronto Marlies to the Memorial Cup championship in 1955 and 1956, and helping produce future Leafs such as Bob Pulford, Bob Baun, Billy Harris, Bob Nevin and Carl Brewer. Despite this impressive record, a much hoped-for job as coach of the Maple Leafs never developed.

Broda was elected to the Hall of Fame in 1967.

Maple Leaf stats:	GP	Wins	Losses	Ties	Shutouts	GA
regular season	629	302	224	101	62	2.53
playoffs	101	59	40	1	13	1.97

Turk Borda was a two-time winner of the Vezina Trophy and a two-time NHL first-team all-star. (HB)

LORNE CARR

RIGHT-WINGER LORNE CARR was kicking around professional hockey for a number of years before he got his big chance with the New York Americans in the 1934–35 season. A native of Stoughton, Saskatchewan, Carr was teamed with fellow westerner Sweeney Schriner and centre Art Chapman to create a line that became the Americans' main threat for the next few seasons. Carr was a consistent player who averaged 14 goals a year, and one season his overtime goal eliminated the arch-rival Rangers in the playoffs. His career was nearly ended by a check from Boston's Eddie Shore: Carr suffered a bad cut on his head when he crashed to the ice, but escaped with a concussion and was back after just a couple of games. By the early '40s the Americans were in trouble (the 1941–42 season was their last in the NHL), but luckily for Carr the Toronto Maple Leafs came along and rescued him.

To secure Carr's services the Leafs entered into an interesting deal in which they lent players Red Heron, Nick Nott and Gus Marker to the New York club for one year. The Leafs also sent the Americans some cash and forward Jack Church to close the "future considerations" portion of the trade. The Leafs reunited Carr with his old linemate Schriner, and he quickly returned to form, helping the Leafs in their unbelievable comeback in the 1942 finals against Detroit. In 13 postseason games that year Carr had three goals and five points, scoring a key goal in the fourth game of the series to keep the Leafs' hopes alive against the Red Wings and assisting on two goals by Schriner in the seventh game. Carr then earned first-team all-star honours in 1942–43 when he had 27 goals and 60 points in 50 contests (good for fifth best in the scoring race), and again in 1943–44 when he produced a 36-goal, 38-assist season and the third-best point total in the league. It was pretty clear the Leafs had stolen a gem from a sinking ship.

At 5'8" and 161 pounds Carr was not a big man, but he had a smooth, gentlemanly style of play and a knack for showing up at just the right moment to score a goal. Above all, he was known as a very hard worker. When the 1944–45 season began, Carr was playing with Gus Bodnar at centre and the combination produced a 21-goal season for the winger, with 46 points in 47 games played. The Leafs took the Stanley Cup once again in 1945 by knocking off Montreal and then Detroit; Carr contributed two goals and two assists in the playoffs that spring, all against the Canadiens. The 1945–46 campaign was his last in Toronto and he played in 42 games, scoring five times and notching his 200th career goal against Boston. He played his last game as a Leaf on March 16, 1946, a 7–3 win over Detroit. After retiring from hockey, Carr ran a hotel in Calgary.

🍁

Lorne Carr led the Leafs in points twice in his career, with 60 in 1942–43 (tied with Billy Taylor) and 74 in 1943–44. (HHOF)

Maple Leaf stats:	GP	G	A	P	PIM
regular season	236	105	121	226	37
playoffs	37	6	7	13	11

BOB DAVIDSON

BOB DAVIDSON was born in Toronto on February 10, 1912, and grew up in the east end of the city. He played junior hockey for the Toronto Canoe Club between 1928 and 1932 while working as an office boy in a meat packing plant. Davidson attended the opening game at Maple Leaf Gardens in 1931 with his father and was very impressed with the bright lights and sight-lines. For the 1932–33 season Davidson split his time between the Toronto Marlboros of the Ontario Hockey Association (21 games) and the Toronto City Services team of the Toronto Mercantile Hockey League (18 games), scoring a combined 19 goals and 32 points. He played briefly for the Marlboro senior team the next season and then spent most of 1934–35 with Syracuse of the International Hockey League, though he did manage to play in five games for the Maple Leafs that year.

When the sturdy 5'11", 185-pound left-winger went to the Leafs camp in 1935 he got a chance to stick with the big club when a knee injury sidelined Buzz Boll. From that time on Davidson was with the Maple Leafs for the rest of his life. He made a name for himself as a steady, dependable checker who could pot the occasional goal — his best goal-scoring year was 1943–44, when he scored 19 times. He was given the assignment of looking out for the Leafs' top player and centre, Syl Apps, on a line that also featured scorer Gord Drillon. Davidson was the digger on the line and he carried out his duties very well by showing good judgement; Davidson was good at avoiding foolish penalties even though he was often cast in a checking role. He was respected as much for his leadership as for his play on the ice, and when Apps went away to fight in World War II Davidson was named team captain, a post he held until Apps returned. In 1945, Davidson's last year as captain, the Leafs won the Stanley Cup.

One of his great moments came in the 1942 playoffs with the Leafs down 3–0 in games to Detroit and losing 2–0 in the fourth. Badly in need of a goal, Davidson got one past Johnny Mowers in the Detroit net and — suddenly — the Leafs had some life. Lorne Carr tied the game and, even though the Red Wings took the lead, goals by Apps and Don Metz brought the Leafs their first win of the series by a score of 4–3. They followed up with 9–3, 3–0 and 3–1 victories to cap an incredible comeback. But it might never have happened if Davidson had not stemmed the tide by scoring that first goal in Detroit.

His last good year with the Leafs was in 1944–45, when he had 17 goals and 18 assists in 50 games. He played 41 games the next year, scoring nine times and earning 18 points, but the Leafs missed the playoffs. Management decided to bring in a lot of new players for the next season and Davidson was out of a job.

He turned to coaching in the minor leagues with St. Louis and Pittsburgh, but found his way back to the Maple Leafs as a scout and stayed there for the rest of his working days. Davidson became the Leafs' chief scout and helped to bring players like Frank Mahovlich to Toronto. His long and meritorious service was recognized by the Leafs in 1995 when he was given the J. P. Bickell Trophy by the board of directors. The award, given in recognition of outstanding contributions by a player or management staff member, was awarded only three times in the '90s.

Bob Davidson was captain of the Leafs between 1943 and 1945. (HHOF)

I played with a great bunch of guys and we had a couple of Stanley Cups.

Being a Maple Leaf is definitely something special.

Bob Davidson, Leafs playoff program, 1995

Leaf file:

As one of the best-checking wingers on the Leafs (and in the NHL), Davidson was frequently assigned to cover the opposition's best player. On the night of March 23, 1944, he had the task of shadowing the great Maurice "Rocket" Richard of the Montreal Canadiens during a playoff game at the Montreal Forum. Halfway through the second period, Davidson was doing just fine and the Rocket had not scored. Then, when the Leafs captain had Richard pinned against the boards, a Canadiens fan reached over and grabbed Davidson's stick. Despite an appeal to referee Eddie Chadwick there was no whistle, and while Davidson was retrieving his lumber, the Rocket got away to score his first of five goals that night. Davidson was on the ice for all five goals that got past Leafs goalie Paul Bibeault. The Habs won 5–1 and took the series in five games.

When Bob Davidson finished his playing career he tried coaching in the minor leagues, then became a scout for the Leafs in 1951. (HHOF)

Maple Leaf stats:	GP	G	A	P	PIM
regular season	491	94	160	254	398
playoffs	82	5	17	22	79

BILL EZINICKI

BY THE MID-40S the Toronto Maple Leafs had a tough hockey club shaped by the philosophy of manager Conn Smythe and coach Hap Day. The team was especially physical along the blue line, with Gus Mortson, Bill Barilko, Jim Thompson and Garth Boesch making life difficult for opposing forwards. The toughness on the forward lines started and ended with Winnipeg native Bill Ezinicki.

Nicknamed "Wild Bill," Ezinicki was as tough as they come in an era when hockey was "a man's game." The bruising right-winger was not very big at 5'10" and 170 pounds, but he was extremely powerful and not afraid to hurl himself into anyone wearing the opposing uniform. He was known for his free skating style and his tremendously strong arms. Ezinicki loved to get in players' faces and thought dishing out a solid bodycheck was as good as scoring a goal. His style of play made him very popular in Toronto and a hated man in every other NHL arena.

Ezinicki left Winnipeg in 1942 to play junior hockey in Ontario for the Oshawa Generals. He was a pretty good goal scorer, with 21 in 16 games in his first season and 38 in 25 games in his second. The Generals lost the Memorial Cup final in 1943 to the Winnipeg Rangers, but took the championship the following year when they beat the Trail Smoke Eaters at Maple Leaf Gardens. The Generals were coached by former Leafs great Charlie Conacher and included players from the St. Michael's Majors. Ezinicki scored just seven seconds into the first game of the 1944 series, setting the tone for a four-game sweep of 9–2, 5–2, 15–4 and 11–4. The tough right-winger contributed 12 postseason goals for the Generals and caught the attention of the Maple Leafs brass, who promptly acquired rights to him. Ezinicki played eight games for the Leafs in 1944–45, scoring one goal and five points; he played 24 games the next year and produced a very respectable 12 points.

The 1946–47 season saw Ezinicki play in 60 contests and start to make his mark on the league by racking up 93 penalty minutes.

He scored 17 times and earned 37 points for the first of three straight Cups Ezinicki won with the Leafs. His penalty-minute totals rose to 97, 145 and 144, which kept his place on the Leafs very secure, especially as he was on the line with captain Syl Apps. Ezinicki was ordered to protect Apps at all times and he did that and more.

His physical play often got him into trouble, but the Leafs were quick to defend their tough guy. One time Ezinicki went after New York Rangers star Edgar Laparde, and the Rangers insisted that the Leafs winger had deliberately elbowed and high-sticked their player with the purpose of injuring him. Conn Smythe, who had arranged for all Leafs games to be filmed, insisted that the check was legal and urged the Rangers to view the film if they wished. "And you might learn how a good bodycheck is delivered," he chortled. The Rangers asked NHL president Clarence Campbell for a suspension but none was forthcoming because Campbell agreed with Smythe. It was a vindication of sorts for Ezinicki, who studied how to deliver a proper check from the front, where he felt he could inflict the most damage. Timing was everything in delivering his hits and his low centre of gravity gave Ezinicki a great platform to launch his assaults. He nailed Metro Prystai of Chicago with a check similar to the one that hurt Laparde and hit Montreal's Maurice Richard so hard that the Canadiens star went wild in a retaliation attempt. Richard earned a one-game suspension and a $250 fine for his actions, right in the middle of a playoff series.

Eventually, the Leafs complained that Ezinicki was spending too much time playing golf and threatened to cut his salary to $7,000. Instead they demoted him to Pittsburgh in the American Hockey League to start the 1950–51 season, then traded him to Boston, where he spent two years as a Bruin. His 16 games with the New York Rangers in 1954–55 were his last appearances in the NHL. His hockey career over, "Wild Bill" returned to the Boston area and became a golf pro.

Bill Ezinicki really did not like to carry the puck, but he loved to use his body on the opposition. He led the Leafs twice in penalty minutes during his career, with 147 in 1948–49 and 145 in 1949–50. (HHOF)

Maple Leaf stats:	GP	G	A	P	PIM
regular season	271	56	79	135	525
playoffs	34	4	7	11	69

THE METZ BROTHERS

BETWEEN THEM, Nick and Don Metz won nine Stanley Cups as members of the Maple Leafs between 1942 and 1949. Born two years apart in Wilcox, Saskatchewan, they both played junior hockey for St. Michael's Majors and did very brief spells in the minors before becoming full-time Maple Leafs. Both played their entire NHL careers in Toronto before returning to Saskatchewan to work together on the family farm.

Nick Metz joined the Leafs as a left-winger on November 8, 1934 when the Leafs beat the Boston Bruins 5–3. He was placed on a line with his former junior teammates Pep Kelly and Art Jackson; the trio had played a large role in St. Michael's march to the Memorial Cup title in 1934. His linemates didn't last long with the Leafs, but Metz stayed until his retirement in 1948. He was important to the team because he was willing to do the unglamorous work of checking and digging the puck out of the corners. A very dependable player, he had his best year in 1944–45 when he scored 22 times and matched a career high of 35 points. He could play in any situation and was very cool on the ice, especially when sent in to kill penalties.

Nick's best moment came in the 1942 playoffs, when he had four goals and four assists and scored the winning goal that got the Leafs past the New York Rangers in the semifinals. Onlookers were surprised to see him shoot the puck when he had marksmen like Syl Apps and Gord Drillon beside him on the winning play, but Metz put it in the back of the net at 19:54 of the third period to knock out the Rangers four games to two. When the Leafs staged a miracle come-

back against Detroit in the finals, it was Metz who scored the winning goal in the fourth game to give the Leafs their first win against the Red Wings. Like teammate Apps, the reliable winger announced that he would retire after the 1948 playoffs. The Leafs won another Stanley Cup and Metz scored his first ever winning-overtime goal in the playoffs, against the Bruins, but he decided to go out on top.

Don Metz was not quite the all-round player his brother was but he, too, was a consistent performer. He came to prominence when coach Hap Day gave him a bigger role in the Leafs lineup after the team had lost the first three games of the 1942 finals against Detroit. He contributed immediately by providing four goals and three assists as the Leafs bounced back to take the Cup. During the 1946–47 season, Metz sidelined Canadiens centre Elmer Lach when he bowled him over with a check. Montreal coach Dick Irvin thought it was a deliberate attempt to injure, but Metz carried on and had a couple of assists in the six-game finals in which the Leafs beat the Habs. Lach was out for the series, but any revenge motive Irvin tried to establish against the Leafs winger failed.

Don had trouble staying with the Leafs (his highest point total was 14 in 1940–41) and often found himself in the minors. The Leafs liked having him around to fill in for injured players, a role Metz filled very well. With Turk Broda and Ted Kennedy, he is one of only three players to have won five Stanley Cups with the Leafs.

Both the Metz brothers served Canada during World War II, missing significant time during the prime of their NHL careers.

❦

Left-winger Nick Metz played with the Leafs from 1934 to 1948, winning four Stanley Cups. (HHOF)

Don Metz (with alternate captain's 'A' on sweater), Wally Stanowski (standing) and Nick Metz admire the Stanley Cup. (HHOF)

Maple Leaf stats:		GP	G	A	P	PIM
NICK METZ	regular season	518	131	119	250	149
	playoffs	76	19	20	39	31
DON METZ	regular season	172	20	35	55	42
	playoffs	47	7	8	15	10

WALTER 'BABE' PRATT

DEFENCEMAN WALTER "BABE" PRATT broke into the NHL with the New York Rangers in 1935 after a junior career with the Kenora Thistles. The big blueliner (6'3", 215 pounds) didn't nail down a regular place until 1936–37, when he contributed eight goals and 15 points during the regular season. He went on to score three times in nine games in the playoffs, and his winning-overtime goal knocked the Maple Leafs out of the postseason. Pratt remained with the Rangers for seven seasons, consistently producing 20-point years, winning one Stanley Cup in 1940 (beating the Leafs in the finals) and helping New York to a first-place finish in 1941–42.

Conn Smythe admired the stylish and colourful Pratt and sought his services for his Maple Leafs club: a few games into the 1942–43 season, Smythe offered Hank Goldup and Dudley "Red" Garrett to New York in exchange. The Rangers wanted to move the somewhat unpredictable Pratt out and took the deal, but the Leafs certainly got the best player in the transaction.

Pratt enjoyed his best years in hockey with the Leafs. He racked up 37 points in his first 40 games with Toronto but saved his best for the next season, 1943–44, when he won the Hart Trophy for the best player in the NHL. Pratt scored 17 goals that year and totalled 57 points in 50 games, a record for defencemen at the time. After his great season he sought a raise in salary to $7,000, but the Leafs would give him only $6,500. This upset Pratt so much that he told a teammate he was going to take the first portion of the season off. Pratt did nothing until Christmas of the 1944–45 season and his point total dropped to 41 (18 goals, 23 assists). He played one more year in Toronto before he was traded to the Boston Bruins.

Pratt was successful with the Leafs because coach Hap Day let him roam free on offence, confident that Pratt was a skilled blueliner who could score goals and put up points. Pratt recorded six assists against the Bruins during a 12–3 Leafs win on January 8, 1944. Off the ice, Day went so far as to become Pratt's roommate on the road so that he could keep an eye on the wayward defenceman. It worked for a while, but during the 1945–46 season Pratt was suspended by the NHL for gambling. League president Red Dutton took into account the fact that Pratt never bet against his own team, yet rightly worried that mounting losses might force a player into a compromising situation. The public outcry on behalf of the popular Pratt forced the league to cut his suspension from 16 games to nine: fans and sports writers saw gambling all around NHL arenas and wondered why Pratt was being dealt with so "harshly." The incident got him a ticket out of Toronto, but the gregarious Pratt never seemed to let it bother him that much.

After a very brief time with the Bruins, he played a few seasons in the minor leagues before retiring. Years later he became an ambassador of sorts for the Vancouver Canucks when they joined the NHL in 1970 and often appeared on *Hockey Night in Canada* broadcasts. In one television appearance during the 1972 playoffs he predicted that Toronto forward Jim Harrison would score an overtime winner against the Boston Bruins; Harrison proved him right, firing a shot past Gerry Cheevers in the Boston net. The Hall of Fame defenceman's son, Tracy, played for the Leafs during the '70s.

Walter 'Babe' Pratt was one of the most colourful and talented players in the NHL. He was a Leaf from 1942–43 to 1945–46. (HHOF)

Babe Pratt won the Hart Trophy as the NHL's best player in 1944–45, when he scored 17 goals and 40 assists as a defenceman. He also earned a place on the first all-star team that year. (HHOF)

They did that to keep me on the straight and narrow, but it was the worst time of my life. We were awake all night, talking hockey. I'd scream at him, 'I could be out drinking and here we are talking hockey!'

Babe Pratt, on having coach Hap Day as a roommate, *Action Sports* magazine, February 1980

Leaf file:

Babe Pratt scored a lot of goals for a defenceman of his era, and none was more important than the Stanley Cup winner against Detroit in 1945. The Leafs took a 3–0 lead in games backed by the stellar goaltending of Frank "Ulcers" McCool, but the Red Wings battled back with three consecutive wins of their own to force a game 7 showdown in the Motor City. It was a close contest that was tied 1–1 in the third period when Detroit's Syd Howe took a penalty for cross-checking the Leafs' Gus Bodnar. Nick Metz set up the winner by carrying the puck up the ice and taking a shot on goalie Harry Lumley. The puck bounced off Lumley's pads to Pratt, who had followed up on the play. He took a couple of whacks at it and it finally slithered under Lumley and into the net. The Leafs protected the 2–1 lead the rest of the way and McCool made great saves on Murray Armstrong and Carl Liscombe of the Red Wings to kill a penalty to defenceman Elwyn Morris.

When the Leafs arrived home, only about 25 people were there to greet their train because most of Toronto thought they had blown the series!

Maple Leaf stats:

	GP	G	A	P	PIM
regular season	181	52	108	160	139
playoffs	24	3	9	12	20

DAVID 'SWEENEY' SCHRINER

DAVID "SWEENEY" SCHRINER was one of the very few NHL players from the '30 and '40s who was not born in Canada. He was born in Saratov, Russia, on November 30, 1911. His family emigrated to Canada and settled in the Calgary area, where he played junior and senior hockey for a number of years. His goal-scoring exploits caught the eye of big-league scouts and he played for the New York Americans in 1934–35, producing 18 goals and 22 points and being named the NHL's best rookie. Schriner was around the 20-goal mark every year (during 48-game seasons) and twice led the NHL in scoring, in 1935–36 (with 45 points) and 1936–37 (46). He also earned two all-star team berths while he was in New York.

At an even six feet and 185 pounds Sweeney was a large man, but he could skate very fast. He had "soft hands" and did not shy away from physical play, but his penalty-minute total was quite low — only 148 in 484 career contests. Conn Smythe was looking for new talent in 1939 and offered the Americans four players for Schriner. Schriner did not have an exceptional year in 1939–40 for the Leafs (11 goals, 26 points in 39 games) but soon became a force for his new club. For the 1940–41 season he was teamed with Billy Taylor and Don Metz and his great 24-goal year earned him a spot on the first all-star team.

Schriner tore his knee ligaments in the next season but still managed 19 goals. He was ready for the playoffs, scoring six goals in 13 postseason games and adding three assists as the Leafs took the Stanley Cup away from Detroit. Schriner had been especially affected by a letter written by a young lady who was very unhappy that her Leafs were down three games to none against Detroit. Coach Hap Day had read the letter to the team before the fourth game and Schriner stood up and told the coach the team would win it for the little girl (he got one assist that game). Schriner's two most important goals in the playoffs came in game 7 of the finals on April 18, 1942, at Maple Leaf Gardens. Before a packed house, he scored the Leafs' first goal to tie the game 1–1 in the third period (Schriner told Smythe not to worry when he saw the Leafs owner fretting in the second intermission), then added an insurance marker to make the final 3–1.

After serving in the Canadian army during World War II, the left-winger returned to the Leafs for the 1944–45 season and scored 22 goals in just 26 games, helping the Leafs win another Stanley Cup. He played one more year in Toronto, scoring his 200th career goal against Boston on March 10, 1946, before returning to western Canada to play and coach senior hockey and then work in the oil industry. Schriner was inducted into the Hall of Fame in 1962.

Leaf Sweeney Schriner was a first-team NHL all-star in 1940–41. (HHOF)

Maple Leaf stats:	GP	G	A	P	PIM
regular season	244	109	83	192	75
playoffs	47	14	10	24	22

HOCKEY NIGHT IN CANADA:
RADIO AND TV, 1927 – 2002

by Frank Orr

A POSTSEASON TOUR of western Canada in the mid-1930s showed the Toronto players who the most popular Leaf was.

"Every place the train stopped and we stepped off, a crowd of people would make a little fuss over myself, Busher Jackson, Joe Primeau and Red Horner," said Charlie Conacher, the team's high-scoring winger of that era. "But they soon were saying: 'Where's Foster?' The biggest ovation and the most attention did not go to big hockey players. Naw — it went to the skinny little guy who never scored a goal."

Foster Hewitt was the Leafs broadcaster on radio and television for almost 50 years and, arguably, the best-known figure in the franchise's history, with a fame that exceeded that of any of Canada's political, entertainment or sports stars. But in the team's history, he was more than the pioneering voice in hockey broadcasting: he played a pivotal role in its ascent from the St. Patrick's of the musty old Mutual Street Arena to the Maple Leafs in that wonder of the Depression, Maple Leaf Gardens.

"I don't think we could have built Maple Leaf Gardens in those terrible economic times if it hadn't been for the clout of Foster's radio broadcasts," said Leafs owner Conn Smythe. "Response to things we tried on the hockey broadcasts told us how popular the game was, a big help in getting investors aboard the Gardens project at a time when people who had any money were sitting on it."

Hewitt became a broadcaster almost by accident. He was a young reporter at the *Toronto Star* in March 1923 when he was assigned to broadcast a junior playoff game on the paper's radio station. From Mutual Street Arena he called the game into a telephone and described the first goal with "He shoots! He scores!" His trademark phrase is used to this day by most of the game's voices.

"I said it that way because it just seemed the thing to say," Hewitt explained.

After Smythe bought the St. Patrick's and changed the name to Maple Leafs in 1927, Hewitt broadcast the NHL games from the old rink. Smythe was trying to raise money for a new building; one on-air mention by Hewitt that Leafs game programs were

available for 25 cents brought orders for more than 3,000. In 1931 Smythe and his assistant, Frank Selke Sr., produced a special program that boosted the need for a new building and contained preliminary drawings of one; Hewitt mentioned it on a Saturday night broadcast and orders for 91,000 copies poured in.

"Smythe knew then that radio could do more than make the team well-known," Hewitt said. "It had money-making potential."

When the Gardens opened in 1931, Hewitt controlled all broadcasting and picked his own broadcast location: "the Gondola," a slender steel tube in the rafters 56 feet above the ice that became the feature many wanted to see on their first visit to the Gardens. Hewitt sold the broadcast rights to an advertising agency and sponsorship cost General Motors $500 per game.

On January 1, 1933, the Leafs broadcast made its coast-to-coast debut. The greeting "Hello, Canada, and hockey fans in the United States and Newfoundland" was born and Foster Hewitt became the Saturday evening guest in most Canadian homes.

"Hewitt was the best free scout any team ever had," Smythe once said. "He made every boy in English Canada want to be a Maple Leaf."

Hewitt continued to call the Leafs games by himself into the 1950s, with the between-periods commentary of the so-called Hot Stove League: sportscaster Wes McKnight, journalists Elmer Ferguson and Bobby Hewitson and former player Harold "Baldy" Cotton. In the 1950s, he also become the voice on the first *Hockey Night in Canada* telecasts, eventually turning that task over to his son, Bill. Foster continued to do the radio call for several seasons until national radio coverage vanished, and the television version became Canada's most-watched program, a position it has now held for close to half a century.

Just as Hewitt became a household name, the Leafs telecasts have also produced several major Canadian broadcast stars. Play-by-play callers Bill Hewitt and Bob Cole, analyst Harry Neale, hosts/interviewers Ward Cornell, Brian McFarlane, Dave Hodge and Ron McLean all became national figures.

But the man who attained airwaves fame that equalled Hewitt's was former minor pro player Don Cherry. His colourful dress and

Foster Hewitt was as popular as any Maple Leaf player during his broadcasting career.
(HB)

outspoken comments on the intermission show *Coach's Corner*, especially against anything he deemed "non-Canadian" in hockey, transformed him from unemployed coach to broadcasting icon.

Watching today's high-tech telecasts with cameras covering the action from every possible angle, including that of the "net-cam" that shows the goalie's view, it is difficult to remember that it all started on a telephone line that was interrupted by other calls on that first night in 1923.

the '50s

The '50s were the best and worst of times for the Toronto Maple Leafs. The decade started out in great fashion, with a Stanley Cup win after a superb 1950-51 season, but the shocking death of defenceman Bill Barilko in a plane crash sent the Leafs reeling. The loss of the overtime hero who had scored the Cup-winning goal left a big hole on the blue line that the Leafs couldn't seem to fill and some of the team's spirit seemed to go with Barilko's unexpected passing. But the problems went deeper than the loss of one player. For the first time since Conn Smythe had assumed control of the team, new prospects were not panning out and management and coaching were in disarray. The Leafs would not start to recover and build another dynasty until the end of the decade. Here is a look at the Leafs' '50s roller-coaster ride.

Left: *Leafs forwards Rudy Migay (centre) and Eric Nesterenko (#16) go on the attack against Detroit's Terry Sawchuk. Migay played in 418 games for the Leafs between 1949-50 and 1959–60, scoring 59 goals and making 92 assists. A native of Flin Flon, Manitoba, Nesterenko scored 43 goals and 79 points in 206 games for Toronto.* (HB)

Right: *Bill Hewitt broadcast Leafs games on television starting in the '50s.* (HB)

Management and Coaching

When the Leafs lost the Stanley Cup in 1950, Hap Day decided it was time to give the coaching reins to former Leafs great Joe Primeau. Day moved into a management role, essentially assisting Smythe in running the team, and Primeau seemed to be a good replacement as the Leafs won the Cup in his first season. But in the long term Primeau was not cut out to be an NHL coach and left the position after the 1952–53 season, albeit with an overall record of 97–71–42. He was replaced by King Clancy, another former Leafs great, but the colourful leprechaun had little to work with. He lasted three seasons behind the bench and made the playoffs each year, but the team lost to Detroit every time.

Yet another ex-Leaf, Howie Meeker, got the job of coaching the team in 1956–57, but he was too young to take it anywhere, as his regular-season record of 21–34–15 shows. Former Montreal Canadien Billy Reay replaced Meeker; the team languished in last place for 14 months before he was let go by the new assistant general manager, Punch Imlach. The unknown 40-year-old Imlach was hired by Stafford Smythe, who had convinced his father it was time he and his management team took charge of the Leafs. The younger Smythe also dismissed Hap Day.

Best Trades and Acquisitions

The Leafs added goalie Al Rollins in a deal with Cleveland of the International Hockey League and another trade with Boston brought tough defenceman Fern Flaman to the club. But the team that won the Cup in 1951 was slowly dismantled and the Leafs lost useful players in forwards like Fleming Mackell and Joe Klukay. Flaman was dealt back to Boston, while Gus Mortson, Cal Gardner and Rollins were lost in a trade with the Chicago Black Hawks, although the Leafs did get back a good goaltender in the deal with the acquisition of Harry Lumley. Just as a young defender named Leo Boivin was gaining experience, he was sent to the Bruins in exchange for a fading Klukay.

These poor trades and the aging of stars such as Ted Kennedy, Max Bentley, Turk Broda and Harry Watson left the Leafs in need of capable replacements, but the cupboard was bare for a few years. Better moves started to happen when Imlach took charge and picked up quality veterans such as Johnny Bower, Bert Olmstead, Gerry Ehman and Allan Stanley, who helped get the Leafs to the finals twice before the decade was over.

Notable Events

The best thing the Leafs did in the '50s was to renew their commitment to developing young prospects, especially those in the Toronto area. While the big team floundered in the mid-50s, junior teams like the Toronto Marlboros and the St. Michael's Majors produced many future Leafs stars including Dick Duff, Bob Pulford, Billy Harris, Bob Baun, Carl Brewer and Frank Mahovlich. Young Leafs included George Armstrong, Tim Horton and Ron Stewart, all of whom would make bigger contributions in the next decade. Older players who consistently produced for the Leafs in the '50s were Tod Sloan, Sid Smith, Jim Thomson and Ted Kennedy, but none of the four were around by the time Imlach took over.

Worst of the Decade

The Leafs were a dull and defensive squad for most of the decade and only some great goaltending from Lumley kept the team record respectable. The biggest disappointment was the poor showing of players who were thought to have great futures when they were signed, including Rudy Migay, Danny Lewicki, Eric Nesterenko, Brian Cullen, Barry Cullen, Ed Chadwick, Hugh Bolton and Jim Morrison. The Leafs were better at tying games than winning them — they had 22 ties in 1954–55 — which made for some terrible hockey.

Leafs coaches came and went, and Meeker became so frustrated that he got into a shoving match with Stafford Smythe over how the team should be managed. Conn Smythe was back in the news when he tried to put the players' movement down in 1957. He was furious when the players defied him and voted to join the proposed association, but he need not have worried: the Detroit Red Wings team backed down and NHL players would not get their union going for another 10 years.

Bill Barilko (diving) scores his famous 1951 Stanley Cup-winning goal in overtime as the Leafs beat the Montreal Canadiens. (HHOF)

The Leafs had other problems. They finished the 1957–58 season at an all-time-low sixth place, with a 21–38–11 record. It was a bad time to be struggling, because games were now being televised on coast-to-coast television. Fortunately, changes were in the works that would make the team a winner once again.

Bottom-line Results

With only one Stanley Cup and a record of 281–282–137 between the 1950–51 and 1959–60 seasons, this was easily the worst decade the Leafs had endured since their formation. The team won 41 times in 1950–51, not getting close to that mark again until they won 35 in 1959–60 (the mark was not broken until the 1992–93 season). The years in between were a wasteland at Maple Leaf Gardens. But as the decade closed, a miracle fourth-place finish to close the 1958–59 season and a second-place finish in 1959–60 led to two trips to the finals. Though both series were lost to Montreal, they were a sure sign of good things to come. Imlach would not stand for anything less.

Best Leafs of the Decade

IN GOAL: Harry Lumley and Al Rollins.

ON DEFENCE: Jim Thomson, Gus Mortson and Fern Flaman.

AT FORWARD: Ted Kennedy, Sid Smith, Harry Watson, Tod Sloan and Dick Duff. (Thomson, Mortson, Kennedy and Watson are also being recognized for their contributions in the late '40s.)

BILL BARILKO

THE MOST TRAGIC FIGURE in Maple Leafs history was born on March 25, 1927, in Timmins, Ontario, a northern breeding ground for many Leafs and NHL players. The Leafs spotted the diamond in the rough when he played for teams like the Porcupine Combines in the Northern Ontario Intermediate Hockey Association between 1942 and 1945. He then went to the Pacific Coast Hockey League for the 1945–46 season and racked up four goals, nine points and 103 penalty minutes in 38 games for the Hollywood Wolves. He added five points in 12 playoff games and was signed to a contract by the Leafs in 1946.

Barilko began the 1946–47 season with the Wolves, but when the Leafs ran into injury problems he was recommended to Conn Smythe by Wolves player-coach Tommy Anderson. He played his first game with the Leafs on February 6, 1947, a crushing 8–2 defeat to Montreal. But Barilko did dish out some great body-checks, a preview of what was to come from the brash youngster. Calling himself "the Kid," he flashed a warm smile off the ice, which the ladies liked, but on ice his toughness made all opposing forwards keep their heads up.

The hard-hitting defenceman was not afraid to crunch players into the boards and did not hesitate to go after established NHLers such as Ken Reardon, Bill Gadsby, Leo Reise Jr,, George Gee and Milt Schmidt. In fact, the Canadiens Elmer Lach said Barilko was "the hardest hitter in the league . . . when he hits you, he hurts you." Barilko always got a piece of the opposition, something the Leafs team had been sorely lacking, and he led the NHL in penalty minutes in his second season with 147. His play caused some injuries, but many opponents ran at him and he never backed down.

Tutored by coach Hap Day and teamed with Garth Boesch on defence, Barilko never returned to the minors. He soon developed a confidence that helped him rise to the occasion more than once. For example, 200 fans from Timmins came to watch Barilko square off against Bep Guidolin of the Black Hawks, another Northern Ontario graduate, in a game against Chicago on March 18, 1950. The Leafs won a tight contest 2–1 and Barilko was named first star. During a playoff contest against Boston in 1951 that ended in a 1–1 tie, he was at his rough, brawling best, racking up four minors and a 10-minute misconduct from referee Red Storey. He had a bit of a scoring touch, with 26 career goals and one Stanley Cup winner in five seasons with the Leafs. But it was his physical presence that served the Leafs so well as they won four Stanley Cups.

The bashing defenceman would have had a long career with the Leafs, but on August 26, 1951, his life came to a dramatic end in a plane crash in northern Ontario, where it had begun 24 years earlier. Conn Smythe offered a $10,000 reward for any information about the whereabouts of the Barilko plane, but the crash site was not found until 1962.

Barilko's death left a large hole in the team and started a long slide that would not be corrected until the end of the '50s. No Leaf has worn his number 5 sweater since, and a photo of a smiling Barilko hangs on a banner in the Air Canada Centre as a reminder of the young man who lived the Canadian dream.

Maple Leaf stats:	GP	G	A	P	PIM
regular season	252	26	36	62	456
playoffs	47	5	7	12	104

Bill Barilko gallops in from the blue line to put the Stanley Cup-winning goal past Montreal goalie Gerry McNeil in 1951. (HHOF)

Facing page: A smiling Bill Barilko in 1951 enjoys his fourth Stanley Cup win in five seasons as a Leaf. (HHOF)

Leaf file:

The most important goal of Bill Barilko's life was also his last. It came in overtime during the fifth game of the 1951 finals against the Montreal Canadiens. The Leafs were up 3-1 in the series and hoping to wrap up the Cup with a win at Maple Leaf Gardens. But the Canadiens would not cooperate and the Leafs needed a last-minute goal with the goaltender on the bench to tie the game at 2-–2. They could sense victory and stormed out to start the overtime session. Howie Meeker, Cal Gardner and Harry Watson were swarming around the Montreal goal when the puck squirted free. Against the wishes of coach Joe Primeau, Barilko charged in from the blue line and lifted a sweeping backhand shot over prone Montreal goalie Gerry McNeil. The Gardens crowd went wild and the Leafs had their fourth Cup in five years. Conn Smythe came into the Leafs dressing room to shake hands with the hero and the two shared a laugh. (It was sweet revenge for Barilko, who had seen a Leo Reise shot deflect off his stick and slither past Leafs goalie Turk Broda to give Detroit a 1–0 game 7 victory in the semifinals the year before. Many Leafs of that era believed they could have been the first team to win five Cups in a row and not the Canadiens, who did it between 1956 and 1960.)

After all the celebrations were over, Barilko walked out of the Gardens for the last time.

FOSTER HEWITT

FOSTER HEWITT was already a broadcasting legend by the '50s and would be on the scene for many years to come. He had established himself as a hockey broadcaster in the '20s and was as much a part of the Leafs as any player, coach or manager. In the minds of many listeners across Canada he *was* the Maple Leafs, and his Saturday night play-by-play radio broadcasts were not to be missed. When hockey superstar Bobby Hull met Hewitt for the first time he said it was like meeting God. Hewitt got much the same reaction wherever he travelled as his familiar "Hello, Canada, and hockey fans in the United States and Newfoundland" rang out happily in homes across our vast country (and overseas during World War II). Future broadcasters took their cue from the pioneering Hewitt and his catchphrases, notably "He shoots! He scores!", still ring out today.

Born in Toronto on November 21, 1902, Hewitt became involved in sports as a boxer while attending the University of Toronto. He was working for the *Toronto Star* newspaper, where his father, W. A. Hewitt, was a sports editor, when he was given the assignment of broadcasting a hockey game at the Mutual Street Arena. He didn't relish the idea but was told there was no one else available. It was the start of a career that would span both radio and television and take Hewitt all over the world to describe hockey games for Canadians. Although he was primarily known as the voice of the Leafs, Hewitt also covered Olympic and world championship hockey games.

Before television, Hewitt's radio broadcasts were tremendously important for hockey fans. He understood that he was really "selling" the game of hockey and thus he chose to describe rather than criticize what he was watching. It has been said that there were two games, the one being played and the one Hewitt broadcast — but he was rarely criticized for his style, as the game he described was often better than the one on the ice. A very astute businessman, Hewitt was also quick to understand the value of sponsors who might be listening to his broadcast. He learned the power of his words during a 1928 broadcast when he announced that a Leafs game program was available for 10 cents by mail. The Leafs received bags of requests, proving to owner Conn Smythe just how valuable Hewitt could be in marketing the club. Little wonder that Smythe gave Hewitt the broadcast rights to all games coming out of Maple Leaf Gardens after it was built.

Although Hewitt received tons of mail from all over Canada and was said to be more recognizable than the prime minister, he was shy and reserved in person. He wrote many books, but did not mix with a large number of people. He was also a very tough negotiator, known to be a little tight with his money; he was one of the few people who could dicker on the same level as Smythe and he even managed to tie up marketing rights for the Leafs players, much to their chagrin. In 1951 Hewitt started his own radio station — called CKFH, the last two letters for his own initials — and took the Leafs games with him to 1430 AM. His son, Bill, became sports director at the station and was playing a large role in Leafs television broadcasts by 1958, when he took over the play-by-play duties.

Hewitt could see that the future of hockey broadcasting was going to be in television, but after trying simulcasts in which he called the game on both radio and television he decided to leave the new medium to his son. Bill was a natural at play-by-play and became the voice of the Leafs to the generation that grew up with television. After the 1967 season, the last with the original six NHL teams, Hewitt took on a smaller role and was heard less and less often, even on the radio; it was said that he did not like the expansion of the NHL, even though he was part of a group that lobbied for a failed Vancouver entry. He did return to broadcast one last Leafs game for television in 1978. A member of the Hall of Fame, he did an estimated 3,000 broadcasts. "The voice of hockey" was forever silenced with Foster Hewitt's passing in 1985.

Foster Hewitt chats with goalie Ed Chadwick (left) and defenceman Jim Morrison. During the '50s Leafs games were aired on television for the first time. Foster eventually turned over those play-by-play duties to his son, Bill, in 1958. (HB)

Facing page: To most Canadians, Foster Hewitt was the voice of hockey. Already a legend, in 1951 he started up his own radio station CKFH and for years broadcast all Leafs games there on 1430 AM. (HB)

Leaf file:

The Maple Leafs made many contributions during World War II, between 1939 and 1945. First, Conn Smythe sent a letter to all his players encouraging them to enlist in the Canadian army, which many did. Then Foster Hewitt took advantage of a Leafs broadcast to ask listeners to send in binoculars because there was a shortage in the services: the response was so overwhelming that in a subsequent broadcast, he had to ask people to stop.

Hewitt went even further by packaging highlights of the Saturday night games so that they could be aired overseas on the BBC short-wave radio, a task that cost him many hours of extra work but demand from Canadians in Europe was very strong. It grew even stronger when the Leafs staged their great playoff resurgence against Detroit in the 1942 finals, capped off with a seventh game win at Maple Leaf Gardens.

TED KENNEDY

ONE OF THE MOST industrious and hard-working Maple Leafs, Ted "Teeder" Kennedy was born on December 12, 1925, in Humberstone, Ontario, near Port Colborne. He never knew his father, who was killed in an accident two weeks before Kennedy was born, but he did not let that deter him as he grew up.

His hockey playing first caught the eye of scouts when Port Colborne won a juvenile championship in 1941. Montreal was tipped off about the good prospect Kennedy was becoming and put his name on its list. The Canadiens knew Kennedy was getting good grooming from former NHL star Nels Stewart and felt the youngster was worth a look. At age 16 he was invited to attend their training camp, but he became homesick and complained that the Canadiens did not provide appropriate accommodation or educational facilities. He knew Montreal was not the team for him, but for a while Kennedy had no idea what was going to happen to his hockey career.

He got a big break at the end of 1942–43 when Stewart told the Maple Leafs about the great season Kennedy had had with the senior hockey Port Colborne Sailors (23 goals and 29 assists in 23 games). The Leafs wanted to take a look at him in NHL action and asked his mother to allow them to pull him out of high school one day and told him to report to Maple Leaf Gardens. He travelled with the team to Madison Square Garden in New York, where the Leafs tied the Rangers 5–5. He played in the next game, another 5–5 tie, in Boston, picking up an assist and impressing the coaches. The Leafs still did not own his rights officially but on September 10, 1943, they sent defenceman Frank Eddolls (at that point in the Canadian army) to the Canadiens to acquire Kennedy.

The deal was made without the knowledge of Leafs manager Conn Smythe, who was fighting in Europe at the time, and he was enraged when he found out about the trade. Smythe later admitted it was the best trade the Leafs had ever made, but he was nonetheless permanently peeved at assistant Frank Selke, and ironically this

would lead to Selke leaving Toronto for Montreal, which he soon built into a powerhouse.

There is no doubt that it was the best trade in Leafs history. Kennedy proved to be a great leader and played on a team-record five Stanley Cup-winning Leafs teams. His main strength was his determination and an intense desire that never waned. Kennedy would not hesitate to tell a teammate to get his game together if he had to, but he also led by example. He was excellent on faceoffs (coach Hap Day placed strong emphasis on getting control of the puck) and excelled at positional hockey, which was perfect for the Leafs' style of play. Kennedy's skating was termed laborious by the writers of the day, but he did not let this perceived deficiency hold him back. When he had the puck few could take it away from the 5'11", 180-pound Kennedy, who would scrap for every inch of ice.

His statistics show that he was an all-round performer. In 1943–44, his first full year with the Leafs, the hard-nosed centre scored 26 times with 23 assists to total one point per game played. He had five seasons of 20 or more goals for the Leafs (29 being his highest total, in 1944–45) and 11 years with 20 or more assists (43 was his highest helper total, in 1950–51). Like many great players, Kennedy saved his best for the playoffs, racking up 60 points in 78 postseason games.

When the Leafs had Kennedy, Syl Apps and Max Bentley as their centres, they had the best trio of pivots in the NHL by a wide margin. In 1947–48, when the Maple Leafs finished first in the NHL, Kennedy had 25 goals and 46 points, while Apps had 26 and 53 and Bentley 23 and 48. When Apps retired in 1948, Kennedy was named team captain at the banquet honouring the 1948 Stanley Cup champions. He was only 23 years old, but there was no doubt that he was the leader of the team.

The NHL did not recognize Kennedy's great play very often (he was a second-team all-star three times), though he did win the

Ceremonial face-off between captain Milt Schmidt of the Bruins and captain Ted Kennedy of the Maple Leafs. Both are Hall of Fame players. (HHOF)

Hart Trophy in 1954–55. He racked up only 10 goals and 42 assists that year, but it was seen as a justified reward to honour a great player near the end of his career. Kennedy retired after his MVP season, but the Leafs coaxed him back in 1956–57 for 30 games, which saw him record 22 points, before letting him retire for good. He was elected to the Hall of Fame in 1966.

Maple Leaf stats:	GP	G	A	P	PIM
regular season	686	231	329	560	432
playoffs	78	29	31	60	32

Leaf file:

Ted Kennedy played a large role when the Leafs won the first of three straight Stanley Cups in 1947. Toronto finished the 1946–47 season in second place with 72 points, six behind Montreal. They knocked off the Detroit Red Wings in six games in the semifinals, while Montreal beat the Boston Bruins to set up an all-Canadian final. The Leafs were wiped out 6–0 in the first game but came back to reel off 4–0, 4–2 and 2–1 victories, which the Habs countered with a 3–1 win back at the Forum. The sixth game was played at the Gardens on April 19, 1947, and Buddy O'Conner scored to make it 1–0 for Montreal in the first. But at 5:34 of the second, Kennedy outfought Toe Blake for the puck and got it out to Vic Lynn, who tied the score. The contest was still tied with just under five minutes to play in the third when Kennedy took a pass from Howie Meeker. The Leafs captain took his time, as coach Nels Stewart had told him to do, waiting until he was about 12 feet out before firing the puck into the corner of Montreal goaltender Bill Durnan's net. It was the Stanley Cup-winning goal as the Leafs hung on to win 2–1.

Facing page: *A determined Ted Kennedy led the Leafs in assists on six separate occasions.* (HHOF)

Ted Kennedy (with alternate captain's A on sweater) leads a Leafs attack on the New York Rangers net. Other Leafs shown are (left to right) Vic Lynn, Garth Boesch (with moustache) and Howie Meeker. (HHOF)

HOWIE MEEKER

FOR THE START of the 1946–47 season the Maple Leafs decided to make significant changes to their lineup and bring in an influx of eager youngsters. None was hungrier than Howie Meeker. The native of Kitchener, Ontario, was just back from a two-year stint in the army, and a wound had affected his legs and feet, but he slowly recovered and was playing senior hockey for the Stratford club by New Year's Day 1946. He scored eight times in seven games and Toronto coach Hap Day, who had scouted Meeker as a junior, suggested that Conn Smythe sign the feisty right winger. The Leafs manager called Meeker in April 1946 and offered him a contract for $4,500 a year plus a $1,000 signing bonus. Meeker gladly accepted.

He not only made the team, he soon made an impression few would forget. He scored his first NHL goal at Maple Leaf Gardens on October 19, 1946, during a 6–3 win over the Detroit Red Wings (who had a rookie named Gordie Howe on the team). Meeker took a pass from linemate Ted Kennedy before beating Harry Lumley in the Detroit net. But Meeker's biggest night was on January 8, 1947, when he put five past Chicago goaltender Paul Bibeault during a 10–4 Leafs win at the Gardens. He did not get immediate credit for the first two goals, which had been chalked up to defenceman Wally Stanowski even though Meeker had redirected them both. But after he scored his third, he casually mentioned that he really had a hat trick already. Day overheard the comment and took it upon himself to get the previous two corrected. Kennedy set up his next two goals and Meeker set a record for first-year players that in 2002 had yet to be broken, though it has been equalled.

Meeker's memorable rookie year saw him score a career-high 27 goals and total 45 points. He displayed a bit of a temper with 76 penalty minutes and especially liked to mix it up with Tony Leswick of the Rangers, whom he once body-slammed to the ice. Speedy and tough, although not very big at 5'8" and 165 pounds, Meeker won the Calder Trophy for best rookie over Leo Gravelle of Montreal and Jim Conacher of Detroit. He capped a great first year with a Stanley Cup win, contributing six points in 11 playoff games, including the over-time winner against Detroit. The Leafs had started the year with seven rookies and it had paid off handsomely.

Meeker's numbers were never as good again, but he was a very efficient up-and-down winger for the Leafs for the next eight seasons. His line with Kennedy and left-winger Vic Lynn was one of the best two-way lines in the league.

Two years after his great rookie season, Meeker went in to negotiate a new contract with Smythe. He thought his demand for a $1,500 raise was very reasonable, but learned that Smythe was tracking his progress when the boss informed him that his plus/minus numbers were not very good. Meeker was not even aware the statistic existed and Smythe had to explain how it was reached: each player on the ice while a goal is scored for or against his team, when both sides are at even strength, is assigned a "plus" or "minus." Smythe said the game films taken by Gardens superintendent Shanty MacKenzie showed that Chicago's Roy Conacher in particular had gotten the better of him during the 1947–48 season. Meeker still got $1,000 out of Smythe, but he asked to see the films so he could improve his game. He learned how to check Conacher from viewing the tapes and ended at "plus five" by the time the 1948–49 season was over.

The Leafs took three straight Cups before losing in the 1950 semifinals to Detroit, then bounced back in 1950–51 to take the Cup from Montreal. Meeker helped to set up Bill Barilko's overtime winner in game 5 by using his speed to chase down a loose puck and getting out in front while he took a hit from big Montreal defenceman Tom Johnson. Meeker played parts of three more seasons with the Leafs before retiring at age 30. He immediately turned to coaching and won an American Hockey League title with Pittsburgh, the Leafs' farm club. Meeker was promoted to the Leafs coaching job for the 1956–57 season (21–43–5) at the age of 32 but was replaced by Billy Reay for the next year. He was even offered the Leafs general manager position, but a severe disagreement with Stafford Smythe left him out of work. A Conser-

Howie Meeker just misses with a shot against Chicago goalie Al Rollins. Meeker scored five goals in one game against the Black Hawks in 1947. (HHOF)

Facing page: Howie Meeker was successful as the coach of the Pittsburgh Hornets of the American Hockey League but had a more difficult time coaching a Leafs team that won only 21 games in 1956–57. (HB)

vative party Member of Parliament for four years, Meeker then went to Newfoundland to coach and play senior hockey for a number of years.

Meeker is best known as a colour analyst on *Hockey Night in Canada* telecasts in the '70s. He stressed the fundamentals of the game and his excellent work earned him a place in the Hall of Fame as a broadcaster, winning the Foster Hewitt Memorial Award in 1998.

The Business of the Maple Leafs:

When Howie Meeker signed his first contract, he understood that if he won the Calder Trophy as rookie of the year the Leafs would pay him a $1,000 bonus. Meeker did win the award but did not get the Leafs money, because that year the NHL decided to give the trophy winner a $1,000 bonus. The rookie thought he was going to double his winnings but Conn Smythe told him the league's money would cover the Leafs' obligation. Meeker was not happy with that line of reasoning, but at the time players had little power to do anything about such arbitrary decisions.

Maple Leaf stats:	GP	G	A	P	PIM
regular season	346	83	102	185	329
playoffs	42	6	9	15	50

GUS MORTSON

LIKE SO MANY OTHER talented players, defenceman Gus Mortson was recruited out of northern Ontario. Born in New Liskeard, he started playing junior hockey for St. Michael's College in Toronto in 1943–44. The Leafs first noticed the rugged blueliner when he played a very good game against the Toronto Marlboros at the Gardens. Mortson won the Memorial Cup with the Oshawa Generals in 1944 and was part of the 1945 St. Michael's team that won the junior title.

Mortson turned professional with the Tulsa Oilers of the United States Hockey League, playing left wing. He went to training camp in the fall of 1946 and was supposed to play for the Pittsburgh Hornets, the Leafs' top farm club. When he heard that the Pittsburgh-bound players were to play the Leafs in an exhibition contest in Hamilton, Ontario, Mortson saw his chance and drove all the way to St. Catharines to get his skates properly sharpened by Leafs technician Tommy Naylor. After playing a terrific game, he was about to board the Pittsburgh bus when he was stopped by Leafs coach Hap Day, who told him to forget about the minors and come join the Maple Leafs.

A sturdy 5'11" and 190 pounds, Mortson built his game around keeping the opposition honest. The tough blueliner recorded over 100 penalty minutes in five of his six seasons as a Leaf. He was a fearless checker who was not above giving a chop across the ankles to stop an opposing attacker. Players who dared go into a corner with Mortson knew they were in for a battle; if all else failed, he would simply use the Leafs' clutch-and-grab style. When he joined Toronto, Mortson was moved back to defence and teamed with Jim Thomson to form the so-called "Gold Dust Twins." Mortson was an excellent skater who liked to carry the puck and join the attack, while Thomson played back. He scored five goals as a rookie in 1946–47, with 13 assists in 60, and led the NHL in penalty minutes with 133. His first of four Stanley Cup victories as a Maple Leaf followed, to finish off a memorable start to his hockey career.

After the 1951–52 season Mortson was traded to the Chicago Black Hawks for goalie Harry Lumley. He thought the Leafs got rid of him because of a jawing session he'd had with owner Conn Smythe after a Toronto loss. Mortson spent the next six seasons in Chicago before one last year in Detroit in 1958–59; he had been offered back to the Leafs, but Toronto coach Howie Meeker refused to part with defenceman Tim Horton, five years Mortson's junior. While he was with the Black Hawks Mortson became the players' representative as talk about a league-wide players' association began. He was not happy when members of the Detroit Red Wings backed out, since that decision crippled the player movement for at least a decade.

🍁

Leafs defenceman Gus Mortson looks up for the puck with goalie Turk Broda in a game against the Boston Bruins. Mortson was an NHL first-team all-star for the 1949–50 season. (AP)

Maple Leaf stats:	GP	G	A	P	PIM
regular season	371	21	71	92	709
playoffs	47	4	7	11	62

TOD SLOAN

ALOYSIUS "TOD" SLOAN was a native of Pontiac, Quebec, who relocated to Ontario to play junior hockey for St. Michael's College in Toronto. An excellent scorer, he helped St. Mike's win the Memorial Cup in 1945 and led the Ontario Hockey Association in goals (43), assists (32) and points (76) during the 1945–46 season. The Maple Leafs could not pass up such a skilled player and signed Sloan on April 30, 1946.

The Leafs were spoiled for centres at the time and it took four years for Sloan to nail down a place with the big club. In the meantime, he gained some pro experience with the Pittsburgh Hornets and the Cleveland Barons of the American Hockey League, and played the odd game for the Leafs, including a 29-game sequence when Howie Meeker fractured a collarbone.

The 1950–51 season saw Sloan play all 70 games for the Leafs, scoring 31 times and racking up 56 points on a line with Ted Kennedy and Sid Smith. Known as "Slinker," the slick centre/winger was great at hanging around the net and knocking the puck in. He was a polished skater and good at handling the puck. While he was not a big man, 5'11" with a slight build, Sloan was aggressive (he had 105 penalty minutes in 1950–51) and played with plenty of grit and determination.

During the 1951 playoffs, his line scored 10 of the 13 Leafs goals in the finals against Montreal and he led the team with seven points in five games. Sloan's best moment came in the Cup-clinching game at the Gardens, when he scored twice. Kennedy helped set up the first goal as Sloan fought off the close checking of Canadiens defenceman Doug Harvey to get one past Gerry McNeil. His second goal tied the game at 19:29 of the third period, when he rapped in a rebound as the Leafs swarmed the Canadiens net with the goalie on the bench. The Leafs won the game and the Cup in overtime on Bill Barilko's famous winner.

Sloan's best year with the Leafs came in 1955–56, when he scored 37 times and added 29 assists. His performance earned him a spot on the NHL's second all-star team and was one of the few bright spots for the Leafs in a dismal year. But when Sloan became involved with the players' association movement, the Leafs shipped him to Chicago in June 1958. Sloan got the last laugh when the Black Hawks won the Stanley Cup in 1960–61, his last year in the NHL. He finished his career with 220 goals and 482 points in 745 games.

Tod Sloan (#15) tries to get the puck past Johnny Bower in the New York net. Known as "Slinker," Sloan won the Bickell Trophy as the Leafs' best player in 1955–56. (HB)

Maple Leaf stats:	GP	G	A	P	PIM
regular season	549	162	184	346	650
playoffs	26	5	6	11	59

SID SMITH

SID SMITH was born in Toronto on July 25, 1925. He played junior hockey for the Oshawa Generals and senior hockey in Toronto and Quebec for various teams. The Maple Leafs had their eye on him and signed him as a free agent on October 8, 1946.

Smith bounced between the Leafs and their farm team in Pittsburgh for the next three seasons. The 1947–48 season saw him score 23 goals for his minor-league team and seven in 31 games for the big club. He was called up again during the 1948 playoffs, which the Leafs won, and played in two games before suffering a knee injury against Boston.

Smith played only one regular season game for Toronto in 1948–49 but was called up for the playoffs. He scored two goals against Boston in the semifinals and a hat trick on April 10, 1949, during a 3–1 Leafs victory against Detroit in the finals. The Leafs swept the Red Wings to take the Cup and Smith had his name on the fabled trophy for a second time. He was through playing in the minors.

Smith won another Cup in 1951. He had a great playoff, with seven goals — including a key overtime winner against Montreal in the finals — and 11 points in 10 games. Between 1949 and 1955, Smith proved that he belonged in the NHL, with goal totals of 22, 30, 27, 20, 22 and 33. The smooth left-winger had a great wrist shot and could deke any goalie in the league. With Ted Kennedy as his centre, Smith's style meshed well with the digging captain and he would often tap in a rebound for a goal. At 5'10" and 173 pounds Smith was a big man, but he played a clean game and twice won the Lady Byng Trophy, in 1952 and 1955.

Smith was a quiet player and did not feel comfortable with the captain's arm band handed to him after Kennedy retired. The pressure seemed to affect his play and he was captain for just one year, 1955–56, scoring only four goals in 55 games. When Jim Thomson took over as captain to start the next season, Smith rebounded to score 17 goals and 24 assists in 70 games. But he got off to a bad start the next season, 1957–58, and the Leafs basically ran him off the team. Considering that he was only 32 at the time, the Leafs treated their former captain poorly, especially as he was one of the few good offensive players they'd had during some dreary years in the '50s.

Smith became a player-coach with the Whitby Dunlops, a senior team, and his play showed that the Leafs might have acted too hastily in dismissing him. The Dunlops won the world championship for Canada that year, with Smith contributing nine goals and 14 points in seven games. He played another year with Whitby before retiring at the end of the 1958–59 season.

Sid Smith looks to check Detroit's Gordie Howe while goalie Harry Lumley makes a save. (HHOF)

Maple Leaf stats:	GP	G	A	P	PIM
regular season	601	186	183	369	94
playoffs	44	17	10	27	2

STAFFORD SMYTHE

BEING THE SON of a man as legendary as Conn Smythe is not easy, but Stafford Smythe eventually found that he could match his father's guile and gumption to lead the Toronto hockey club to many of the same heights. The older Smythe treated his son as little more than an employee for a long time, but Stafford persevered and showed he could also succeed in the hockey business, even if he was never as colourful as his outspoken father. However, Stafford did not have Conn's morals about how to live life, and eventually this got him into big trouble and led to his untimely death at the age of 51.

Stafford Smythe started out as an 11-year-old "stick boy" for the 1931 Stanley Cup-winning Maple Leafs. He also played some hockey in the Toronto Marlboros development chain as a youngster before World War II. Smythe joined the Canadian navy during the war years and was captain of the senior hockey team. Because he weighed only 130 pounds and could not play in a very aggressive manner, Smythe tried playing in the gentlemanly style of his hero, Joe Primeau, but it became clear that his future in the game was not going to be as a player. He turned to managing and coaching, first with the Varsity Blues while attending U of T and then for the junior Marlies, where he worked with Harold Ballard. Like his father, Smythe soon learned he was better at managing than coaching.

As the Leafs floundered in the '50s, the Marlies were doing quite well and Stafford was proving to his father that he could develop young talent. When the moment was right, Smythe finally made a pitch to his father, proposing that the Leafs be run by a committee ("the Silver Seven") and that he head the group while Conn retained the ultimate say on all hockey matters. Sensing that his time was up, the elder Smythe agreed to his son's wishes. In 1957 Stafford basically told Hap Day, whose methods he saw as outdated, that his services were no longer required. He also dumped Howie Meeker as coach and then as general manager because he felt Meeker was too inexperienced for either job. A new Smythe was in place, running the Leafs on a day-to-day basis.

Stafford's efforts to recruit new players into the Leafs system started to pay dividends: Billy Harris, Bob Baun, Bob Pulford, Carl Brewer, Dick Duff and Frank Mahovlich were all with the big club by 1958. He then made his most important decision by bringing in George "Punch" Imlach to manage (and later coach) the team while Stafford settled into the role of team president. It was the beginning of some very triumphant times for the Leafs. In 1962 the team brought the Stanley Cup home to Toronto and three more championships followed during the '60s.

In November 1961, just before the Leafs' first Cup win, Stafford bought his father's shares in the team and Maple Leaf Gardens. He had two partners, Harold Ballard and John Bassett, though this was not disclosed to Conn at the time of purchase. The good times rolled until the taxman got involved. Not content to enjoy their good fortune, Stafford Smythe and Ballard tried to beat Revenue Canada as well. The elder Smythe felt his son was being pursued so vigorously in the tax matter because of Conn's criticism of the Liberal government in Ottawa during the war years, but both father and son lost the battle. Stafford's problems led him to drink, which gave rise to a bleeding ulcer and other health problems that eventually killed him.

Bassett could not wedge himself into a position of power and sold his share of the Leafs to Ballard. The Smythe family tried to raise enough money to keep Ballard out of the picture, but failed. The dream of having Stafford's son, Tommy, running the Leafs one day was over and the Leafs ownership passed to Harold Ballard. It would prove to be a fateful turn of events.

I **was** 11 years old when I assembled a minor bantam team called, of course, the Toronto Maple Leafs. [Former Leaf] Billy Taylor helped me to organize it and we made the city finals the first year. That was in 1953 and the following year we won the title.

Stafford Smythe, Leafs program, February 21, 1968

Inset: *Stafford Smythe (standing) learned the hockey business from his famous father Conn (seated). (HHOF)*

Stafford Smythe (centre) and John Bassett (right) enjoy the Leafs' 1962 Stanley Cup victory. (HHOF)

JIM THOMSON

THE MAPLE LEAFS defence of the mid '40s and early '50s was one of the most formidable in the history of the game. Bill Barilko, Garth Boesch, Fern Flaman, Bill Juzda, Gus Mortson and Wally Stanowski were all top drawer, but the man who held it all together was Winnipeg native Jim Thomson. The other blueliners could play their game safe in the knowledge that the ever-reliable Thomson would be back to make sure the Leafs zone was cleared. All Leafs players of that era would agree that without him the team would never have won four Stanley Cups between 1947 and 1951.

Thomson first arrived in Toronto to play junior hockey for St. Michael's Majors in 1943. A top scholar, he played two seasons for the Majors and won the Memorial Cup in 1945. Thomson's play impressed the Leafs, who signed him in October 1945; he made the team as a 19-year-old the following year. The Leafs quickly saw that he could go up against the best players in the league and was a perfect partner for the attacking Mortson. Thomson would not score much — he had six seasons with the Leafs without a single goal — but his defensive play was among the best in the NHL.

Thomson had good size at an even six foot tall and 190 pounds and played it tough without going overboard. He was exceptional at implementing coach Hap Day's clutch-and-grab style, which became the Leafs' trademark. This lead to a few penalties, but also stopped many goals from being scored.

Like many other players Thomson once upset Conn Smythe, and he certainly heard about it. One night during the 1947 playoffs against Detroit, "Black" Jack Stewart of the Red Wings decked Thomson and the Leafs defenceman did not retaliate. Smythe was livid and told Thomson he'd better get Stewart back. Thomson harassed the Detroit player non-stop for the rest of the series. The Leafs won in five games and went on to take their first of three straight Cups when they beat Montreal in the finals.

If Thomson was not a goal scorer, he was good at setting up plays and led the team with 29 assists in 1947–48. He recorded over 20 assists five times in his career with the Leafs, and in eight years had 70 or more penalty minutes. His all-round play was recognized with a berth on the NHL's second allstar team in 1950–51 and 1951–52 and his leadership skills made him a natural to be named team captain in 1956–57. The captaincy was a reward for a loyal and strong soldier, and when former captain Ted Kennedy came out of retirement during the season Thomson insisted that Kennedy take back the "C."

By that time Thomson had other matters on his mind. Conn Smythe was none too pleased to find out that his captain was helping to organize the first players' association. Doing so wasn't easy for Thomson — he had to make a friend out of a longtime rival and bitter enemy, Detroit's Ted Lindsay — but he got involved because he wanted to improve working conditions for his fellow players.

Smythe was furious at this turn of events and called Thomson in to berate him. He seemed especially angry that the Leafs captain would be involved in union activities. He called Thomson "disloyal" and "thankless" after all that the Maple Leafs had done for him, and also accused Thomson of being a poor influence on his younger teammates. He let it be known that he had never wanted Thomson as captain, but was talked around by general manager Hap Day and new coach Howie Meeker. To his credit Thomson did not back down, but decided he did not want to play for the Leafs again if his loyalty was being questioned. Smythe picked up the phone and sold him for $15,000 to Chicago, where he played the 1957–58 season.

Thomson's playing rights reverted to the Leafs the following season but there was no way they would have him back. At age 31 his career was over. Luckily he had a great business opportunity with his father-in-law and eventually became president of a home heating oil company. Thomson was as successful in business as he had been in hockey and apparently resisted a Leafs offer to manage their minor-league team some years after his retirement.

Jim Thomson (#2) is strong along the boards against the Boston Bruins. He was a second-team NHL all-star selection in 1950–51 and 1951–52. (HHOF)

If he felt any bitterness toward Smythe there was no evidence of it in 1980 at Smythe's funeral, when Thomson joined other former Leafs captains in carrying the casket. Thomson died in Toronto in 1991 at age 64.

Jim Thomson comes back to clear a loose puck in front of goalie Harry Lumley in a game against the Detroit Red Wings. (HHOF)

Maple Leaf stats:	GP	G	A	P	PIM
regular season	717	15	208	223	846
playoffs	63	2	13	15	135

HARRY WATSON

ONE OF THE BEST deals the Toronto Maple Leafs ever made was getting left-winger Harry Watson from the Detroit Red Wings in 1946. The little-known Watson went on to help the Leafs win four Stanley Cups by adding some toughness and scoring on the wing. The rugged 6'1", 207-pound native of Saskatoon was one of the NHL's most feared fighters, although he did not get into many tussles since the opposition usually avoided him. For more than nine seasons Watson was a steadying influence on the Leafs.

His professional career began with the Brooklyn Americans in the 1941–42 season. When the team was disbanded, Watson went to Detroit, where he scored 13 goals in 50 games in 1942–43 and won the Stanley Cup. He joined the army during the war years but returned to Detroit for the 1945–46 season, managing 14 goals in 44 games before heading to Toronto.

The arrival of Watson brought the Stanley Cup to Toronto in each of his first three seasons. Watson became a consistent goal scorer with totals of 19, 21, 26, 19, 18, 22, 16 and 21 marking his time with the Leafs. He patrolled the wing with a strong skating stride, had a hard shot and was a good finisher for a playmaker like Apps in his early years as a Leaf. Watson was outstanding during the 1948 finals, when the Leafs swept Detroit in four straight games. He opened the Leafs' scoring in the first game in a 5–3 Toronto win and scored the winner in the third game, a 2–0 triumph. In the fourth and decisive game, Watson put in two more in the 7–2 Leafs rout.

Watson was tough along the boards and could handle the rough stuff with ease. In the second game of the 1948 semifinal series, Boston Bruins defenceman Murray Henderson went after Watson and learned to regret it as the normally mild-mannered winger dropped his gloves in an instant and pummelled Henderson fast and furiously, smashing his nose with one of his punches. The Bruins player was humbled in front of his home crowd and had to go off for repairs. The fight earned Watson a reputation as a heavyweight who was not to be messed with. His all-round game made him one of the first "power forwards" in the NHL.

By the 1954–55 season the Chicago Black Hawks were struggling so badly that the NHL decided all other teams should send players to help them out. The Leafs offered Watson and sent him to Chicago on December 10, 1954. He played three years with the Black Hawks and another season with the Buffalo Bisons of the American Hockey League before going into coaching.

Since his retirement, Watson has been a great ambassador for hockey and gives his time generously for many charitable causes. A true gentleman, his outstanding career was recognized with a selection to the Hall of Fame in 1994.

Harry Watson keeps his eye on the puck against Detroit defenceman Bob Goldham and goalie Terry Sawchuk. The Leafs acquired Watson from Detroit in exchange for Billy Taylor on September 21, 1946. (HB)

Maple Leaf stats:	GP	G	A	P	PIM
regular season	500	163	122	285	111
playoffs	50	14	9	23	27

BILL BARILKO'S FINAL TRIP

by Kerry Banks

THE DISCOVERY of a skeleton inside the crumpled wreckage of a single-engine plane in the spring of 1962 was front-page news. It provided the answer to hockey's most haunting mystery: the fate of "Bashin' Bill" Barilko. The hard-hitting defenceman, whose tale is immortalized by the Tragically Hip in their song "Fifty-Mission Cap" and whose number 5 is one of only two uniforms officially retired by the Toronto Maple Leafs, scored one of the most famous Stanley Cup-winning goals in history in 1951. Sadly, Barilko's finest hockey moment was also his last.

Born to parents of Russian heritage in the gold-mining town of Timmins, Ontario, the free-spirited Barilko was called up from the Hollywood Wolves of the Pacific Coast Hockey League by the slumping Leafs late in the 1946–47 season. Arriving in Toronto during a terrible snowstorm, the 19-year-old rookie entered the dressing room for his first practice with such legends as Syl Apps, Ted Kennedy and Turk Broda and boldly proclaimed, "Boys, the sun is shining!"

Barilko's optimism and confidence were infectious and he made an immediate impact, fearlessly scrapping with anyone and dishing out punishing bodychecks. As teammate Howie Meeker later recalled, "When he bodychecked someone it was like being hit with the end of a pickaxe or an anvil." With Barilko patrolling the blue line, the Leafs won four Cups in five years. The most dramatic was the fourth, in 1951: all five games in the finals series against the Montreal Canadiens were decided in overtime, the only time that has ever occurred, and the entire country was caught up in the excitement.

In the fateful fifth game at Maple Leaf Gardens, Montreal led 2–1 entering the final minute, only to watch Toronto pull its goalie and tie the score with 32 seconds remaining. The overtime ended suddenly at 2:32, when Barilko impulsively dashed in from the point to lift a loose puck over goalie Gerry McNeil's shoulder. The moment, frozen in time by Nate Turofsky's camera lens, shows Barilko in full flight, soaring through the air as the black disc enters the net.

The goal ignited a wild celebration. Barilko's jubilant mother rushed out onto the ice to kiss her son and the grinning youngster was hoisted atop his teammates' shoulders. Kennedy, the Leafs' captain, called it his greatest thrill.

Barilko was still basking in his newfound fame four months later when he left Timmins on August 24 for a weekend fishing trip with Henry Hudson, a dentist and amateur pilot. Their destination was Seal River on James Bay. The pair never returned.

On August 29 a search was mounted. Lasting 30 days and involving 28 planes covering 840,000 square kilometres, it became the largest search-and-rescue operation in Canadian history. Conn Smythe, the Leafs' notoriously tight-fisted owner, posted a $10,000 reward for his star blueliner. Reflecting the public interest, the *Globe and Mail* ran six articles on the mystery in two weeks. One story quoted witnesses who claimed they saw a plane matching the description of the missing aircraft at dusk on August 28 over Timmins. It buzzed low over the Hudson home and revved its engines as if trying to attract attention before swinging toward Porcupine Lake, where Hudson often landed. Mrs. Hudson was one of those who saw the phantom plane. She rushed to the lake to meet her husband, but found nothing.

Bizarre rumours circulated about the missing men. One asserted that Barilko was a Russian spy and had fled back to his ancestral homeland over the North Pole. Another contended that he and Hudson had been smuggling gold and that the weight of bullion had brought down the plane.

As the weeks passed and speculation grew, psychics were consulted, a fitting touch for a case with so many eerie facets: the 24-year-old blond hockey hero had vanished in a yellow plane called a Fairchild 24 and Barilko's pilot had the same name as the British explorer who had disappeared in the area in 1611, cast adrift by his mutinous crew.

According to the police account, Barilko and Hudson left Seal River on Sunday, August 26. At noon they landed at Fort George on James Bay, where they unloaded sleeping bags, a tent and cooking gear in an apparent bid to lighten their load. They next set down at Rupert House, a Hudson's Bay Company depot 260 kilo-

The Leafs celebrate Bill Barilko's famous 1951 Cup-winning goal. (HHOF).

metres farther south. Dan Wheeler, the depot clerk, warned them of a storm brewing to the south, but Hudson said they had 120 pounds of fish in the plane's pontoons and wanted to get back to Timmins before the catch spoiled. As the plane was refuelled, Barilko stood silently on the dock, staring at the horizon. Witnesses reported that as the aircraft took off it seemed to labour as if weighed down with something heavier than 120 extra pounds. That was the last anyone saw of them.

In late September, as the saddened Leafs gathered at training camp, the search was finally called off. So reluctant was the club to accept Barilko's loss that when the 1951–52 season opened his equipment was placed in his dressing-room stall. Barilko's absence hung over the team like a curse; after capturing four Cups in five years, the Leafs had lost their magic. Over the next seven seasons the club missed the playoffs three times and once finished dead last. In the three years that it made the postseason, Toronto won only two playoff games. As the drought reached 10 years many were convinced the Leafs would never again win the Cup unless Barilko was found. But on April 22, 1962, 11 years and one day after his famous goal, Toronto defeated the Chicago Blackhawks to claim the crown. The jinx was over.

Five weeks later, Gary Fields, a Lands and Forests helicopter pilot, spotted the wreckage of a plane in the muskeg north of Cochrane, Ontario. A search was launched and on June 6 the missing Fairchild 24 was located. Its ghostly occupants were identified as Barilko and Hudson by their watches and other personal items. The Search and Rescue report blamed the crash on pilot inexperience combined with bad weather, but that was only a guess: there was little evidence to support any definite conclusion. Intriguingly, the report did not say why no trace of fish or anything else was found in the sealed pontoons, nor why the police investigation was shrouded in such secrecy. Peter Worthington of the *Toronto Telegram* called the operation a "hush-hush assignment" and wrote: "Although the bush had surrendered the victims, the mystery still lingers."

A strange convergence of fives is connected with the tale. Barilko, who wore number 5, was in his fifth season. His Cup winner was scored in game 5 of the '51 playoffs, and it was the fifth overtime goal of the finals. It was also his fifth career playoff goal and his fifth point of that year's postseason. And Fields, the chopper pilot, was five days into his summer contract when he spotted the downed Fairchild near Highway 5.

THE '60S WAS A GREAT TIME to be a fan of the Toronto Maple Leafs. The club won four
Stanley Cups, in 1962, 1963, 1964 and 1967. Being a constant contender for the Cup made
coach and general manager Punch Imlach the toast of Toronto and the players were heroes
to all of English Canada, much as they had been in the '40s. The new
manager was instrumental in making the Leafs farm system one of
the best in the NHL once again. Before Imlach entered the scene,
the Leafs had only 22 players under contract. He soon had
that number up to 140, although in the late '60s the
organization made a huge mistake in selling off two
minor-league teams, the Victoria Maple Leafs in
British Columbia and the Rochester Americans.
Imlach reaped the benefits of the seeds the club
had planted in the early '50s, but he was
not well liked by his players.

Coach Punch Imlach (right) was not considered a great strategist, but he was an excellent motivator and knew who could play well together. Here he is shown with players Ron Stewart (left) and the bespectacled Tim Horton. (HHOF)

Eddie Shack scored the winning goal in the fifth game of the 1963 finals and then carried off the Stanley Cup. (York University Archives)

Still, he had a knack for making the right personnel moves and did not hesitate to pull the trigger on a trade if he felt it would make the Leafs stronger. He was loyal to a core group of players who enjoyed winning championships together — nine Leafs won all four Cups. Here is a look at how they did it.

Management and Coaching

The major change in the club management was the takeover by Stafford Smythe, Harold Ballard and John Bassett. The trio bought out Conn Smythe's shares in the team and Maple Leaf Gardens. Stafford was now firmly in control and his father was denied any say in player movement by November 1961, when the sale was completed. The outspoken Conn continued to air his opinions about hockey matters on and off the ice until the day he died.

Punch Imlach was the only coach and general manager the Leafs had until 1969. He was assisted by King Clancy, who had hung around the team since leaving the Leafs coaching job. Clancy filled in for Imlach behind the bench on occasion, including a 10-game stretch in 1966–67 when Punch was sick. Clancy was the perfect foil to the stern taskmaster by keeping things light.

Imlach and Stafford Smythe were never great friends and their relationship was often tense, but as long as the Leafs were winning everything was tolerated. When they lost — such as the time lowly Boston beat the Leafs 11–0 at the Gardens on January 18, 1964 — Imlach suffered Smythe's sarcasm. By the end of the decade, Stafford decided it was time for younger men to take over. He fired Imlach moments after a playoff loss to the Bruins in 1969 and brought in Jim Gregory as general manager and John McLellan as coach. It was the end of an era.

Best Trades and Acquisitions

Imlach's initial moves to shore up the Leafs in the late '50s were incredibly astute (the best was the deal that brought Allan Stanley to Toronto) and he kept it up in the early '60s. First he landed Red Kelly to play centre and then he took a chance and traded for Eddie Shack. He added depth by acquiring Don Simmons as backup for Johnny Bower and found good supporting defenders in Kent Douglas, Larry Hillman and Al Arbour and extra forwards in Eddie Litzenberger and John MacMillan. In the middle of the decade Imlach added Andy Bathgate and Don McKenney from New York and Terry Sawchuk, Marcel Pronovost and Larry Jeffrey from Detroit. All the players he brought in contributed to at least one Stanley Cup win. But as the decade ended, the Leafs were getting older and Imlach's trading abilities seemed to be declining as well. Some of the young players he gave up in deals might have helped the Leafs in the future.

Notable Events

The Leafs' development system was producing a strong group of players including Dave Keon, Bob Nevin, Ron Ellis, Brit Selby and Jim Pappin. They joined a solid core already in place by the late '50s to turn Toronto into an NHL powerhouse. The team that won the Cup in 1967 could not have done so without Peter Stemkowski, Mike Walton and Brian Conacher, all Toronto Marlboro graduates.

The Leafs were a difficult team to play against. They won their first Cup in 11 years at Chicago in front of rabid Black Hawks fans, and came through in the seventh game at the Montreal Forum in 1964 to keep alive their hopes for three straight championships.

The Toronto-Montreal rivalry was intense and made for great television viewing between 1958 and 1967. Hockey fans would tune in to see Leafs games every Saturday and Wednesday night, watching NHL all-stars like Frank Mahovlich, Tim Horton, Carl Brewer, Allan Stanley, Dave Keon and Bower lead the team to many victories. Keon, Kelly, Douglas, Selby, Johnny Bower and Sawchuk also won major awards during the decade.

Worst of the Decade

The bad things that happened to the Leafs in the '60s did not really hit home until the decade, and the Imlach years, came to an end. After the 1967 surprise win over the Montreal Canadiens in the finals, the team missed the playoffs the next season even though it was an expansion year. It soon became evident that

Toronto had no new stars on the horizon and that many of its veterans were on their last legs.

As Bower and Sawchuk faded, the Leafs were forced to use journeyman Bruce Gamble in net after losing future Hall of Famer Gerry Cheevers to the Bruins (Imlach got nothing in return). In another trade he lost Dick Duff, Arnie Brown, Rod Seiling and Bob Nevin. Subsequent deals cost Toronto the services of Jim Pappin (in exchange for a used-up Pierre Pilote) and youngster Garry Unger, who was thrown into an arrangement with Detroit.

That deal was the infamous Mahovlich trade that also had the Leafs losing Stemkowski and the rights to Brewer, who simply refused to play for Imlach. Mahovlich had been badly treated by Imlach for over 10 years and needed a change, but the Leafs lost their best player. Norm Ullman and Paul Henderson, acquired from the Red Wings in the deal, played well but Toronto fans missed the "Big M" badly. It got to the point where the Leafs virtually gave away Horton, their defensive stalwart, in a deal with the New York Rangers toward the end of the 1969–70 season in the hope that a couple of marginal prospects might come through.

Bottom-line Results

The Leafs won 337 games and lost 258 between the 1960–61 and 1969–70 seasons, with 121 draws. They finished first once, second twice, third three times, fourth twice, in fifth spot once and bottomed out in 1969–70 with a sixth-place finish in the Eastern Division. They won over 30 games in nine of the 10 seasons, with a top mark of 39 in 1960–61, and lost over 30 just once (34 in 1969–70).

The franchise really started to see increases in the team's profitability. When the new owners had taken over in 1961 they had quickly set out to reduce the debt. Seating capacity at the Gardens was increased from 12,737 to 16,700 (with an estimated 15,700 seats reserved for season-ticket holders) and a restaurant, the Hot Stove Lounge, was added. The building hosted more concerts, political conventions and other forms of entertainment than ever before.

In February 1965 the Leafs sold their radio, television and program rights to MacLaren Advertising for $9 million over six years. They got $2 million for the six-team expansion of the NHL in 1967 and took in just under $1 million for the sale of two farm teams. Gardens stock that had sold for 94 cents in 1935 was up to $80 a share by 1947, when the stock split four for one. In November 1965 the stock split again, this time five for one, when the price hit $93 a share: an investor who had held one 94-cent Maple Leafs Gardens share since 1935 would have had $30,000 by 1969. By April that year the profit for the previous six-month period at the Gardens was $810,000. The big-money era had arrived, but for a couple of the Leafs owners it was still not good enough. Greed would soon win out.

Best Leafs of the Decade

IN GOAL: Johnny Bower and Terry Sawchuk.

ON DEFENCE: Tim Horton, Allan Stanley, Carl Brewer and Bob Baun.

AT FORWARD: George Armstrong, Dave Keon, Red Kelly, Frank Mahovlich and Bob Pulford.

Toronto captain George Armstrong looks at a Maple Leafs game program with some wide-eyed youngsters at Maple Leaf Gardens. (HB)

GEORGE ARMSTRONG

GEORGE ARMSTRONG was born on July 6, 1930, in Skead, Ontario, to an Irish father and an Algonquin First Nations mother. He was always proud of his heritage and became known as "Chief," a moniker he never seemed to mind. Armstrong began his hockey career with the Cooper Cliff Redmen in a northern Ontario junior league for the 1946–47 season. The next season he moved to another junior team, the Stratford Kroehlers, and produced 33 goals and 40 assists in just 36 games. Scout Bob Wilson told the Maple Leafs about the strapping 6'1", 184-pound right-winger and they invited him to Toronto to play for the Marlboro junior team for the 1948–49 season. He scored 29 times in 39 games and racked up an impressive 62 points.

Armstrong quickly became the Leafs' best prospect, but did not get into the big-league lineup on a full-time basis until the 1952–53 season. In the meantime, he played senior hockey for the Marlies and scored an amazing 85 goals in 75 regular-season and playoff games. He turned professional with the Pittsburgh Hornets of the American Hockey League where he scored 45 goals over two seasons.

Armstrong was finally promoted to the Leafs for the 1951–52 season and scored a goal in his first game, a 3–2 win over Montreal on February 9, 1952. He didn't score again until the last game of the season, when he bagged two in a 4–2 loss at Boston to finish the year with three goals and three assists in 20 games. In 1952–53, Armstrong suffered a separated shoulder at training camp, but still managed to play 52 games and score 14 times. He would never return to the minors.

The Leafs teams of the '50s were never great on offence but it also became evident that Armstrong was not going to be a prolific goal-scorer at the NHL level. He didn't score 20 goals in one season until 1958–59, hitting his career high of 23 a year later (when he also had a career-best 51 points). Still, he was a very diligent worker who could handle the puck well in tight quarters; his shot was not overpowering, but he had very good hands and was incredibly strong along the boards. These skills kept the plodding

skater in the NHL until the 1970–71 season. The gritty Armstrong was clearly a leader on and off the ice. Conn Smythe recognized these skills and made him the last captain he had a hand in selecting, for the 1957–58 season. He thought Armstrong represented all that was great about Canadian hockey players. It was a good choice: Armstrong's sense of humour was just the buffer the players needed between themselves and management. He was equally at ease speaking to his teammates or to a rough-edged coach like Punch Imlach. During the volatile '60s, "Army" Armstrong kept the Leafs team on the straight and narrow even when a revolt against Imlach methodology seemed inevitable. He was the backbone of the Leafs and everyone respected his quiet leadership and practical jokes.

By the end of his career, Armstrong had played in a team-record 1,187 games and captained the Leafs to four Stanley Cups. His work in the playoffs was always superior and he was not afraid to show his emotions when the Leafs lost a series. He was around the 20-goal mark year after year, and his most famous was an empty-netter against the Montreal Canadiens to seal a 3–1 win in the 1967 finals. This was the last goal of the NHL's "original six" era and many thought Armstrong would retire.

But he kept coming back. The captaincy was given to Dave Keon in 1969 but Armstrong wanted to stay on and was welcomed. He contributed seven goals and 25 points in 59 games at the age of 40 in 1970–71, his last year as a Leaf. He turned to coaching and won two Memorial Cups with the Toronto Marlies (1973 and 1975) with some of the greatest teams ever seen in junior hockey history.

When the Leafs changed coaches in 1977 they did not offer the job to Armstrong, who was scouting for the team at the time, and soon stopped paying him a salary. He went to work for the Quebec Nordiques but returned to Toronto in the late '80s. He did not want to take over from Leafs coach John Brophy in 1989, yet owner Harold Ballard insisted he do so if he still wanted a job. His heart not in it, Armstrong essentially let assistant Garry Larivere

run the team and was relieved when Doug Carpenter was hired to replace him. Armstrong went back to scouting, a position he still held in 2002. He was elected to the Hall of Fame in 1975.

George Armstrong gives chase to defenceman Wayne Hillman of the New York Rangers. (HB)

Maple Leaf stats:	GP	G	A	P	PIM
regular season	1,187	296	417	713	721
playoffs	110	26	34	60	52

Leaf file:

George Armstrong scored only two career hat tricks but the first was one of the most important in Leaf history. It came on March 15, 1959, in a 6–5 victory over the New York Rangers at Madison Square Garden. The Leafs were chasing the Rangers for the fourth and final playoff spot but were trailing "the Blueshirts" by seven points with just five games remaining; a weekend home-and-home series would go a long way toward settling the issue. When the Leafs won the first game 5–0 on Saturday night it gave them some hope, but taking the Sunday night contest in the Big Apple was not going to be easy. However, Armstrong put three past Gump Worsley in the Rangers net and Bob Pulford scored the winner on a long, bouncing shot the Ranger netminder missed. The Leafs won 6–5 and had a sweep. They won their last three games, including a 6–4 victory over Detroit on the last night of the season, to sneak past the Rangers by one point. A Leafs dynasty was in the making and the captain's contribution was substantial.

Left: *George Armstrong puts a shot past Boston goalie Eddie Johnston.* (HB)

Above: *Detroit goalie Terry Sawchuck tries to hold up George Armstrong before he can pick up the loose puck.* (HB)

BOB BAUN

WHEN MIKE NYKOLUK (a future coach of the Leafs, between 1981 and 1984) was asked to try out for the Toronto Marlboros junior "B" affiliate, the Weston Dukes, the right-winger insisted that his good friend Bob Baun go along with him. The Marlie managers agreed. This turned out to be a great move, not only for the terrific Marlboro clubs of the mid-50s but also for the Toronto Maple Leafs as they rebuilt their sagging team with youngsters such as Baun. The chunky defenceman (5'9", 182 pounds) played in 16 games for the junior "A" Marlies in 1952–53 and then enjoyed two Memorial Cup seasons in 1954–55 and 1955–56. By the 1956–57 season Baun was ready for pro hockey, but he began the year with Rochester of the American Hockey League despite a good training camp with the Leafs.

Baun got the call to join the Leafs on November 29, 1956, for a game against the Canadiens at the Montreal Forum. The Leafs lost 4–2, but Baun made his presence known by going after Montreal stars Jean Beliveau and Henri Richard. He ended up playing in 20 games for the Leafs that year (no goals, five assists) and learned what was needed to play in the NHL. He became a full-time Maple Leaf in 1957–58, scoring one goal in 67 games and working hard on his game. Baun came to realize that he couldn't just dart around the ice trying to nail people, but had to pick his spots and stay under control without taking himself out of the play. He also spent time working on his shot by taking a bucket of pucks after practice and just shooting away from the point until his arms were tired. Although he scored only occasionally (37 career goals), his point shot was effective and accurate and handy at times. Baun also worked diligently to improve his passing and backwards skating.

If Baun was known for anything, it was toughness. Using his stocky body and low centre of gravity, he could dish out some devastating bodychecks and kept the opposition wary. The Leafs defenceman was not especially fast on his skates, but he could close in on an opponent very quickly to hand out some heavy punishment: his battles with Chicago's Bobby Hull are the stuff of legend. His bow-legged skating stance helped Baun throw some fierce (and clean) hip checks, a lost art today. He was fearless in blocking shots and suffered a great deal of pain throughout his career because of his style. When the Leafs paired him with Carl Brewer, the team had a formidable combination that helped it win three straight Stanley Cups.

Baun's most famous moment as a Leaf came in the 1964 finals against Detroit, when he broke his ankle during the sixth game of the series. The Leafs were facing elimination and were tied 3–3 in the third period at the Detroit Olympia when he was injured blocking a Detroit shot. He couldn't skate and was taken off on a stretcher, but returned before the third period was over. The game went into overtime and Baun was given a shot of painkiller, then went out to take his shift with his ankle heavily taped. Red Wings defenceman Al Langlois shot the puck blindly around the boards and right to Baun, who immediately fired a shot from the point. The puck hit Red Wing Bill Gadsby's stick and flew over the shoulder of helpless Detroit goalie Terry Sawchuk: the Leafs had tied the series. Baun also played in the seventh game at Maple Leaf Gardens, not missing a shift while enduring incredible pain as the Leafs won 4–0.

Like other Leafs, Baun had his share of battles with coach and general manager Punch Imlach, usually about money. Before the 1965–66 season he asked for a $10,000 raise. Imlach would offer him only $2,000, but when Brewer suddenly retired, Imlach upped this by $8,000. The money battles were not over, especially when Imlach heard that Baun had offered a younger Leaf advice on how to negotiate; Baun had plenty of interests outside hockey and could wheel and deal with ease. But Imlach decided Baun had become expendable after expansion in 1967–68 and his limited role in the Leafs Cup win the previous spring.

Baun returned to the Leafs during the 1970–71 season and helped a young blue-line corps develop; he also broke Serge Savard's leg with a clean hip check at the Montreal Forum during

Bob Baun (#21) ties up Dave Balon of the Montreal Canadiens after a faceoff in the Leafs end. (HB)

a 5–4 Leafs win over the Canadiens on January 30, 1971. Baun was named the Leafs MVP that year, but was forced to retire in 1972 after a hit from Mickey Redmond of Detroit seriously injured his neck. Leafs owner Harold Ballard once said in an interview that nobody remembered Baun, but the bombastic one was wrong again: Baun remains one of the most popular Leafs of all time.

The Business of the Maple Leafs:

On December 7, 1963, the Maple Leafs and the Chicago Black Hawks staged a wild donnybrook at the Gardens as a 3–0 Toronto victory was winding down. Reggie Fleming of Chicago speared Eddie Shack of the Leafs and Bob Baun went after him in the penalty box. This started a wild melee that ended up costing Baun $2,800 in fines, at a time when he was earning only about $12,500. Former Leafs owner Conn Smythe was so pleased that Baun had stood up for a teammate that he sent Baun and his family a cheque for $2,800 as a "gift" just before Christmas. In a letter that accompanied it, Smythe wrote: "Men must stand up and be counted."

Maple Leaf stats:	GP	G	A	P	PIM
regular season	739	29	140	169	1,155
playoffs	92	3	12	15	165

JOHNNY BOWER

BORN IN PRINCE ALBERT, Saskatchewan, Johnny Bower did not have much as a child. He was always worried about going hungry yet had a tremendous desire to succeed. His first idol was a local hockey goaltender named Don Deacon. Bower carried Deacon's skates to games and generally hung around his hero. One day, when Bower was 10 years old, Deacon gave him a pair of his old skates. They were too big, but Bower found a way to wear them and a hockey career was born: Bower and a friend made pads out of mattresses and he was all set to be a goalie. He began playing junior hockey with various teams in his hometown, including the Prince Albert Black Hawks, before turning professional in 1945.

After spending most of the 1945–46 season with the Providence Reds of the American Hockey League, Bower played for the AHL Cleveland Barons until 1954. He led the AHL in wins three times and was named to the first all-star team in 1952 and 1953. His good play was noticed by the New York Rangers, who acquired his rights from Cleveland in exchange for cash and two players, including goaltender and future Rangers general manager Emile Francis.

Bower played in all 70 games with the Rangers in 1953–54 and posted a respectable 29–31–10 record, with five shutouts. But the next season saw him back in the minors, this time in the Western Hockey League for the Vancouver Canucks, for all but five games in New York. He split the next two years between Cleveland and Providence and seemed happy in the minors despite suffering his fair share of injuries. He would not wear a mask until the 1968–69 season and one night an AHL opponent's skate tore into Bower's jaw, hooked around a molar and ripped the tooth out of the socket, leaving a hole in his cheek. There was a lot of blood, but Bower was stitched up and went out to finish the game.

Eventually, his toughness and perseverance paid off. The Maple Leafs were not happy with their goaltending in the summer of 1958, so when Bower caught the attention of coach Billy Reay the Leafs drafted his playing rights away from the Barons. The

two-year deal, and the urging of Cleveland owner Jim Hendy, gave Bower the impetus he needed to try the NHL one more time. He played in 39 games (15–17–7) for Toronto in 1958–59 and got the Leafs into the playoffs, where they lost in the finals to Montreal. In the next season Bower was the Leafs' number 1 goalie and won 34 of his 66 appearances. In 1960–61 he won the Vezina Trophy as the NHL's best netminder, with a 33–15–10 record and a league-leading 2.50 goals-against average.

By the 1961–62 season, in which Bower had 31 wins, the Leafs were primed to win their first Stanley Cup since 1951. He led the team past the New York Rangers in the semifinal and played the first four games of the finals against Chicago. During the fourth game, Bower stretched to stop a Bobby Hull blast and pulled a muscle; he finished the game but was done for the series. Backup Don Simmons took over in goal and won the last two games to bring the Cup back to Toronto. For Bower, who had been set to finish his career in the minor leagues only a few years earlier, winning the fabled trophy was a dream come true.

The Leafs breezed to another Cup in 1962–63, finishing in first place and wiping out Montreal and Detroit in just 10 games. They took the Cup again in 1963–64, but the going was harder and questions were raised about Bower's performance during the playoffs. He struggled at the start of the semifinals against the Montreal Canadiens but won a crucial contest at the Gardens with a 3–0 shutout to tie the hard-fought series at three games each. The final game was played at the Forum and Bower was excellent, allowing only one goal, in the third period, while Dave Keon scored three to give Toronto a 3–1 win.

In the finals against Detroit, the Red Wings had a 3–2 lead in games going home. Bower bent in game 6 but did not break and the Leafs won a close contest 4–3 in overtime. The seventh game in Toronto was 1–0 going into the third period when the Leafs popped in three more and Bower kept Detroit at bay. Bower had proved his worth. A very competitive player who stayed in excel-

Johnny Bower tries to use his famous poke check on Chico Maki of the Chicago Black Hawks, with Red Kelly looking to lend a hand. (HB)

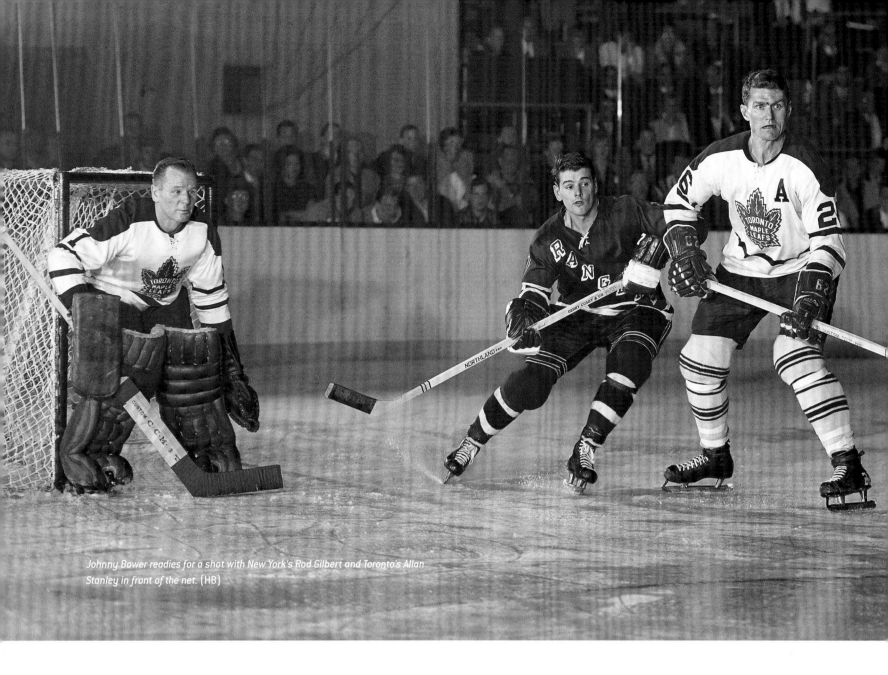

Johnny Bower readies for a shot with New York's Rod Gilbert and Toronto's Allan Stanley in front of the net. (HB)

lent shape, he had more than four more seasons left in his aging body (nobody was quite sure of his age, although his birthday is listed as November 8, 1924).

Terry Sawchuk came to the Leafs to split the netminding duties for the 1964–65 season and the two shared a Vezina Trophy and a Stanley Cup in 1967. Bower won two games in the finals against Montreal, the first a 3–0 shutout at the Forum in the second game.

His second win came in the following game in Toronto, when he was brilliant in turning back the Canadiens during a long over-time battle that the Leafs finally won 3–2. Bower pulled off one trademark move during the game when he poke-checked the speedy Yvan Cournoyer as the Habs player was poised to score. It was the final hurrah for Bower — a fitting way to remember the Hall of Fame goaltender.

Maple Leaf stats:	GP	Wins	Losses	Ties	Shutouts	GAA
regular season	472	220	161	79	33	2.51
playoffs	74	34	35	–	5	2.58

I never enjoyed being scored on by anyone regardless of the situation. During practice it was all business for me. Because of my age, I was constantly working on my angles and I took a lot of pride in making saves against my teammates or any opponents. Johnny Bower, Leafs program, January 2, 1984

Johnny Bower makes a save against Ab McDonald of the Pittsburgh Penguins with Larry Hillman of the Leafs moving in. Hillman was a valuable member of the 1967 Stanley Cup-winning team. (HB)

CARL BREWER

DEFENCEMAN CARL BREWER was born in Toronto on October 21, 1938, and was a good all-round athlete. He excelled at football and baseball but was even better at hockey. Given a chance to try out for the Cleveland Indians, he decided to play hockey instead. Brewer came to the attention of the Leafs' local talent scouts when he made the Weston Dukes in 1955–56. He moved to the Toronto Marlboros in 1956, winning the Memorial Cup with them that year. He spent two more years with them before moving straight to the Maple Leafs in 1958–59.

The strength of Brewer's game was his great skating. He could take the puck and carry it up the ice at top speed. He displayed many of these skills as a top rookie in 1958–59, with three goals and 21 assists. He finished second to Ralph Backstrom of the Canadiens in voting for the Calder Trophy and also showed a bit of a temper, with 125 penalty minutes. In 1959–60 he upped his penalty-minute total to 150, top in the NHL, while scoring four times and recording 23 assists. By this time Brewer was showing all-star talent — he made the first team in 1963 and the second team in 1962 and 1965 while he was with the Leafs — and a certain unpredictability that would be his trademark.

Brewer's problems seemed to start and end with coach and general manager Punch Imlach. It all began with his first contract, although Brewer did pretty well by getting an estimated $16,500 over two years, with a $4,000 bonus thrown in. A few years later he fought with Imlach for a difference of barely $100 and enrolled in university to prove his point; Imlach's assistant, King Clancy, had to retrieve Brewer before the season began. Another time, Brewer was upset that the Leafs would not pay him extra money after he broke his arm during the 1963 Stanley Cup finals against Detroit and could not work during the summer as a result. The issue was resolved once again but Brewer, though happy playing pro hockey, was unhappy with the Leafs. He could be moody and a little distant from teammates from time to time, but his extraordinary talent made him very valuable.

Bob Baun was the perfect defensive partner for Brewer, who could charge around the ice knowing that "Boomer" was behind him to back him up. The blue line pairing was essential to the Leafs' winning three straight Stanley Cups in 1962, 1963 and 1964. But Brewer was not long for the Leafs.

After an all-star season in 1964–65 when he had a career-high 27 points, he was in a cantankerous mood at the Leafs' 1965 training camp. He had a run-in with goalie Johnny Bower in the dressing room during an exhibition game and did not join his teammates for the next period. Imlach confronted him and told Brewer to take off his uniform: it was the end of Brewer's career as a Leaf. In 1968, his rights were traded to Detroit and he promptly regained his all-star status in 1969–70.

Brewer also played for the St. Louis Blues and for Canada in the world championships in Winnipeg in 1967. He came back to Toronto with the World Hockey Association in 1973 and then rejoined the Leafs in an ill-advised return to the NHL during the 1979–80 season. He was not especially welcome in the dressing room but felt he could not turn down the opportunity to finish his career as a Maple Leaf — an offer made by one-time nemesis Punch Imlach.

Years later Brewer played a large role in bringing former friend and NHL Players Association executive director Alan Eagleson to justice over his management of the players' pension fund, and in helping members recover the money owed them. Brewer asked many of the questions that got the ball rolling and went to the lawyer who won the case for the retired players. Some were upset that Brewer did not make a financial contribution to the cause, but without the start he provided the entire case might never have come together.

Brewer died suddenly in the summer of 2001.

Carl Brewer (#2) of Toronto ties up Detroit's Alex Delvecchio (#10). (HB)

Leaf file:

When the Maple Leafs and the Chicago Black Hawks staged a wild brawl at the Gardens on December 7, 1963, Carl Brewer was pivotal. Earl Balfour was bent on getting at Brewer and scrapped with him twice during the bench-clearing fight. At one point Balfour managed to manoeuvre Brewer along the boards and the Leafs defenceman fell through the open gate onto the Leafs bench. Balfour pro-

ceeded to pummel him before a number of others pulled the Black Hawk off.

Brewer claimed he was never the same after this brawl. He may have been trying to protect the arm he had broken the previous spring, but probably was being too hard on himself as he was never a fighter and had a reputation for using his stick.

Maple Leaf stats:

	GP	G	A	P	PIM
regular season	473	19	136	155	917
playoffs	63	3	15	18	136

DICK DUFF

DICK DUFF was born in Kirkland Lake, Ontario, on February 18, 1936, the sixth of 13 children. A bright pupil, he was an even better hockey player. The Maple Leafs recruited him for St. Michael's high school in Toronto for the 1952–53 season and he started out playing for the Buzzers in the junior "B" loop. Duff was promoted to the Majors that year and scored three goals in 16 games. The next season Toronto hockey fans saw a glimpse of the team's future when Duff scored 35 times in 59 games and totalled 75 points. He played one more year for the Majors and kept up his scoring with 33 goals in 47 games, making enough of an impression to get a brief three-game trial with the Leafs in 1954–55. They signed the spunky left-winger on September 23, 1955.

In 1955 the Leafs were so desperate for attackers that Duff was not given any time to learn the pro game in the minors. He proved he didn't need any seasoning, scoring 18 times and making 19 assists in 68 games. The next two years saw Duff record consecutive 26-goal seasons, and he had raised his points total to 49 by 1957–58. The team was still floundering in the early going of the 1958–59 campaign, but Duff came up with a career-high 29 goals and a miracle finish to the regular season secured the final playoff berth. Duff was instrumental in nailing down the playoff spot by scoring the winning goal on the last night of the season, a 6–4 win over Detroit. Centre Larry Regan told Duff he was going to break a 4–4 tie late in the game and set up the left-winger for the important marker. In those playoffs Duff had seven points in 12 games, including an overtime game winner in the third game of the finals against Montreal with the great Jacques Plante in net.

Duff's goal-scoring started to decline the following season and he would never again score over 20 goals as a Leaf. In 1959–60 Duff bagged his 100th career goal during a 3–0 win over Boston on October 17, 1959, assisted by Ted Hampson, but totalled only 19, with his points falling from 53 to 41. In the next three years he scored 16, 17 and 16 goals during the regular season but he came up big in the playoffs.

In the 1962 finals against Chicago it was Duff who scored the Stanley Cup-winning goal in the sixth game of the series. The Leafs were up 3–2, but the Black Hawks were tough on home ice and opened the scoring in the third period when Duff lost the puck to sharpshooter Bobby Hull. After a wild celebration by the Chicago crowd, Bob Nevin tied the game for the Leafs and Tim Horton set up Duff to blast the winner past Glenn Hall. In the 1963 finals against Detroit, Duff opened the series with two goals in 1:08, using his speed to escape the attentions of Floyd Smith and a sleepy Red Wings defence; this speed record for a pair of goals at the start of a playoff game still stands. It was Duff's last shining moment as a Maple Leaf.

Small but scrappy at 5'9" and 165 pounds, Duff was as tough as nails and never hesitated to drop the gloves if he had to. He was simply determined to score goals. His good looks and cheery personality made him very popular in Toronto, so it was a great shock when he was dealt to the New York Rangers in 1964 in a trade that brought Andy Bathgate to the Leafs. He did not thrive in New York, but found his game with Montreal and went on to play for Los Angeles and Buffalo before retiring after the 1971–72 season. He finished with 283 goals and 572 points in 1,030 games.

Duff returned to the Leafs, working as a scout for many years and then going into management, though he never rose to a position of great prominence in the organization. Bad investments hounded him for many years, but he recovered and is still remembered for his drive and competitive spirit as a Leaf.

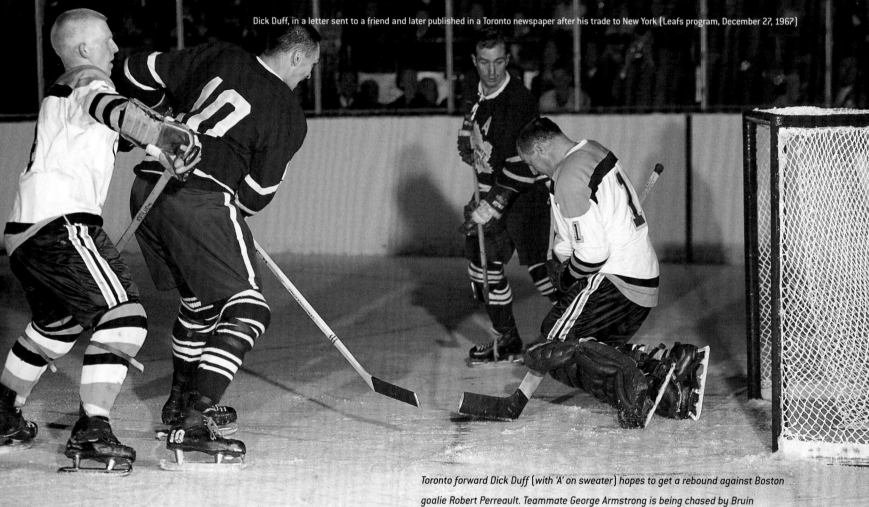

... I thank the Maple Leafs management for their deep personal interest in my development, first as a man and then a National Leaguer. Their organization has my highest endorsement for any young boy wanting to play in the National Hockey League.

Dick Duff, in a letter sent to a friend and later published in a Toronto newspaper after his trade to New York (Leafs program, December 27, 1967)

Toronto forward Dick Duff (with 'A' on sweater) hopes to get a rebound against Boston goalie Robert Perreault. Teammate George Armstrong is being chased by Bruin defenceman Pat Stapleton. (HB)

Maple Leaf stats:	GP	G	A	P	PIM
regular season	582	174	165	339	535
playoffs	54	14	23	37	40

RON ELLIS

IF THERE IS ONE Maple Leaf who epito-mizes consistency and solid two-way play, it's Ron Ellis. His first NHL coach, Punch Imlach, once said he wished he had a team filled with players like the sturdy right-winger. Ellis was no superstar, but Imlach recognized that he was the type of player a coach could use in any situation. To date, Ellis is the last player to start and end his career as a Maple Leaf, a fitting epitaph for a great Toronto hockey legend.

Ellis was born in Lindsay, Ontario, on January 8, 1945, and nearly became the property of the Detroit Red Wings, who showed an interest in him as a youngster. He turned down a $10,000 scholarship offer to study engineering at Michigan Tech to con-tinue his hockey career and pursue his dream of playing for the Maple Leafs. By 1960–61 he was with the Toronto Midget Marlboros and made the junior "A" team the next season, scoring 17 times in 33 games. His best year with the Marlies was in 1963–64, when he scored 46 goals and helped the powerful team take the Memorial Cup. Future Leafs forwards on the Marlie squad included Peter Stemkowski, Brit Selby, Mike Walton and Wayne Carleton. Ellis was the best of the group and the Leafs decided to give him a try in the NHL at the age of 19.

Considering his tender age, Imlach would have been happy if Ellis had scored 10 goals in 1964–65. But the smooth skater sur-prised everyone by netting 23 as a rookie and lost out on the Calder Trophy only to a spectacular season by Detroit goalie Roger Crozier. Ellis was given an introductory elbow by Gordie Howe of the Red Wings in his first game with the Leafs, a 5–3 Leafs win in Detroit. He was not deterred and scored his first goal in the next game, against Eddie Johnston of the Bruins, during a 7–2 Leafs win on October 17, 1964.

Ellis scored 19 in the next season and 22 in 1966–67 to lead the team in goals. In the Leafs' magical '67 playoffs he produced two goals, opening the scoring in the sixth and last game of the finals against Montreal when he put home a Red Kelly rebound over Canadiens goalie Gump Worsley. The team declined severely after the Cup win but Ellis continued to flourish. Starting with the 1967–68 season, he began a string of nine consecutive years of 20 or more goals, giving him a club record for most career 20-goal seasons with 11. His best year was 1969–70, when he scored 35 times for a team that did not even make the playoffs. Coach John McLellan thought Ellis could have bagged even more goals if he had just shot the puck more often.

Ellis had a powerful shot and his speed allowed him to track down many loose pucks. His stocky build (5'9", 195 pounds) made him tough to knock off his skates and he was a good, clean checker. He could read the play as well as anyone and only a lack of finishing touch held down his goal-scoring. Ellis was named to Team Canada for the historic 1972 Summit Series and played bril-liantly in defence by watching the highly skilled Valeri Kharlamov.

Ellis played three more years with the Leafs after the Summit Series before suddenly retiring for personal reasons after the 1974–75 season, when he had posted a career-best 61 points (32 goals, 29 assists). He was coaxed back to play at the 1977 world championships and rejoined the Leafs for the 1977–78 season. His 50 points and 26 goals — including his 300th, when he blasted a shot past Kurt Ridley of Vancouver on March 4, 1978, in a 4–3 Leafs win — contributed a lot to the team that upset the New York Islanders in the '78 playoffs.

Ellis stayed with the Leafs until the 1980–81 season when he was dropped from the team (after two goals and five points in 27 games) by Punch Imlach, the man who had given him his start in 1964. Ellis remains one of the most popular alumni members of the Leafs and works at the Hockey Hall of Fame in public relations.

Ron Ellis (#11) scores his first NHL goal, beating Boston goalie Eddie Johnston (#1) on the night of October 17, 1964. Ted Green is the Bruins defenceman. (HB)

Leaf file:

When Ron Ellis began his career in 1964–65 the Leafs gave him sweater number 11, which he wore in his great first season in the NHL. At the start of the next season, superstitious coach Punch Imlach asked Ellis to give number 11 to newcomer Brit Selby, so he could debut with the "lucky" sweater Ellis had worn the year before. Ellis agreed and switched to wearing number 8 that year, while the new number 11 scored 14 goals and won the Calder Trophy for best rookie. Former Leaf Ace Bailey was so impressed with Ellis that he asked for his sweater number 6 to be taken out of retirement and given to the Leafs winger. Ellis started wearing number 6 for the 1968–69 season and kept it as long as he was with the Leafs. Number 6 has not been worn since Ellis played his final game as a Leaf on January 14, 1981.

Maple Leaf stats:	GP	G	A	P	PIM
regular season	1,034	332	308	640	207
playoffs	70	18	8	26	20

TIM HORTON

A NATIVE OF Cochrane, defenceman Tim Horton was one of many young players from northern Ontario to join the Maple Leafs. He was scouted by Bob Wilson and signed to a binding C-form. The organization took him to Toronto in 1947 and placed him at St. Michael's, which was turning into a factory for future Maple Leafs. He played two seasons at St. Mike's and was playing pro hockey by the 1949–50 season. Toronto owner Conn Smythe felt Horton was the best defensive prospect in Canada, but still sent him to Pittsburgh to play in the American Hockey League for the Hornets, where he earned about $4,000 a year. He stayed there for three seasons and won a championship in 1951–52. Then a trade opened a spot on the Toronto roster and Horton joined the big club.

When the Leafs sent defenceman Gus Mortson to Chicago they believed Horton could easily step in and take his place, especially since he played a similar type of game. Horton proved he belonged in the NHL by playing all 70 games in the next two seasons, wracking up 47 points. He was named a second-team all-star after the 1953–54 season.

But disaster struck at Maple Leaf Gardens on March 12, 1955, when he took a thunderous bodycheck from Bill Gadsby of the New York Rangers as he was carrying the puck near his own blue line (Horton's skate may also have caught a rut on the ice). Horton's jaw and leg were broken and it was said that the cracking sound could be heard all over the Gardens. The devastating injuries forced Horton to miss most of the following season and many feared his career was over. His salary was cut and the Leafs thought long and hard about dealing him to Chicago (for Mortson), Boston (for defenceman Bob Armstrong) or even Montreal. Luckily, they hung onto the powerful defenceman and he bounced back to have a Hall of Fame career. There is little chance the Leafs would have won four Stanley Cups without him.

Horton's game was built around his great strength. Although he stood just 5'10" and weighed 180 pounds, his body was solid and his ability to lift weights was amazing. His strong upper body allowed him to crunch the opposition and he could apply a death-like bear hug to an unruly foe, as he did to Phil Esposito in the 1967 playoffs. Horton rarely fought, because few dared to challenge him (Derek Sanderson of Boston and Dave Schultz of Philadelphia tried but failed), so he could concentrate on playing his game. He was a good skater with decent speed and could fire a shot from point with the best in the league. Horton was so good at both ends of the ice that he was sometimes sent up to right wing, where he was quite effective. Despite his legendary strength he was not a bodychecker, but when he did hit someone it was like being whacked by a tree trunk.

As the Leafs improved under coach Punch Imlach, Horton regained his all-star status. He was a first-team all-star in 1963–64 and runner-up for the Norris Trophy as the NHL's best defenceman twice — to many, it's something of a travesty that he never won it. He produced around 20 assists a year and scored 10 times in 1961–62. In the '62 playoffs, Horton set a record for a defenceman with 16 points (three goals and 13 assists) as the Leafs regained the Stanley Cup.

Horton and defensive partner Allan Stanley were the glue that held the Leafs together throughout the '60s. In 1964–65 Horton scored 12 goals; four years later he set a career high for points with 40. He got even better with age and started to get recognized for his performances in the late '60s, earning two first-team all-star berths alongside the new star defenceman of the NHL, Bobby Orr. By 1969–70 Horton was earning about $70,000 a year, a much more appropriate wage for a player of his stature.

As Horton aged, the Leafs were in a severe decline and started to move out some of their veterans. He was highly regarded both on and off the ice, so his teammates were shocked when Horton was dealt to the New York Rangers in March 1970. Toronto did not receive much in return (role players Guy Trottier and Denis Dupere) but did acquire goalie Jacques Plante in the transaction via St. Louis. The Leafs were never the same without him.

Tim Horton was a four-time NHL first all-star team member as a Maple Leaf in 1963–64, 1966–67, 1967–68 and 1968–69. (HB)

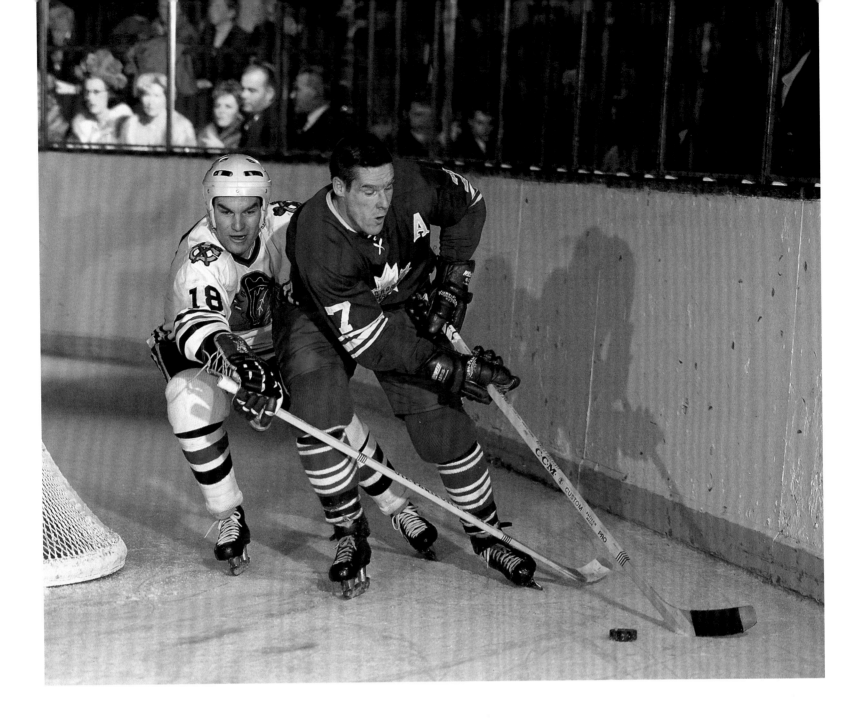

Horton could not resist the great money on offer and kept playing until the age of 44, ending his career with Pittsburgh and Buffalo; in his last years he was earning close to $100,000. He was all set for retirement after founding a successful business venture selling doughnuts, when he died in a car accident on February 21, 1974. Fittingly, his last game was against the Leafs at the Gardens and he was named one of the three stars.

Tim Horton pulls away from Chicago's Andre Boudrias. (HB)

Facing page: Tim Horton makes sure Detroit's Parker MacDonald is not going anywhere. (HB)

Maple Leaf stats:	GP	G	A	P	PIM
regular season	1,185	109	349	458	1,389
playoffs	97	9	32	41	135

GEORGE 'PUNCH' IMLACH

GEORGE IMLACH was born in Toronto on March 15, 1918, to parents of Scottish descent. He was raised in the working-class neighbourhood of Riverdale and played hockey as a youngster. Though never good enough to turn professional he was not a bad player, skating for various teams in the Toronto area and contesting a few games at Maple Leaf Gardens. He got the nickname "Punchy"—eventually shortened to "Punch"—after he was knocked out in a fight and came to swinging, as if the battle was still going on.

After a stint in the Canadian army, where he developed a strong military approach to life and sport, Imlach became involved with senior hockey in Quebec. He was coach, manager and eventually part owner of the Quebec Aces, whose star player was Jean Beliveau; Imlach often referred to the future Canadien as the best player he ever coached. Imlach then joined the Boston Bruins organization as coach and manager of the Springfield Indians in the American Hockey League and led the team straight to the finals. That caught the attention of Stafford Smythe, who was now running the Maple Leafs. Smythe offered him the assistant general manager's position (there was no official general manager at the time) and Imlach joined the Leafs in the summer of 1958.

Asked why the Leafs were doing so badly in the first two months of the 1958–59 season, Imlach replied in his famous blunt manner that the team was not playing well for coach Billy Reay. Imlach refused to say or do any more unless he was given full authority. After some discussion, the management committee gave him the power he wanted, including Conn Smythe's approval to fire Reay, and he promptly made himself coach as well as general manager.

Suddenly the Leafs had a leader who wasted no time in promising his players they would make the playoffs. This seemed a ridiculous statement at the time, but the team staged a miraculous turnaround and qualified, beating the New York Rangers into last spot by one point. In 50 games, Imlach had posted a 22–20–8 record. After upsetting the Boston Bruins in the first round, the Leafs lost to the mighty Montreal Canadiens in the 1959 finals. The young club was on its way, after so many years of underachieving.

Although Imlach was pleased with the young talent, he knew he needed some veteran help. He began by bringing in Allan Stanley (a steal from Boston in exchange for Jim Morrison) and picking up winger Gerry Ehman from the minors. This was just the beginning for the master trader, who loved the business side of hockey. He then added Red Kelly from Detroit, for spare defenceman Marc Reaume, and spiced up the team with the unpredictable Eddie Shack from the Rangers, again giving up extra players in return. Other additions included Al Arbour, Kent Douglas and Larry Hillman, minor-league defencemen who gave the Leafs great depth throughout the '60s, and Don Simmons, Bruce Gamble and Terry Sawchuk, experienced goalies brought in to help Johnny Bower in net.

Most important of all, Imlach gave his young players the chance to play. The holdovers and veterans mixed well with the newcomers in a revitalized team that won the Stanley Cup for three straight years from 1962 to 1964.

It was not easy to play for Imlach the coach and even harder to negotiate with Imlach the general manager. First, he believed in a "defence first" mentality that frustrated some of his more creative athletes such as Frank Mahovlich and Carl Brewer. The positionally sound Leafs won many games using this strategy, which was ideal for the playoffs but difficult to keep up throughout a long season. Second, Imlach skated his team into the ice during practice and many players felt they were just too tired to play the games well. Third, he had trouble dealing with players as individuals and offended many with his vulgar approach to them. When it was time to discuss contracts, Imlach guarded the Gardens vault as if it were his own, which pleased the Smythes but caused more acrimony with the players. If Imlach was cruel to some, he got a taste of his own medicine when Stafford Smythe fired him on the spot moments after the Leafs lost four straight playoff games to Boston in April 1969.

Imlach's strength as a coach was his ability to organize his

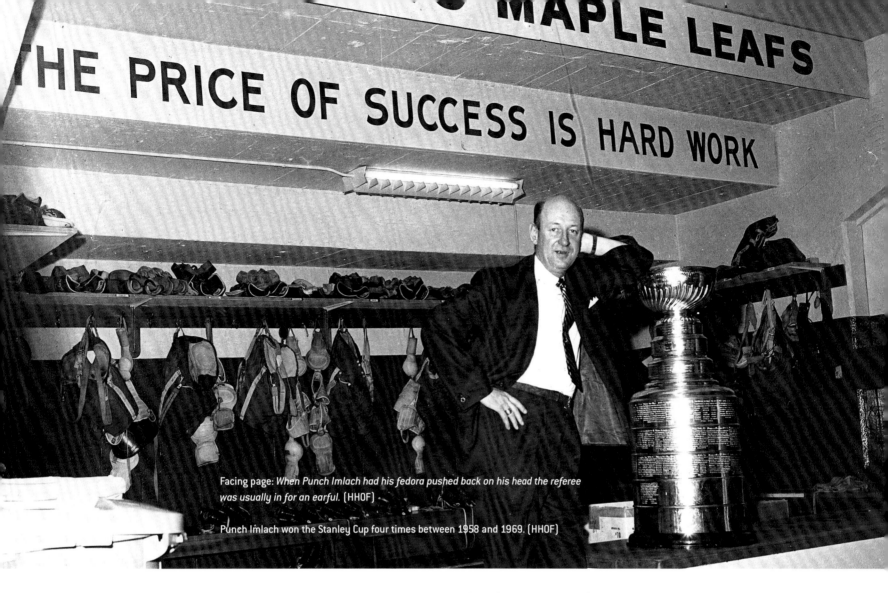

THE PRICE OF SUCCESS IS HARD WORK

Facing page: *When Punch Imlach had his fedora pushed back on his head the referee was usually in for an earful.* (HHOF)

Punch Imlach won the Stanley Cup four times between 1958 and 1969. (HHOF)

players properly and get the right matchups on the ice. Conn Smythe claimed Imlach was the best coach he had ever seen at managing a game. Imlach was no teacher of skills — he expected his players to be ready for the NHL — but was good at getting the most out of his team. He did not hesitate to use any motivational tactic, including drawing upon the teachings of Dr. Norman Vincent Peale's book, *The Power of Positive Thinking.*

Incredibly superstitious, Imlach had some quirky habits — such as starting with five defencemen for the opening faceoff — which drove players to distraction but kept his name prominent in the news. He battled for every inch if it meant winning a game and wasn't shy about giving the referee a cussing out. Love him or hate him, Imlach led his team to four Stanley Cup wins and six appearances in the finals from 1958 to 1969. His place in Leafs history cannot be denied.

However, Imlach did a lot to tarnish his legacy when he returned to manage the Leafs in 1979 after a good run with the Buffalo Sabres, and the feuding with his players reached almost comic proportions. He cost the Leafs many great players such as Lanny McDonald and Darryl Sittler and set the team back at least a decade with some ridiculous moves. After suffering a heart attack he was pushed out of the general manager's job by Harold Ballard, who told him he was gone by taking away his parking spot. It was a sorry end to Imlach's career as a Leaf.

Maple Leaf stats:		GP	Wins	Losses	Ties	Winning %
As Coach and General Manager:						
regular season		760	365	270	125	.563
playoffs		92	44	49	–	.473
Stanley Cups	4					

L E O N A R D   ' R E D '   K E L L Y

WHEN LEAFS GENERAL MANAGER and coach Punch Imlach heard that Detroit's Leonard "Red" Kelly was available in a trade, he quickly pursued an opportunity the Leafs had passed up years earlier. Now, Kelly had been dealt to the New York Rangers, but had refused to report and announced that he was "retired." In a very smart move, Imlach sent assistant general manager King Clancy to talk to Kelly about becoming a Leaf: Clancy and Kelly were both Catholics and Imlach's helper turned on the Irish charm. It helped that Detroit wanted nothing more to do with Kelly, so all the Leafs had to offer was journeyman defenceman Marc Reaume.

Kelly agreed to terms with the Leafs and played his first game on February 10, 1960, at the Gardens against the Montreal Canadiens. He was given number 4 because trainer Tommy Naylor said that many other great Leafs, including Hap Day, Bob Davidson and Harry Watson, had worn that number with distinction, so it would suit the former Red Wings star. For the next seven years, Kelly proved he was worthy of the jersey.

Red Kelly was born on July 9, 1927, in Simcoe, Ontario, and attended St. Michael's College in Toronto. It cost his father $600 a year to send him to the prestigious high school and to help pay the costs young Kelly earned about $200 as a waiter for college students. Former Leafs great Joe Primeau coached him at St. Mike's and steered Kelly away from his urge to fight the way he had in midget hockey: the fiery Irishman could get riled up, but Primeau knew he had more valuable skills. Primeau also taught Kelly how to defend, showing him how to skate backwards, break up opposition rushes and turn properly.

The Leafs scouted St. Mike's closely but turned down the chance to enlist Kelly as a recruit, also ignoring St. Mike's alumnus Ted Lindsay, a longtime teammate of Kelly's. But Carson Cooper, a Red Wings scout, put Kelly's name on his list and even took a $20 bet from someone in the Leafs organization who said the young defenceman would never make the NHL.

The Leafs were very wrong in their assessment of Kelly. He never played a game in the minors, starting his career with Detroit in 1947–48 and staying with the Red Wings until the 1959–60 season. The blueliner filled out to be an even six feet tall and a robust 190 pounds and soon displayed a flair for offence. He scored only 11 goals over his first two years, but then never scored less than 10 in any season in Motown: his highest total was 19 goals, in 1952–53. His point total was usually between 35 and 50 and he was a first-team all-star for six straight seasons from 1951 to 1957. Along the way the Red Wings, a powerful team for most of the '50s, won four Stanley Cups with Kelly anchoring the blue line.

But Detroit manager Jack Adams became disenchanted with his star defender and blamed Kelly for the Red Wings' failure to make the playoffs in 1959, even though he had played with an injured ankle for most of the year. After the botched deal with New York, Toronto swooped in and scooped up a player who had grown up listening to Foster Hewitt's radio broadcasts and always wanted to be a Maple Leaf.

The Leafs had a solid defensive group by 1960, so they didn't really need the former Norris Trophy winner to play defence. Instead, Imlach turned Kelly into a centreman. With Dave Keon and Bob Pulford already on form, the Leafs suddenly found themselves with the strongest trio of middlemen in the NHL. Kelly proved as deft at his new position as he was defending. He helped winger Frank Mahovlich become the goal scorer everyone thought he could be (48 in 1960–61) while keeping up his own production with 22, 20 and 20 goals in his first three years as a Leaf. His point totals over the same time frame — 70, 49 and 60 — were equally impressive. More importantly, the Leafs were ready to challenge for the Stanley Cup. By the time Kelly's career in Toronto was over the Hall of Famer had won four more Cups, ranking him as one of the all-time best Maple Leafs.

More than just an accomplished hockey player, Kelly also served in Canada's Parliament while still playing for the Leafs between 1962 and 1965. As a member of the minority Liberal

Facing page: *Red Kelly in a game against Montreal.* (HB)

Red Kelly has good position on Boston's Irv Spencer. Kelly won the Lady Byng Trophy in 1960–61. (HB)

government of Lester Pearson his attendance in Ottawa was crucial, which created a gruelling schedule. He kept up both roles for three years, but decided not to run again when his work as an MP became too much and his play suffered.

When he left the game as a player, Kelly became a coach with the expansion Los Angeles Kings in 1967. After a spell with the Pittsburgh Penguins, the Canadian hero came home to coach the Leafs from 1973 to 1977. His clubs had some moderate success during that time and under his leadership the Leafs played some exciting hockey, though he is probably best known for introducing "pyramid power" and "positive-negative ions" as gimmicks to get his crew going in the playoffs. The psychological ploys might have worked to some extent, but the lack of postseason success led to Kelly being replaced as coach by Roger Neilson.

Red Kelly was one of the first players to wear a helmet in the NHL. (HB)

Leaf file:

One of the most significant goals Red Kelly scored as a Leaf came in the 1962 semifinals against New York. The series was tied at two games each when the fifth game at Maple Leaf Gardens went into overtime. The Leafs put a shot on Ranger goalie Gump Worsley and a crowd gathered around the net. Worsley thought he had the puck covered, but *when he lifted his head the disc was lying on the ice. Kelly swatted it home and the Leafs won the game 3–2. They went on to defeat the Rangers 7–1 to clinch the series and took the Stanley Cup when they beat Chicago in the finals.*

Maple Leaf stats:	GP	G	A	P	PIM
regular season	470	119	232	351	74
playoffs	70	17	38	55	16

Red Kelly of the Leafs chases down a
puck against Boston's Bob Pennington.
(HB)

My first Cup (1962) with the Leafs was really something. I'll never forget it, all those people coming out to the airport to greet us. It must have been three or four o'clock in the morning but there were thousands there, cheering, grabbing and picking us up on their shoulders when we got off the plane. Red Kelly, Leafs program, April 18, 1967

DAVE KEON

IT'S A GOOD THING Vince Thompson, the Maple Leafs' scout in Quebec, had a keen eye for talent. After watching Dave Keon play, Thompson wrote a letter urging the Leafs to "come get this boy or he'll hurt you for a long time." Chief scout Bob Davidson heeded the call: The Leafs moved to sponsor Keon's midget hockey team in Noranda and gained the rights to the smooth-skating youngster. Assured that he could continue his education at St. Michael's College high school, Keon became a Leaf.

The 16-year-old was sent to the Majors junior "B" squad for the 1956–57 season, scoring 20 goals and 43 points in 36 games. For the next three seasons, Keon scored no fewer than 72 goals and had 166 points in 138 games for the Majors "A" team in the Ontario Hockey Association. The Leafs weren't sure if he was ready for the NHL, but a terrific performance at their 1960 training camp convinced them he deserved a try.

Keon was the perfect player for coach Punch Imlach's system. Dedicated to solid defensive play and always ready to sacrifice for the team, Keon became a loyal soldier for the organization for many years. Despite his small stature (5'9", 165 pounds) the centreman had learned how to check while he was at St. Michael's, getting help from people like Father David Bauer and former Leafs defenceman Bob Goldham, who knew how important this was in surviving in the NHL.

Keon had other important qualities that allowed him to adapt to life in the big league. He could skate as well as anybody in hockey. His longtime friend and hockey analyst Harry Neale summarized it best: "It looked like Keon invented skating." The diminutive centre also knew how to avoid danger on the ice and miss getting nailed by bigger foes. He was hit on occasion but was never seriously injured because his sense of anticipation was always sharp. He checked cleanly without slashing or trash-talking and his clean style of play earned the admiration of everyone, especially Leaf fans. Most importantly, Keon scored more than his share of goals, many of them in the most important games.

The 1960–61 season saw Keon and winger Bob Nevin join the team. Both passed the 20-goal mark and were considered for the Calder Trophy; Keon, who had racked up 45 points, took the award and edged his teammate into second place. That was just the beginning for Keon. The next season saw him score 26 times and 61 points in 64 games. He then added eight points in 12 playoff games as the Leafs claimed the Stanley Cup for the first time since 1951. He was awarded the Lady Byng Trophy, the first of two in a row. and a spot on the second all-star team. Keon was just as brilliant in 1962–63, notching up 28 goals, including one that clinched top spot for the Leafs in a game against Montreal on March 20, 1963. Toronto needed one point but was down 3–2 to the Habs with seconds remaining. Keon got the puck from a faceoff in the Montreal end and came out in front of the net to slip a backhand shot past Jacques Plante. The Toronto crowd went wild and the Leafs had their first first-place finish since 1947–48.

In the playoffs Keon saved his best performance for the last game of the finals against Detroit, when he scored two shorthanded goals in a 3–1 win during the clinching game for a second straight Leafs Cup win. He was the first player to bag two such goals in one playoff game.

The Quebec native twice broke the hearts of the Montreal Canadiens. In the 1964 semifinals he scored all three goals at the Montreal Forum in a 3–1 Leafs win during the seventh game of the series. Keon had scored 23 times in the regular season, but these were his first goals in the entire playoff series; he was inspired to perform for his ailing father. He then scored five times in the finals against Detroit as the Leafs won a third straight Cup.

The Canadiens got their revenge in the next two seasons, but in the 1967 playoffs Keon was back at his skating best. As broadcaster Bill Hewitt said in a television broadcast, "Keon is here, there and everywhere." Constant and relentless, he led the Leafs as they checked the Montreal squad into the ice. Toronto won its fourth Cup of the decade and Keon was rewarded with the Conn Smythe Trophy as top performer in the playoffs.

Dave Keon tries to swat the puck past Eddie Johnston (#1) of the Boston Bruins while defenceman Tom Johnson (#10) moves in. (HB)

Dave Keon works to beat Boston goalie Robert Perreault to a bouncing puck. Keon wore number 14 throughout his great career as a Leaf. He had actually wanted number 15, to honour his cousin and former Leaf, Tod Sloan, but that was worn by Billy Harris. Keon settled on 14 and it became synonymous with the slick centre. (HB)

Toronto never reached those heights again for the rest of Keon's career there. Many older Leafs retired; others such as Frank Mahovlich and Tim Horton were traded away, but Keon stayed on. In fact, he scored more goals than ever. In 1970–71, for example, he had 38 goals (his best total as a Leaf) and 38 assists while playing on a line with Garry Monahan and Billy MacMillan, two hard workers who nonetheless could not compare to the Hall of Famers with whom Keon was used to playing.

It may have been difficult for a perfectionist like Keon to accept the new realities of the expanded NHL and the struggling Leafs. He expected his teammates to play all out every game, as he did, but the new generation did not have the same desire or discipline as its leader. The Leafs could never get far in the playoffs during the early '70s but Keon continued to produce: in 1974–75, his last season as a Leaf, he still managed 59 points in 78 games.

Now the all-time leading goal scorer and point leader for the team, Keon wanted to stay put but Leafs owner Harold Ballard — who had never given the captain his just rewards financially — wouldn't offer him an acceptable contract. So Keon headed to the World Hockey Association where he played in the new pro league with Minnesota, Indianapolis and New England, before returning to the NHL with the Hartford Whalers in 1979.

The Leafs had blocked his first attempted return to the NHL with the New York Islanders by demanding a first-round draft choice, even though they had let Keon go to the rival WHA. He was justifiably upset and made the most of his return to Maple Leaf Gardens on October 31, 1979: he scored on Leafs goalie Mike Palmateer by rapping home a Blaine Stoughton rebound to give his team a 2–1 lead. The Toronto crowd gave Keon a standing ovation and he was chosen as the first star in Hartford's 4–2 win.

Prior to that game, former Leafs owner Conn Smythe had paid a special visit to the Whalers dressing room. He thanked Keon for all he had done for the Leafs and told him that he should have been treated better by the team — truer words were never spoken.

Keon played two more seasons with the Whalers and finished with 498 pro goals and 1,277 points (NHL and WHA totals combined). He was elected to the Hall of Fame in 1986.

Dave Keon was not a large man but he never shied away from physical battles such as the one he is having here with Bill Gadsby of Detroit. (HB)

Leaf file:

Dave Keon recorded only 75 penalty minutes during his career with the Leafs. He picked up two of those on the night of January 12, 1963, against Detroit, when he scuffled with Red Wings tough guy Howie Young. It was Keon's only penalty of the season and he actually had to explain his actions to a curious media after the game: Keon said Young was holding him and he was trying to break away. Ironically, just before the game Keon had been presented with the Lady Byng Trophy for sportsmanship and gentlemanly play, which he had won for his clean behaviour the previous year. The brilliant centre scored both goals in a 2–1 Leafs win that night. Years later, on April 7, 1974, Keon recorded the only major fighting penalty of his career when he had a dust-up with Gregg Sheppard of the Bruins. When the "fight" was over, Keon asked linesman John D'Amico, "Where do I go now?"

If you were an English-speaking boy growing up in Canada, that was the ultimate, to face off at the Gardens at eight o'clock on Saturday night and have Foster Hewitt call your name. Dave Keon, Leafs program, December 9, 1991

Above: *Dave Keon was the NHL's best rookie in 1960–61.* (HB)

Maple Leaf stats:

	GP	G	A	P	PIM
regular season	1,062	365	493	858	75
playoffs	89	32	35	67	6

Frank Mahovlich tries to shed the close checking of Boston defenceman Warren Godfrey (wearing helmet). (HB)

FRANK MAHOVLICH

No PLAYER WAS MORE scrutinized as a Maple Leaf than Frank Mahovlich between 1957 and 1968. From the day he was recruited in northern Ontario until the day more than a decade later that he was traded to the Detroit Red Wings, no other Toronto player was so carefully watched by Maple Leaf fans. The big left winger was often a hero and a villain at the same time to a critical public: it was only after he was gone that people began to fully appreciate what he had done for the team and understand what a truly great player Mahovlich had been.

Leafs scout Bob Davidson worked very hard to convince the Mahovlich family that the Leafs were the best organization for their son. The Red Wings were also hot on the trail of the six-foot, 205-pound teenager, but the opportunity for Frank to go to St. Michael's College seemed to convince his father, Peter, that the Leafs were going to be the best team for his son. Mahovlich went to St. Mike's for the 1954–55 season and scored 12 goals in 25 games. He added 14 the next year and then an Ontario Hockey Association-best 52 goals in 49 games during the 1956–57 season.

The goal-hungry Leafs could hardly wait to get Mahovlich onto the big team and gave him three run-outs at the end of the 1956–57 NHL season, allowing him to score his first NHL goal. The team was having a terrible time in the mid-50s and hoped that Mahovlich could help them turn the languishing club around. In 1957–58 the left-winger scored 20 goals and 36 points to take the Calder Trophy as the best rookie in the league, beating out Chicago's Bobby Hull for the award. The Leafs had found their superstar.

Mahovlich moved like a thoroughbred, with a strong, fluid style that made it look as if he was galloping through the opposition. In full flight, he was an imposing figure. An explosive skater, Mahovlich could spot the right moment to turn it on and burst in on goal. He had a great move where he would take the puck off the wing, cut into the middle of the ice and try to bust through two defencemen for a chance on goal. He didn't always get through but when he did he scored some memorable goals. His style of play on offence caused teammate Dave Keon to remark: "Nobody scores better goals than Frank."

However, coach Punch Imlach did not endorse Mahovlich's attacking style of play. The Leafs mentor wanted players who were defensively minded first and foremost, and he did everything to rein in Mahovlich. Imlach wanted him to pick his moments to burst forward instead of attacking all the time. Mahovlich did this very well, but the waiting often made it look as if he was not going all out, and the fans booed him on many occasions. Imlach was not very sympathetic and did nothing to dispel the notion that his star was not always giving his absolute best. A sensitive man, Mahovlich needed a coach who would stroke him rather than whip him. In that regard Imlach was a complete failure.

For the 1960–61 season everyone was happy when Mahovlich scored 48 times and finished third in NHL scoring, with 84 points. Imlach liked the fact that the "Big M" was very aggressive that season — he recorded 131 penalty minutes. Mahovlich would have scored more than 50 if he hadn't tired from all the scrutiny of chasing Rocket Richard's record (50 goals in 50 games).

He never again scored more than 40 as a Leaf but had seasons of 33, 36, 26, 23 and 32 to bring to six in a row his years of leading the team in goals scored; he also led the team in points five times. Mahovlich was also strong in the playoffs, notably in 1962 (12 points, six goals and six assists in 12 postseason games) and 1964 (15 points in 14 games). But the Leafs star's relationship with Imlach was beginning to wear thin.

In 1964–65 Mahovlich had to take some time away from the team to recover from a bout of depression. He still had 51 points in 59 games, but his time in hospital was a sign of things to come. A doctor urged him to draw a curtain around himself when Imlach was around and it seemed to work in 1965–66, when Mahovlich bounced back to score 32 times and earn a spot on the second all-star team. A mediocre 1966–67 season (only 18 goals) was saved by a Stanley Cup win in the playoffs, but his career in Toronto was coming to an end.

Frank Mahovlich moves in front of Gump Worsley in the New York net. (HB)

Mahovlich entered hospital once again early in the 1967–68 season when he was not feeling well, and Imlach felt it was time to finally trade him. He had tried to move Mahovlich earlier but had not found the right deal; that changed when Detroit offered Norm Ullman and Paul Henderson in a trade. Many Leaf fans were livid, but after the initial shock wore off Mahovlich realized it was the best thing that had happened to him. He had not been happy in Toronto for a number of years and now had the opportunity to revive his career.

Detroit was a breath of fresh air for Mahovlich and he scored a career-best 49 goals in 1968–69 playing alongside Alex Delvecchio and Gordie Howe. Things got even better when the sad sack Red Wings sent him to Montreal and he won two more Cups there, in 1971 and 1973, playing with his younger brother, Peter. He recorded a career-high 96 points for the Habs in 1971–72 and stayed in Montreal until the end of the 1973–74 season. Mahovlich finished his Hall of Fame career back in Toronto, with three seasons for the Toros of the WHA (they later moved to Birmingham, Alabama). His NHL totals include 533 goals and 1,103 career points.

The Business of the Maple Leafs:

Frank Mahovlich did pretty well when he signed his first contract with the Leafs. He got a two-year deal that paid $10,000 a year plus a $10,000 bonus, a generous offer for a man billed as "the future of the franchise" (not even Bobby Hull earned as much). Mahovlich used $3,200 of his bonus money to buy a 1957 Buick. He added to his earnings with $1,000 for winning the Calder Trophy and also had a verbal agreement with Conn Smythe that he would get a $1,000 bonus if he scored more than 35 goals.

When Mahovlich scored 48 in 1960–61 he assumed that the bonus

would be paid, but general manager Punch Imlach refused because it was not written in the contract. This put a strain on an already shaky relationship between coach and player. In October 1962 the Chicago Black Hawks offered the Leafs $1 million for the rights to the as-yet-unsigned Mahovlich. The Leafs accepted the offer initially (Harold Ballard doing the honours) but later changed their mind at the urging of Conn Smythe, who pushed his son Stafford to decline the offer. He did, and abruptly signed up Mahovlich for the amount he was asking — $25,000.

Frank Mahovlich looks to get going against Wayne Connelly (#14) of the Detroit Red Wings. (HB)

Maple Leaf stats:	GP	G	A	P	PIM
regular season	720	296	301	597	782
playoffs	84	24	36	60	135

BOB PULFORD

As a youngster Bob Pulford suffered from a spinal condition and was told that he should consider not playing sports. Luckily, exercise and normal growth corrected the problem and the native of Newton Robinson, Ontario, went on to have a Hall of Fame career in the National Hockey League. For 16 seasons, Pulford was a solid two-way centre for the Toronto Maple Leafs (1956 to 1970) and the Los Angeles Kings (1970 to 1972). He has stayed involved in hockey in a variety of coaching and management positions with the Kings and the Chicago Black Hawks since his retirement as a player. Quite an achievement for someone once told to stay away from sports.

Like many other Leafs recruits in the '50s, Pulford began with the Weston Dukes and then moved up to the Toronto Marlboros in the Ontario Hockey Association's major "A" circuit. He was a top player on the Marlie team that won the Memorial Cup in 1955 and 1956 and a scoring star in the '56 Cup playoffs, netting 10 goals in the final four games of the decisive series. He scored 54 goals in his last two years as a junior and the Leafs looked forward to having the sturdy centre (5'11", 188 pounds) join the big team as soon as possible.

Pulford never played a game in the minors and appeared in 65 games during his rookie season with the Leafs in 1956–57, scoring 11 goals and making 11 assists. Two years later he had upped his goal total to 23 and become a consistent player who was always around the 20-goal mark. In 1965–66, his best year, he scored 28 goals and 56 points.

Pulford was the anchor of the Leafs' third line. Everyone in the NHL knew his value to the team and his name constantly came up in trade talks, but the Leafs also knew they had a solid performer in "Pully" and turned down all offers.

Pulford was a good defensive player and a top penalty killer for the Leafs: he scored six short-handed goals in 1959–60. A very versatile player, he could also play on left wing, but he was probably best known for his penchant for scoring timely goals. When the Leafs were making their miracle run for a playoff spot in 1959, it was Pulford who scored the winning goal to give them a very important 6–5 win over the team they were chasing, the New York Rangers. Without that victory it is unlikely the Leafs would have reached the post-season and their first finals appearance since 1951.

When the Leafs needed to steal back the momentum from Chicago in the 1962 finals, Pulford scored three goals in an 8–4 Toronto win in the fifth game of the series. In 1964 he netted the winner in a 3–2 victory in the first game of the finals against Detroit, with two seconds to play while the Leafs were short-handed. In the sixth game of the same series, the Leafs were facing elimination and the end of their two-year reign as champions when Pulford came to the rescue again by scoring two goals in a 4–3 overtime win. The Leafs won their third straight Cup on home ice two nights later.

By 1966–67 Pulford's play had declined slightly, though he still scored 17 goals and 45 points. The Leafs almost traded him to the Boston Bruins, but an injury to a Bruin player scuttled the proposed trade. Then King Clancy took over from Punch Imlach behind the Leafs bench for a few games and decided to play Pulford on left wing, with linemates Peter Stemkowski at centre and Jim Pappin on the right flank. The line caught fire and scored many key goals in the playoffs, including a game winner by the opportunistic Pulford: The finals series was tied 1–1 when the third game went into double overtime at Maple Leaf Gardens. Pulford ended the thrilling contest when he took a Stemkowski pass and knocked it into the cage behind Montreal goalie Rogie Vachon.

Pulford's last great moment as a Leaf came in the sixth game of the same series, when Imlach chose him to defend Toronto's one-goal lead with 55 seconds to play. The faceoff was in the Leafs end and Red Kelly, Tim Horton, Allan Stanley, George Armstrong and Pulford stopped the six Canadien attackers cold, preventing them from getting a single shot on Leafs goalie Terry Sawchuk. Kelly then got the puck out to Pulford, who slid it out to Armstrong so that the Leafs captain could fire it into the open Montreal net. It was a moment Pulford would cherish forever.

In 1967–68 Pulford scored 20 goals and 50 points, playing on a

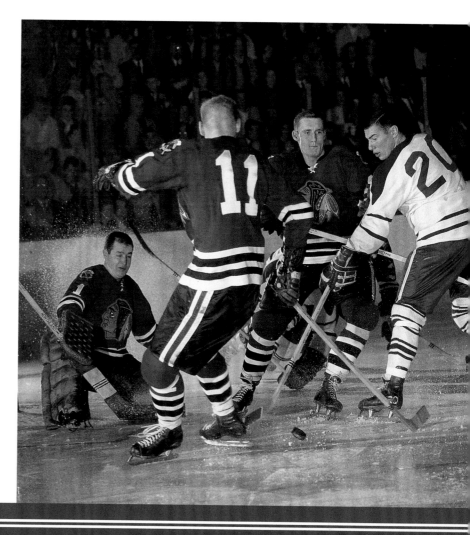

Bob Pulford (#20) tries to find the puck in front of the Chicago goal in a battle with Bill Hay (#11), Wayne Hillman and goalie Glenn Hall. (HB)

line with Dave Keon and Murray Oliver, but the Leafs missed the playoffs. In his final year in Toronto Pulford had 18 markers, but another year out of the playoffs meant changes. He was dealt to Los Angeles (for Garry Monahan and Brian Murphy), where he was named captain of the Kings. He played for two seasons there before being named coach. He had some good seasons coaching the Kings and later the Black Hawks but never took a team to the finals.

Pulford has been entrenched in Chicago since 1977 and was general manager for many years, with only moderate success. His induction into the Hall of Fame as a player in 1991 was not well received by everyone, but there is little doubt that he is one of the all-time best Maple Leafs.

Leaf file:

Bob Pulford was a bright, educated man who earned his Bachelor of Arts in 1963 and was interested in doing well off the ice. He became friends with lawyer Alan Eagleson and together they formed an investment club to help some of the other young Leafs players who were concerned about life after hockey. It was only natural that Pulford would be strongly involved when Eagleson formed the Players Association in 1967; Pulford was named the first president of the new group.

This did not sit well with Toronto coach and general manager Punch Imlach, who hated the idea of players having any power and had a particular disdain for Eagleson in the mid-60s. Imlach went so far as to treat players as either union supporters or nonunion supporters: the Leafs boss took

the "A" from Pulford's sweater, stripping him of his status as alternate captain , an honour he had held since the 1962–63 season. Pulford got the message and gave up the presidency and Imlach put the "A" back on his sweater for the 1968–69 team photo — Imlach's last with the Leafs.

When Pulford joined NHL management, he was still quite close to Eagleson and did not support the NHL alumni as they battled him for their pension-surplus compensation. This did not make Pulford a popular figure among his old teammates, and some, such as Carl Brewer, suggested he give his own windfall ($110,044) from the subsequent lawsuit to a fund to help out retired players in dire need of financial assistance.

Maple Leaf stats:

	GP	G	A	P	PIM
regular season	947	251	312	563	691
playoffs	89	25	26	51	126

TERRY SAWCHUK

DURING NHL MEETINGS in June 1964, Leafs coach and general manager Punch Imlach was on the hunt for a seasoned goaltender. He knew the aging Johnny Bower needed help to get through a long season and had lost faith in perennial backup Don Simmons, especially after an 11–0 loss to Boston the previous season. He was all set to select Gump Worsley from the Canadiens when the Detroit Red Wings suddenly announced that Terry Sawchuk, the all-time shutout leader, was available. The Leafs quickly grabbed the goalie they had just beaten to win their third straight Stanley Cup and Imlach was all smiles. Many of the other general managers moaned at how lucky the Leafs had been in scooping up the 35-year-old Sawchuk for a mere $20,000. Time would prove them right.

Nobody was more surprised he was let go than Sawchuk. After all, he had just taken the Red Wings to the 1964 finals and only a lucky goal by the Leafs' Bob Baun had stopped Detroit from winning the Cup on home ice in the sixth game of the series. But Detroit wanted to make room for rookie goalie Roger Crozier and was happy with its other netminder, George Gardner. The Red Wings gambled that Sawchuk might get through the intra-league draft, but Imlach was not about to let that happen.

Once he had recovered from the shock, Sawchuk began to see the benefits of moving to the Leafs. His first year with Toronto was a good one as he shared the netminding duties with Bower; Sawchuk played in 36 games to Bower's 34 and posted a 17–13–6 record, with a 2.56 goals-against average and one shutout, the 97th of his already great career. The two goalies gave up a total of 173 goals and took the Vezina Trophy over the Detroit Red Wings by two goals.

They clinched the Vezina on the last night of the season with a 4–0 win over the Red Wings (who had beaten the Leafs 4–1 the previous night in Toronto) with Bower in net at the Olympia. The two hugged after the game was over and Sawchuk insisted that both names should go on the trophy. The NHL complied and a trend was started.

Although he was happy with his season and elated at winning the

Vezina, the aging Sawchuk was not exactly an agreeable person. He was a loner and kept aloof from his teammates. A bad drinker and a wayward husband, Sawchuk was usually in a sour mood. He often challenged fans to fights and did not shy away from confrontation, even arguing with hockey writers who had quoted him accurately about his retirement plans. Unlike Bower, he hated practice and gave an earful to any teammate who put the puck too high.

Some observers felt Sawchuk was a different man after he lost a lot of weight in a serious bout of mononucleosis. His numerous injuries—including an estimated 400 stitches in his face—also took their toll. Sawchuk's 1965–66 season was not as good as the previous year, with only 27 appearances for a 10–11–4 record and a 3.16 goals-against average, and he gave serious consideration to retiring.

Punch Imlach talked Sawchuk into returning for the 1966–67 season. The veteran goalie felt much better after a back operation that summer that had added two inches to his height and allowed him to stand straighter than he had in years, but when the season began he suffered back spasms during a game in Montreal and was forced out of the lineup for several months. He played well enough to post a 15–5–4 record in the regular season and recorded his 100th shutout against Chicago. He saved his best for the play-offs that spring, with a superb performance against the Black Hawks in the semifinals and another in the final against Montreal.

Sawchuk lost the first game 6–2 at the Montreal Forum and Imlach turned to Bower for the next two games, both Leafs victories. The night before the fourth game Sawchuk was out drinking, not at all worried about playing the following evening. But just before the game began, Bower pulled up with a bad leg, his season over. Thrust into the breach unexpectedly, Sawchuk had a terrible game and again lost 6–2.

After the game, he was furious when he received a telegram from a fan who suggested he had taken a dive; the same fan had congratulated him after his shutout against Chicago. If Sawchuk

Detriot's Parker MacDonald (#20) hopes for a rebound from Toronto netminder Terry Sawchuk. MacDonald played with the Leafs in 1954–55. (HB)

needed any motivation, he certainly had it now. He was virtually unbeatable in the next two games and the Leafs took the Cup with 4–1 and 3–1 wins to close out the "original six" NHL era. Sawchuk's performance in the last game was so remarkable that television commentator Brian McFarlane suggested that he should get all three stars of the game.

Sawchuk probably should have retired after the '67 Cup win, but the lure of some of the best money of his career was too much to resist. With seven children to look after, he could not refuse when the Los Angeles Kings took him in the expansion draft and

offered a three-year deal that would take him to age 40 at $40,000, $38,000 and $35,000 a year — he was making between $18,000 and $25,000 with the Leafs in 1966–67. He played one year in Los Angeles and liked it there, but was then sent to Detroit and on to New York, where he recorded his 103rd and final shutout.

The Hall of Fame netminder died of internal injuries suffered in a scuffle with former Leaf Ron Stewart, in part because his ravaged body could not take the operations that had to be performed to try to save his life. He was only 40 years old when he died on May 31, 1970. Stewart was later cleared of any wrongdoing.

Leaf file:

Terry Sawchuk's greatest game as a Leaf came against the Chicago Black Hawks on April 15, 1967, during the fifth game of the semifinal series. Nobody had given the Leafs a chance against the powerful Chicago club that had finished first in the NHL during the 1966–67 season, but the teams were tied at two games each going into the fifth. Chicago had won the last game 4-3 in Toronto and was now back home in front of its loud and boisterous fans.

Johnny Bower started the game and looked bad, giving up two goals in the first period. Punch Imlach called him over and asked if he wanted to come out. Normally Bower would rather have died than leave a game, but he knew he didn't have it and told his coach, "Well, there's a lot at stake." Imlach looked at Sawchuk, who said he would prefer to start the second period. Bower finished the first period and the Leafs managed to tie the score 2–2.

Sawchuk then faced a tremendous assault from the Black Hawks, who knew he was incredibly bruised and battered. Bobby Hull got the puck at the faceoff dot in the Leafs end and blasted a drive that nailed Sawchuk on the shoulder. The Leafs goalie dropped like a stone and trainer Bob Haggert came out to check Sawchuk's condition. The Black Hawks, pretending to show concern, were actually circling, taunting and laughing at the veteran goalie. Chicago defenceman Pierre Pilote "suggested" Sawchuk stay down so he wouldn't have to face any more. Sawchuk got angry: When Haggert asked him how he was, Sawchuk replied, "I stopped the (expletive deleted) shot, didn't I?" He gathered himself back up and shut out the Hawks the rest of the way, stopping 37 shots while the Leafs scored twice to win 4–2. Two nights later, he was great again as the Leafs took the series with a 3–1 win at home.

Maple Leaf stats:

	GP	Wins	Losses	Ties	Shutouts	GAA
regular season	91	42	29	14	4	2.81
playoffs	13	6	7	—	—	2.73

EDDIE SHACK

THE NEW YORK RANGERS thought they were getting a potential scoring star when Eddie Shack joined the team for the 1958–59 season. After all, the native of Sudbury, Ontario, had scored very well as a junior with the Guelph Biltmores in the Ontario Hockey Association. In 1956–57, his last season in Guelph, Shack had netted 47 goals in 52 games and led the league in assists with 57. A year in the minors with Providence of the American Hockey League saw him score 16 goals in 35 games and he was expected to do the same with the Rangers the following year. But Shack managed to score only seven times in 67 games as a rookie and eight times in 62 appearances during the 1959–60 season. Those numbers earned him some more time in the minors and eventually a ticket out of New York.

Rangers coach Phil Watson did not like Shack — the feeling was mutual — and saw the 6'1", 200-pound winger as nothing more than a good skater. With over 100 penalty minutes in both seasons with the Rangers Shack was aggressive, but the Rangers wanted more goals from him and thought they would never come. So they traded him to Toronto, where Punch Imlach was willing to give the youngster a fresh start; the Leafs gave up only spare parts in forwards Johnny Wilson and Pat Hannigan, so it wasn't much of a gamble. For Shack it was a new lease on life with a more talented team, where there was much less pressure to perform. It was a great move and he made the most of it for many years.

Imlach did not know what to do with Shack, so decided to wait and see where he fitted into the team. He soon realized the young player was unpredictable and reckless, qualities that did not sit well with the Imlach mode of discipline, but the Leafs coach seemed to understand that Shack could bring a certain energy to the game and tried to place him accordingly. Toronto fans took to him instantly despite their generally conservative nature and he became a cult hero.

Shack often provided a kind of comic relief when he came off the bench because he didn't hesitate to take on the stars of the opposition. He became known as "The Entertainer." He assumed a policeman's role on the team and did a fair amount of fighting on ice, but he showed some skill, as well. He had a very good shot and could skate with just about anybody in the league. His willingness to use his body kept the opposition on their toes and the Gardens crowd on the edge of their seats.

He suffered knee injuries in his first two years with the Leafs but still managed 21 goals in limited appearances. In 1963 he scored the Stanley Cup-winning goal when he tipped home a Kent Douglas shot past Terry Sawchuk in the Detroit net during the fifth game of the finals. He had scored a career-high 16 goals in 1962–63, but dropped back to 11 in 1963–64. When he scored just five times in 1964–65, he found himself back in the minors to start the next year.

The Leafs got off to a 2–4–1 start without Shack and quickly called him back from Rochester, where he had been sent to boost attendance and interest in the team. He went on to produce 26 goals and 43 points that year, both career highs with Toronto. "The Entertainer" stayed with the Leafs for their fourth Cup in 1967, before being dealt to Boston for Murray Oliver and $100,000 US.

Shack did well with the Bruins in his first year there, scoring 23 goals, but was dealt to the Los Angeles Kings after two seasons. He also played for Pittsburgh and Buffalo and rejoined the Leafs in 1973 before leaving the NHL. Shack's career goal total is a very respectable 239, with 465 points in 1,047 games.

After retirement, he continued to hawk any product or service he could to make money. He knew his name was still popular in Toronto and was happy to cash in on his fame, not being afraid to take a ribbing about his large nose if it meant a good payday. Leaf fans still recall the popular song "Clear the Track, Here Comes Shack." He had also been very astute in buying and selling real estate while he was moving around the NHL and that helped him get ahead financially. For a man with no formal education who has trouble reading and writing, Shack has done remarkably well and should serve as an example for anyone in similar circumstances.

Facing page: *Eddie Shack in a game against the New York Rangers.* (HB)

Eddie Shack (#23) lets Pierre Pilote (#3) of Chicago know he is in for a battle. (HB)

Leaf file:

Eddie Shack was very good at riling the opposition, often to get the Leafs going, and he was known for never backing down against even the best players in the NHL. He had a particular feud going with Gordie Howe of the Detroit Red Wings. The superstar was used to being left alone, but this did not stop Shack from nailing him on January 4, 1961, during a game at the Gardens. Shack had just arrived in Toronto and this hit on Howe, which left the Red Wing with a concussion and a 10-stitch cut from Shack's stick and glove, helped to build his reputation.

He also went after Stan Mikita of the Black Hawks (Shack claims this is why the Chicago superstar changed his game and went on to become a Lady Byng Trophy winner) and Doug Harvey and Henri Richard of the Canadiens. He head-butted the latter in the 1964 play-offs, enraging brother Maurice Richard, who told Shack it was a good thing he hadn't hit his little brother with his nose or he would have split it. Shack also had a running battle with Chicago tough guy Reggie Fleming, who speared him in a game at the Gardens on December 7, 1963: after Shack had been a pain in the side of the Black Hawks all night long and even scored a beautiful goal, Fleming had seen enough and hunted him down late in the game. The Leafs were furious and made Fleming pay in a full-scale brawl.

Maple Leaf stats:	GP	G	A	P	PIM
regular season	504	99	96	195	676
playoffs	57	6	3	9	107

143

ALLAN STANLEY

FORMER LEAF Harold "Baldy" Cotton, who became a scout with the Boston Bruins, first noticed Allan Stanley playing in a juvenile game at Maple Leaf Gardens. The native of Timmins, Ontario, attended the Bruins training camp in 1941 but did not turn professional until the 1946–47 season when he played for the Providence Reds of the American Hockey League. Stanley also played some senior hockey in the Bruins system for a team called the Boston Olympics.

He stayed in Providence for two seasons before being traded to the New York Rangers for three players and $75,000 in cash, a significant sum at the time. His contract was purchased for the 1948–49 season but he didn't join the Rangers until partway through the year. His arrival was greeted with much anticipation in New York, but Stanley couldn't live up to expectations and was roundly booed in Madison Square Garden. After nearly six years as a Ranger he was dealt to the Chicago Black Hawks, where he spent the better part of two years before moving back to Boston. He was with the Bruins for another two seasons, making the finals both times, but was on the move again when Leafs coach Punch Imlach wanted to shore up his leaky defence.

Imlach knew Stanley from his days at the Bruins and saw potential in the 6'1", 190-pound, slow-footed defenceman. Many thought the Leafs had made a mistake when they sent Jim Morrison to Boston in exchange for the 32-year-old Stanley in 1958, but Imlach knew what he was doing: Stanley became a force on the Leafs for the next 10 years, helping them to win four Cups.

Quiet and laid-back off the ice but always intense on it, Stanley was a very experienced player by the time he got to Toronto. His game was all about angling the opposition off. He was slow on his feet — they called him "Snowshoes" because his skating was so laborious — but did not let this hamper his ability to defend. He used his smarts to survive and his offensive skills got the Leafs a fair few goals.

Stanley had five seasons of more than 20 assists with the Leafs

and scored 10 goals in 1959–60. But his real value was his strength and size, which he used to clear the opposition from in front of the goal. He was not overly physical in doing this, never tallying more than 60 minutes in penalty time while with Toronto. When he was teamed with Tim Horton, the Leafs had a pair of reliable defencemen who could be counted on in any situation. Stanley's sense of anticipation was extremely sharp and helped him to survive in the NHL for over two decades. He was named a second-team all-star three times with the Leafs (1960, 1961, 1966), quite an achievement for a player few had appreciated.

Stanley's greatest benefit to the team may have been his experience. He had seen it all before, and nothing — not even a demanding coach like Imlach — was going to faze him. He urged his teammates to win in spite of the coach and was strong enough to withstand just about anything, including having his face sliced by the skate of Montreal's Bill Hicke in 1960–61. The blow broke his jaw, but he was only slightly surprised that Imlach wanted him to play in the next game. Stanley realized that veterans like Red Kelly, Bert Olmstead, Johnny Bower and himself thrived under Imlach's system, so the complaints were never too loud. It was no accident that the Leafs improved when veterans like Stanley showed the way. He was an effective defenceman for the Leafs until the day he left the team.

Stanley took the final faceoff in the last game of the 1967 finals against Montreal's Jean Beliveau; Imlach had his defencemen take the draws in the Leafs end, including all faceoffs in the sixth and final game of the series against the Habs, so Stanley was ready when called upon. He tied up Beliveau nicely and the rest of the Leafs got the puck out of danger to sew up the last Cup of the "original six" era.

"Silent Sam" played one more year in Toronto, getting one goal and 14 points in 68 games. Then he was selected by the Philadelphia Flyers in the reverse draft and played one more season to bring his career totals to 1,244 games played, with 100 goals and 433 points. He was elected to the Hall of Fame in 1981.

Facing page: *Allan Stanley (#26) uses his size and strength to take an opposing forward into the boards.* (HB)

Detroit's Gordie Howe is stationed close to the Leafs net, where goalie Terry Sawchuk (#30) is sprawled and Allan Stanley (#26) is moving in to take charge after a save. Howe said Stanley was the toughest defenceman he faced. (HB)

Maple Leaf stats:	GP	G	A	P	PIM
regular season	633	47	186	233	318
playoffs	82	4	27	31	60

BEHIND THE BENCH: 75 YEARS OF LEAFS MANAGEMENT

by Jim Kernaghan

ANY HISTORY of the Toronto Maple Leafs could well be subtitled *The Proud and the Profane* and find its tone in the roar of a circus minibike.

It is the dead of night in the empty Maple Leaf Gardens. Owner Harold Ballard is at the tiny bike's controls. In the nude. With an equally *déshabillé* lady perched on his shoulders as they zoom, well-refreshed, around the Gardens' corridors. The circus is in town, of course. Fact is, it never really left in those days.

Go forward or backward from the Ballard era, back to the stern reign of founder and builder "Major" Conn Smythe, ahead to the current reserved and reticent regime of Steve Stavro, and it all pales by comparison.

But more on the ringmaster of the hockey circus in a minute. Others made more substantial contributions to the legendary team during its 75 years, none more than Clarence "Hap" Day. At the outset Smythe decided to anchor his team around Day, his first captain. As it turned out, the former pharmacy student would be central to Leaf fortunes after his playing days were over. In Day's decade (1940–50) behind the bench the Leafs won five Stanley Cups, in '43, '45, '47, '48 and '49. Only Smythe did more to install the Toronto Maple Leafs among the pantheon of storied North American sports franchises. It is no coincidence that the season-tickets phenomenon — they are still left in wills — began in the fabulous '40s.

But by the late '50s on-ice fortunes had waned. It would turn out to be a blip when George "Punch" Imlach took over as general manager and launched the second of the Leafs' two great eras. He did it through bold moves, starting with firing coach Billy Reay and taking over behind the bench. He then added rookie defenceman Carl Brewer, a 33-year-old rookie goaltender named Johnny Bower, veterans Allan Stanley and Eddie Shack and installed Dave Keon at centre. The team was coming together.

Imlach brought in Detroit defensive star Leonard "Red" Kelly and, with typical audacity, turned him into the centre that extravagantly talented left winger Frank Mahovlich required. It was a stroke of genius, as that pair, helped by Bob Nevin or another right-

winger, became one of the most dangerous lines in the league.

If the '40s were Day's Decade, the '60s were Imlach's. His teams won four Stanley Cups, including the franchise's last in 1967. But by '69 Imlach was gone, fired by Stafford Smythe, whose consortium bought the Gardens from his father, Conn. Punch would be back later, but not before the Ballard reign wrought havoc with the franchise.

Ballard and Stafford Smythe were charged with tax evasion in 1969. Smythe died before sentencing, but after Ballard got out of the slammer, he bought control of the club — only to lose 14 players to the upstart rival World Hockey Association. General manager Jim Gregory and coach John McLellan clutched at straws and a 20-year spiral began.

Red Kelly's most memorable contribution as coach was, alas, arcane. He introduced "pyramid power," placing pyramids under the player bench to "energize" them. His replacement, Roger Neilson, took the team to the 1978 semifinals with a stunning victory over the New York Islanders. Ballard fired Neilson late the next season — then, when he couldn't replace him, asked if he'd return to the bench with a paper bag over his head at the next home game, for drama. Neilson refused to wear it.

In 1979 Ballard went back to an old strength, Punch Imlach, but times had changed and Imlach's autocratic 1960s player-relations style failed abjectly. Once, when Imlach's car battery was dead upon the team's late-night return, defenceman Dave Hutchison streaked by in the darkness, laughing and waving jumper cables. Hutchison was central to another telling vignette: when he was traded, a number of teammates gathered at a bar near the Gardens, put Imlach's photo on a dartboard and blazed away. Imlach was next to go.

A succession of coaches followed as Ballard became increasingly out of touch. First Gerry McNamara was named general manager, then untried 30-year-old Gord Stellick. A woman named Yolanda McMillan found her way into Ballard's heart after showing up at his apartment with a cake and she usurped some influence.

The Leafs won five Stanley Cups in the 1940s. This photo shows the victory parade to celebrate their 1948 championship. (HB)

When Ballard died in 1990 the franchise was in tatters, having run up a record of 255 wins and 432 losses in the previous decade. Supermarket mogul Stavro, a longtime director, gained control of the financially successful but competitively moribund team and wasted no time in hiring Cliff Fletcher to rebuild it. Fletcher started by trading for Doug Gilmour and Mats Sundin as cornerstones. Pat Quinn became coach in 1998 and added the general manager's portfolio the following year. After the 2002 playoff run, long-suffering Toronto fans hoped it was the dawn of a third great era. One without the circuses.

The '70s was the first full decade in Toronto Maple Leaf history in which they did not win a single Stanley Cup. In fact, the team did not even come close, though in 1978 it seemed capable of winning it all. But as nice as the first-round upset of the New York Islanders was in the spring of '78, in reality Toronto was no challenger to the Montreal Canadiens for hockey supremacy. The Leafs' best players between 1975 and 1979 were as good as any in the NHL, but that small group of six or so individuals had virtually no supporting cast except for a bunch of grinding checkers. The decade started off with a surprising team in 1970–71, but declined for the next two years before rebounding under the leadership of Darryl Sittler and coaches like Leonard "Red" Kelly and Roger Neilson. It closed on a bad note with the hiring of George "Punch" Imlach as general manager, a role to which he was no longer suited . The '70s saw the Leafs win as many games as they lost. Here's how they did it.

Facing page: Maple Leaf rookies for the 1973–74 season: (left to right) Inge Hammarstrom, Bob Neely, Ian Turnbull, Lanny McDonald and Borje Salming. Hammarstrom had three seasons of 20 or more goals for Toronto, getting 20 goals and 23 assists in 1973–74, his best year as a Leaf. Neely got 36 goals and 89 points in 261 games as a Leaf. (HB)

Brian Spencer (#15) and Jim Dorey (#8) of the Maple Leafs stop St. Louis Blues forward Garry Unger in his tracks. Spencer played for three seasons with the Leafs and scored 10 goals and 30 points, with 192 penalty minutes, from 1969 to 1972. Dorey played in 231 career games for Toronto and scored 25 goals and 99 points to go with 553 penalty minutes. (HHOF)

George Ferguson was the first draft choice (11th overall) of the Maple Leafs in 1972. He played in 359 games for Toronto, scoring 57 goals and 110 assists. The former Marlie had his best year with the Leafs in 1974–75, when he had 19 goals and 49 points in 69 games. (DM)

Management and Coaching

As the '70s began, Jim Gregory was firmly in place as the team's general manager. He had been given the job in 1969 after being in the Leafs organization for some time as the successful coach and manager of the junior Marlboros and he seemed a bright executive. He was Leafs manager from 1969 to 1979 and posted a 334–324–130 record, good but not awe-inspiring. His trading record was uneven but he had his good moments, such as stealing goalie Bernie Parent from Philadelphia and converting aging netminder Jacques Plante into a top draft choice that gave them Ian Turnbull. Some of his other deals were flops, but it was difficult trying to manage around owner Harold Ballard's whims.

Leaf coaches in the decade included nice guy John McLellan, offensive-minded Red Kelly and defensive-oriented Roger Neilson. All had some success, but for every step forward there were several steps back. A key moment for the team came after the upset of the New York Islanders, when it looked as if the Leafs might be on the verge of something special, but Gregory and Neilson decided to add checkers and defencemen when they needed goals. The Leafs could have made a move to sign free agents Anders Hedberg and Ulf Nilsson (who wanted to come to Toronto) but did not even make the effort. A year later Ballard was tired of Gregory and Neilson and brought back Imlach, who made Floyd Smith coach for the 1979–80 season.

Best Trades and Acquisitions

In acquiring Parent the Leafs had the best young goalie in the game (though they could not sign him to a new contract) to go with a great veteran in Plante (also obtained in a deal). Toronto made a very good move in getting Bob Baun back to give the young defenders some guidance and leadership during the 1970–71 season. When the team was going nowhere near the end of a horrible 1972–73 season (27–41–10) it traded Plante to Boston for goalie Ed Johnston and a number 1 draft choice. The Leafs added that choice to two others and made three selections in the first round of the 1973 draft.

Their drafting record in the '70s was pretty good, given that they picked quality NHL players like Darryl Sittler, Lanny McDonald, Errol Thompson, Ian Turnbull, Rick Kehoe, George Ferguson, Pat Boutette, Dave Williams, Mike Palmateer, Doug Jarvis, John Anderson, Randy Carlyle, Joel Quenneville and Laurie Boschman. Unfortunately, many of those players were traded away (some by a vindictive Imlach). The Leafs also added two free agents from Sweden, defenceman Borje Salming and forward Inge Hammarstrom, who helped turn fortunes around in the 1973–74 season. The only good trade Imlach made was the acquisition of Dave Farrish and Terry Martin from Quebec late in 1979 for the rights to Reg Thomas.

Notable Events

Sittler was superb for the entire decade, especially in 1976 when he capped a great year by scoring 10 points in one game. Defenceman Turnbull set an NHL record with five goals in one game in 1977, an example of how offensive-minded the Leafs were between 1973 and 1977; they were very exciting to watch while Red Kelly was coach. The Leafs-Flyers playoff series in 1976 was a bitter battle that saw three Philadelphia players charged by Toronto police after one contest. The Leafs played the Flyers in three straight years in the postseason and lost every series.

The hiring of coach Roger Neilson was an innovative move — his original teaching techniques were not widely used in pro hockey at the time — that led to the Leafs winning a seven-game series for the first time since 1967. The coach was willing to do just about anything to help the Leafs win. His firing was just as unique; it happened twice, once on national television.

Jacques Plante and Dave Keon were second-team all-stars for their performance in the 1970–71 season, while Salming was a six-time all-star (once on the first team) during the decade. Sittler and McDonald also appeared on the second team, but no player won a major award. Sittler finished as high as third in scoring one year (1977–78) and was the first Leaf to record 100 points in a season. On January 2, 1971, the Leafs recorded their largest shutout victory when they shellacked Detroit 13–0 at Maple Leaf Gardens.

Toronto goalie Doug Favell (#33) gets help from defenceman Brian Glennie (#24) against the Minnesota North Stars. Favell posted a 26–26–16 record with the Leafs between 1973 and 1976. He was acquired in the deal that saw the rights to Bernie Parent go back to Philadelphia. (DM)

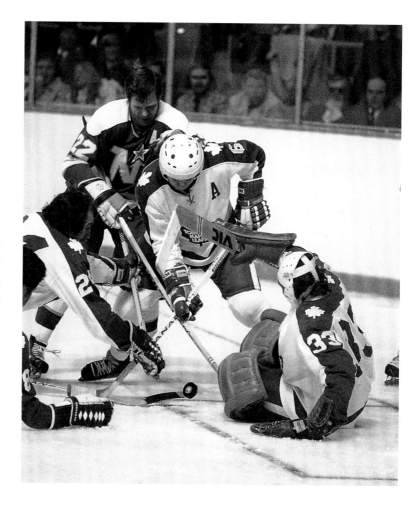

Worst of the Decade

Harold Ballard spent a year in jail for tax evasion but returned to wreak havoc on the once-proud organization built by the Smythe family. He ran a bare-bones operation and was prone to changing his mind at a moment's notice. He refused to compete with the World Hockey Association when the rival league started signing NHL players; as a result the Leafs lost Jim Harrison, Rick Ley, Brad Selwood, Guy Trottier, Jim Dorey (who was traded to New York) and Bernie Parent prior to the 1972–73 season. Paul Henderson and Mike Pelyk went to the new league a little later.

Ballard fired his coach while leaving the Montreal Forum, telling his journalist friend Dick Beddoes that Neilson was through while TV cameras captured the conversation, then changing his mind two days later. But his worst move was bringing back Imlach to manage the club, a catastrophe that set the team back at least a decade.

The Leafs also made some very poor trades, losing the likes of Kehoe, Jarvis, Parent and Carlyle for practically nothing. They overpaid mightily for Dan Maloney and Imlach topped it all off by trading future Hall of Famer Lanny McDonald to the Colorado Rockies to get back at Sittler, who had a no-trade clause in his contract that Ballard respected. Poor draft choices among the top 25 players selected in their respective years included Dave Fortier, Bob Neely, Jack Valiquette, Don Ashby, Trevor Johansen and Bob Gladney.

Bottom-line Results

The Leafs record for the decade from 1970–71 to 1979–80 was 340 wins, 330 losses and 122 ties. The team missed the playoffs once in the decade (1972–73) but won only one seven-game series. They did win five preliminary-round best-of-three series, defeating Los Angeles in 1975 and 1978, Pittsburgh in 1976 and 1977 and Atlanta in 1979, but their one and only appearance in the semifinals was a 4–0 wipeout to the Montreal Canadiens in 1978. The

Leafs produced a 41-win season to equal a club record at the time in 1977–78 but won more than 35 games only one other time (37 in 1970–71).

The early '70s saw the Leafs beaten by New York (who made the finals one year) and the Boston Bruins (who won two Stanley Cups in the decade), while the mid-70s saw them lose to Philadelphia (who won two Stanley Cups). The final years of the decade saw the club twice ousted by the Canadiens (who won six Cups in the '70s). The Leafs were a decent team for most of the decade, but they could not compete with the championship clubs of the era.

Best Leafs of the Decade

IN GOAL: Mike Palmateer, Jacques Plante and Bernie Parent.
ON DEFENCE: Borje Salming and Ian Turnbull (honourable mention to Brian Glennie and Jim McKenny for enduring so much).
AT FORWARD: Darryl Sittler, Lanny McDonald, Errol Thompson, Ron Ellis, Paul Henderson, Norm Ullman and Dave Williams.

PAUL HENDERSON

WHEN PAUL HENDERSON was still with the Detroit Red Wings, Toronto coach and general manager Punch Imlach told him he would one day be a Maple Leaf. Imlach was always a fan of fast skaters and there was none faster than the speedy left-winger. Henderson dismissed the manager's words as just talk, but when Imlach had a chance to get his man he did so very quickly, in the trade that sent Frank Mahovlich to the Red Wings on March 3, 1968.

The deal was almost scuttled when a newspaper scooped it and printed all the details before it was even announced: Henderson learned he was bound for the Leafs when Audrey MacGregor, the wife of his Detroit teammate Bruce MacGregor, phoned him with the news. But Imlach and Detroit manager Sid Abel decided to go through with the deal anyway. A Red Wing for many years, Henderson was shocked, but he soon came to enjoy playing in Maple Leaf Gardens and basking in the hockey-rich tradition of Toronto.

Longtime Detroit coach and manager Jack Adams, Abel's predecessor, once called Henderson the best prospect the Red Wings had seen in years. The swift, hard-shooting winger was first scouted after a newspaper story detailed how he had scored 18 goals in one game in juvenile hockey. Detroit, Boston and Toronto all showed interest but he settled on the Red Wings when he made their junior "A" squad during a stopover in Hamilton, Ontario: he had been on his way to the Bruins' junior camp in Niagara Falls.

Henderson didn't see full-time duty with the baby Wings until the 1961–62 season but made quite an impression when he did, scoring 24 times in 50 games and then helping the Hamilton club win the Memorial Cup with seven goals in 14 post-season games. His last season of junior in 1962–63 saw him score a league-leading 49 goals to go along with his 76 points. He also played in a couple of games for the Red Wings, both in a weekend series against the Leafs, in which he did nothing notable except rack up nine penalty minutes. After he fought with Dick Duff and slashed Frank Mahovlich, the Leafs were ready to lynch the brash youngster.

Henderson's minor-league career lasted all of 38 games with the Pittsburgh Hornets of the American Hockey League before he got the call to join the Red Wings in 1963–64. In 32 games Henderson scored three times with three assists, then scored two more goals in the playoffs that saw Detroit lose the Cup in seven games to Toronto. After an eight-goal season the following year, playing mostly as a penalty killer and extra forward, he had a major breakthrough in 1965–66 when he scored 22 times. The Red Wings lost in the finals once again, with Henderson recording six points in 12 playoff games. He followed up his good season with a nice salary increase and proved he was worth it by scoring 21 goals in 1966–67 for the rapidly fading Detroit club. He had added 18 more in 1967–68 when he was sent to Toronto in one of the biggest trades in NHL history.

Henderson was very nervous before his first game at the Gardens. He proved his mettle by scoring a goal, as did the two other newcomers, Norm Ullman and Floyd Smith, in a 7–2 win over Philadelphia.

Speed and an excellent shot were the strengths of Henderson's game. His sense of anticipation was also very helpful, and he seemed to feed off the pressure to score goals. He was fortunate to play with Norm Ullman as his centre and when Ron Ellis joined them on right wing the Leafs had one of the best lines in the NHL. Henderson scored 27 in his first full year as a Leaf, but injuries hurt him in 1969–70 and his total dropped to 20. But for the next two seasons he was one of the top wingers in the league, with 30 goals in 1970–71 and a career-best 38 in 1971–72. Henderson had always believed he could score 40 goals a year and now he was almost there.

His impressive performance earned him an invitation to Team Canada's training camp in August 1972 for the long-awaited Summit Series against the Soviets. He made the team and was soon playing with Ellis and Bobby Clarke of the Philadelphia Flyers in one of the most consistent lines. Henderson scored the winning goal in every one of the last three games of the series, including the series winner

Facing page: Paul Henderson came back to Maple Leaf Gardens as an Atlanta Flame in 1980 and scored a couple of goals against Mike Palmateer in a 5–1 win. He was named first star. (DM)

Paul Henderson (#19) played through some tough injuries in 1969–70 and scored only 20 goals. When the Leafs offered the speedy winger a token $1,500 raise his fury made the team reconsider.

with just 34 seconds left in the final match. It was a moment no Canadian who was watching at the time will ever forget.

Henderson went through some hard times when he returned home as Canada's hero. He questioned everything in his life and decided to make some major changes. His conversion to Christianity in 1975 gave him a renewed sense of what his life meant and the calmness he needed to adjust to his sudden celebrity. On the ice, Henderson had a miserable 1972–73 season (18 goals in 40 games) but rebounded the following year with 24 goals and 55 points in 69 games for a Leaf team on the way back up.

Harold Ballard was no fan of any player who declared himself a Christian, so when the Toronto Toros of the World Hockey Association offered to double his salary Henderson was seriously tempted. He consulted Frank Mahovlich, who told him there was no point playing for the Leafs under Ballard; after much hesitation, Henderson joined Mahovlich on the Toros. He stayed in the WHA until the 1979–80 season, when he made a brief return to the NHL with the Atlanta Flames.

Maple Leaf stats:	GP	G	A	P	PIM
regular season	408	162	156	318	166
playoffs	19	6	6	12	12

LANNY McDONALD

THE TORONTO MAPLE LEAFS had a terrible season in 1972–73 and finished out of the playoffs. Their only reward was the right to select fourth overall in the 1973 entry draft. Denis Potvin was selected first overall by the New York Islanders, and the Atlanta Flames followed by taking Tom Lysiak. Vancouver then took Dennis Ververgaert, which meant the Leafs could select hard-shooting winger Lanny McDonald. Toronto scout Torchy Schell had been following McDonald closely, even giving helpful advice to the native of Hanna, Alberta. Leafs general manager Jim Gregory knew there was a lot riding on this selection, but Schell was right to recommend the six-foot, 194-pound right-winger. It was a move the Leafs would not regret.

It somehow seemed right that McDonald would end up as a Maple Leaf: He recalled a time as a youngster when he waited outside a Calgary arena for an hour to get the autograph of former Toronto great Frank Mahovlich. McDonald had a strong sense of what it meant to play for the Leafs. When he arrived at Maple Leaf Gardens to sign his contract, he sat in the dark arena just soaking in the atmosphere. The club was looking to get back on track, and expected a lot from the young prodigy.

McDonald's junior credentials were impressive. He had scored 112 goals in his last 136 games with the Medicine Hat Tigers of the Western Hockey League, playing alongside centre and fellow draftee Lysiak. But with Lysiak in Atlanta, McDonald's debut as a Leaf was less than stellar. He struggled badly for two seasons, scoring only 31 goals in 134 games, and the Leafs nearly traded him to Atlanta. Luckily, they changed their minds.

McDonald made a few adjustments (to his skate blades, for example) and got help from teammates like Ron Ellis, a seasoned right-winger. But the biggest change was leaving Dave Keon and George Ferguson to become linemates with centre Darryl Sittler and Errol Thompson. Suddenly everything seemed to click. McDonald scored 37 goals in 1975–76 and followed that with seasons of 46, 47 and 43, earning a place on the NHL's second all-star

team in 1976–77. By then McDonald was the second-best right-winger in the league, after Montreal star Guy Lafleur. The patience of Leafs coach Red Kelly had paid off.

McDonald appreciated the faith Kelly had shown in him and even thanked Toronto hockey writer Frank Orr, who had urged fans to wait for the real McDonald to emerge. Legendary coach Scotty Bowman recognized McDonald as one of the most complete players in the game and saw that he played flat out all the time. McDonald played for Team Canada when it won the 1976 Canada Cup tournament under head coach Bowman.

More than just a hard worker, McDonald also had a blistering slapshot he would unleash as he came down the wing; often the puck would end up in the far corner of the net after McDonald had taken a pass from Sittler or left-winger Errol Thompson. The threesome comprised one of the top lines in the NHL during the 1975–76 season. Strongly built, McDonald was never really a fighter but did not hesitate to drop the gloves if he had to. He was a great scrapper who never gave up on a game no matter what the score. McDonald grew a ridiculously large moustache that became his trademark, as did his sweater number 7. It seemed he was born to be a Maple Leaf.

But when Punch Imlach returned to manage the Leafs in 1979, McDonald's days in Toronto were numbered. After feuding with the winger's great friend Sittler, Imlach traded McDonald to the Colorado Rockies, essentially out of spite. The Leafs gave up defenceman Joel Quenneville and future Hall of Famer McDonald for Wilf Paiement (a good player) and Pat Hickey (an average one). It was a sad day for Leafs supporters and the protests were loud and long — upset fans rallied outside the Gardens to show their displeasure. But the damage was done. Players with McDonald's talent and heart are just not traded away, but it was remarkable to see how many of Imlach's old media friends defended the vindictive general manager. Still, the game had passed Imlach by and this deal was all the proof most people needed.

McDonald eventually found his way to the Flames, who had left

Atlanta for Calgary. He scored a career-best 66 goals in 1982–83 and finished his great career with 500 goals and a Stanley Cup win, secured in his last NHL game. He scored a key goal to help Calgary capture the title at the Montreal Forum, the same building where he had scored his first goal as a Leaf in 1973. It was a fitting farewell for one of the most popular players to ever skate in the NHL.

Lanny McDonald fights along the boards against the Detroit Red Wings. McDonald recorded his first hat trick late in his rookie year, on March 30, 1975, in a 7–3 win against the New York Rangers. (DM)

Leaf file:

Lanny McDonald's greatest moment as a Maple Leaf came against the New York Islanders in the 1978 playoffs. In a hard-fought and often bitter series, the two clubs battled to a seventh game that went into overtime. The Islanders had won the previous two overtime games in the series, but the Leafs were determined to win. At 4:13 of the first overtime period, the puck squirted free to McDonald just over the Islander blue line and he tore in alone on goalie Chico Resch.

McDonald had a serious cut near his eye and a broken nose, which he protected by wearing a football-style face-mask helmet. He was also nursing a broken bone in his wrist, but that did not stop him from picking out the far side of the net with a quick flick of the stick. He leaped all over his teammates in pure joy and Leaf fans celebrated a trip to the semifinals, the farthest they had been since their Stanley Cup win in 1967.

Maple Leaf stats:

	GP	G	A	P	PIM
regular season	477	219	240	459	372
playoffs	45	20	17	37	22

The Business of the Maple Leafs:

The Maple Leafs had to fight off the advances of the Cleveland Crusaders of the World Hockey Association to get Lanny McDonald to sign a contract with Toronto. McDonald earned about $500,000 over five years, the most lucrative deal given to a Leafs first-round draft choice at the time. But it turned out that the Leafs winger had been fleeced by a corrupt agent, Richard Sorkin. Revenue Canada demanded $40,000 in unpaid taxes, which the Leafs agreed to advance him; McDonald appreciated general manager Jim Gregory's help in this tough situation. Unfortunately, he was not the only NHL player Sorkin hurt during his time as an agent.

Montreal goalie Ken Dryden keeps a close eye on Lanny McDonald, whose 219 career goals as a Leaf rank him 11th overall on the team's all-time scorer's list. [DM]

*Lanny McDonald had his best goal-scoring year with the Leafs in 1977–78,
when he had 47. (DM)*

I truly
enjoyed my years with the Leafs
because we had so many good times with so many good people. There were a lot of great memories.

Beating the Islanders and getting close to the Stanley Cup showed what you could accomplish when you hung together as a team.

Lanny McDonald, Leafs program,
1994–95 season

JIM McKENNY

ANYONE WHO WATCHED the Leafs on television in the '70s remembers play-by-play announcer Bill Hewitt saying in a high-pitched scream: "Right in front of the net!" Invariably he was talking about Leafs defenceman Jim McKenny carrying the puck out of his own end by cutting across the front of the Toronto goal. Everyone held their breath for a few seconds as the danger passed and McKenny left the Leafs end. Sometimes the puck-lugging defenceman didn't make it, but that's just the way the talented but enigmatic McKenny played the game, on and off the ice.

McKenny became Leafs property in June 1963 as one of four players the team selected in the first draft held by the NHL. His high school team, the Neil McNeil Monarchs, was no longer going to compete in the Ontario Hockey Association, so all its players were available in the draft. The Leafs took McKenny with their third choice (17th overall) and also selected teammate Gerry Meehan (21st).

McKenny and Meehan became Toronto Marlboros and were looked at as future Leafs. McKenny was a Marlie for three seasons and scored a total of 28 goals and 126 points. After his junior career, McKenny spent four seasons in the minors and scored two goals in 20 games with the Leafs. He finally made the big club for good in 1969–70, scoring 11 goals and 44 points. His point total was the second-best for an NHL defenceman that season (Bobby Orr led the league with 120!) and his future looked bright.

But the Leafs were not a strong team and came to rely far too much on McKenny's dedicated service. He enjoyed the high life off the ice and became one of the NHL's legendary drinkers. His lack of preparation frustrated many of his teammates. McKenny produced some respectable point totals as a Leaf — he was never below 30 — and played in the 1974 all-star game, but he could have done so much more if he had taken things more seriously.

At six feet and 185 pounds, McKenny was not a large defenceman. He wasn't very physical, either, although he once got the better of Andre "Moose" Dupont of Philadelphia in a scrap. McKenny's game was one of finesse, moving and passing the puck precisely. He had a decent shot from the point, accurate but not overpowering, and twice scored 14 goals in a season. When his defensive play declined, McKenny was moved to right wing, where he showed he could survive as a forward. But coach Roger Neilson decided he had seen enough of McKenny 15 games into the 1977–78 season: he called the longtime Leaf into his office and told him he was going to Dallas, where the Leafs had their farm club. McKenny told Neilson he would be back, but the coach told him he wouldn't. His career as a Leaf was over.

The Leafs traded his rights to Minnesota in 1978 and he played in 10 games as a North Star. After he retired from hockey, McKenny turned his life around through Alcoholics Anonymous and became a respected sportscaster at CITY TV in Toronto, where he still amuses viewers with his fast one-liners. McKenny is fondly remembered for his endearing personality. He is also recalled for his role as the double for actor Art Hindle in the hockey movie *Face-Off*, which features a Maple Leaf player much like McKenny.

Maple Leaf stats:	GP	G	A	P	PIM
regular season	594	81	246	327	292
playoffs	37	7	9	16	10

Leafs defenceman Jim McKenny (#18) rushes with the puck against the St. Louis Blues.
McKenny was known as "Howie" for his resemblance to former NHL bad boy Howie Young. (HHOF)

MIKE PALMATEER

THE MAPLE LEAFS had few successes with low-draft choices in the '70s but the 1974 entry draft was an exception. Using the 85th pick overall, they selected goaltender Mike Palmateer from the Toronto Marlboros. The Leafs should have been familiar with Palmateer, since he had played his entire junior hockey at Maple Leaf Gardens with the Markham Waxers and then the Marlies. Born in Toronto on January 13, 1954, Palmateer got a taste of winning in Toronto when the Marlies won the Memorial Cup in 1973 and he came close to experiencing similar success with the Leafs. Palmateer remains one of the most popular goalies in Toronto history.

Leaf fans loved him for his style. Brash, cocky and a gambler in net, the 5'9", 170-pound goalie was all reflex. Like his childhood hero Roger Crozier, Palmateer did everything he could to get a glove or pad out to stop a puck, and if he was all over the ice doing it, so much the better. He also had a way of making routine saves look spectacular, which endeared him to the Gardens crowds and irritated the opposition. His quickness and self-confidence made up for his lack of size.

After his junior career, Palmateer played for the Saginaw Gears of the International Hockey League and the Oklahoma City Blazers of the Central Hockey League before being called in to help a struggling Leafs team. Toronto goalie Wayne Thomas was having a difficult time after a good year in 1975–76, and the Leafs, desperate after starting 1976–77 with a 1–5–3 record, decided to give "the Popcorn Kid" a chance. Palmateer told general manager Jim Gregory not to worry; the Leafs' search for a goalie was over.

In his first game as a Leaf, the roly-poly goalie won a 3–1 decision over the Red Wings, right in Detroit. The Leafs then went 7–2–1 in the next 10 games and Palmateer was there to stay. He was in 50 games that year and posted a 23–18–8 record, with four shutouts. The Leafs were knocked out of the playoffs by Philadelphia, but Palmateer had established himself as the number 1 goalie and the first important netminder developed solely by the Leafs organization.

The 1977–78 season was his best with the Leafs. Toronto was one of the better teams in the NHL that year and he won 34 games, lost 19, tied nine with a 2.74 goals-against average and recorded five shutouts. New coach Roger Neilson was a big proponent of defensive hockey and defencemen Borje Salming and Ian Turnbull were having top years, which made life much easier for the goalie.

In the playoffs, the Leafs wiped out the Los Angeles Kings in two straight games. In the next round Palmateer was outstanding against the heavily favoured New York Islanders, turning them back time after time. He was especially good in the seventh game, when the Leafs knocked off the Islanders with a well-earned 2–1 overtime win. It was the Leafs' greatest moment since 1967 and would not have been possible without Palmateer.

The Leafs thought they were on the verge of winning the Stanley Cup, but the next season was only mediocre (34–33–13, although Palmateer did win 26 games). They were dispatched in the playoffs by the Montreal Canadiens in four straight games once again, as they had been the previous year when they were swept in the semifinal. The loss brought in new management, who were not nearly as enamoured of Palmateer.

New coach Floyd Smith stressed offence and Palmateer was soon suffering from a porous defence and a knee injury. In 38 games he still posted a winning record of 16–14–3, but general manager Punch Imlach had already made up his mind and talked owner Harold Ballard out of re-signing Palmateer. He was dealt to the Washington Capitals for defenceman Robert Picard (who did not last a year in Toronto), ending a promising Leafs career that had started only four years earlier. The Leafs made the deal without another goalie ready to take Palmateer's place.

Things did not go well for Palmateer in Washington. He had always been in a hockey environment and the Capitals were well off the sports radar screen. He won 18 games over two years before the Leafs brought him back for the 1982–83 season. Palmateer posted a respectable 21–23–7 record for a poor club and

Mike Palmateer (#29) makes a save against the Philadelphia Flyers with help from defenceman Borje Salming. Palmateer's childhood hero was former Detroit goalie Roger Crozier and the Leafs netminder copied Crozier's style. (DM)

managed to play in 34 games the next season, though his knees were getting worse. He wanted to play in 1984–85, but insisted he needed a day off after every game; coach Dan Maloney refused the request and Palmateer's career was over.

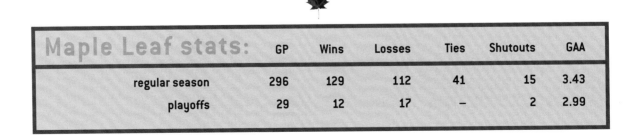

Maple Leaf stats:	GP	Wins	Losses	Ties	Shutouts	GAA
regular season	296	129	112	41	15	3.43
playoffs	29	12	17	–	2	2.99

BERNIE PARENT

TORONTO GENERAL MANAGER Jim Gregory and coach John McLellan were about to leave their Montreal hotel room on January 30, 1971, for a game against the Canadiens when the phone rang. On the other end was Philadelphia Flyers general manager Keith Allen, offering them goalie Bernie Parent in a deal. The Leafs duo could not believe their luck: they had been pursuing Parent for some time and suddenly he was available.

A deal was quickly worked out. The Leafs gave Mike Walton (who they wanted off the team, anyway) and a first-round choice to the Flyers for Parent and a second-round choice who turned out to be Rick Kehoe. It was by far the best deal Gregory made as Leafs general manager.

The Leafs wanted Parent because he was young yet experienced — he had been in the NHL since 1965–66, when he started with Boston — and had the stand-up style so eagerly sought in goaltenders of the '70s. Current netminder Jacques Plante, already 42 years old, would be a perfect mentor for Parent and teach him all the tricks of the trade, such as how to handle the puck outside the crease and how to develop a "book" on opposing shooters.

Things started well, with Parent earning his first win as a Leaf on February 7, 1971, in a 4–3 win over Buffalo. He ended the 1970–71 season at 7–7–3 and should have started the playoff series against the New York Rangers; instead, Plante played net in the opener, a 5–4 loss. Parent won the next game 4–1, but lost his mask during a wild melee toward the end of the contest after he stepped in to help out his friend and teammate Vic Hadfield in a fight with Jim Harrison. Somehow his mask was ripped off and tossed into the crowd. When fans wouldn't give it back, Parent refused to continue and Plante had to finish the game. Parent won the next game, but the Rangers came back to knock out the Leafs in six.

Despite the playoff loss the future for the Leafs seemed bright, especially with Parent in goal. But then the World Hockey Association came knocking: The new professional league was targeting Leafs players and Parent, whose contract expired at the end of the season, was at the top of its list. In February 1972, he took a plane down to Florida and signed a deal with the Miami Screaming Eagles for the 1973–74 season. The Leafs lost the top goalie in hockey.

Parent was worried about his teammates' reaction, but they were surprisingly easygoing about it — defenceman Jim McKenny suggested Parent take the Leafs out to dinner, and rugged blueliner Bob Baun tried to hit him up for a loan! The players were obviously glad to see some big money coming their way and others would follow the goalie to the new league in the months ahead. Parent finished the 1971–72 season with a 17–18–9 record for the Leafs and played well in the playoffs against Boston, though the Bruins knocked the Leafs out in five tough games and went on to win the Stanley Cup.

He never played in Miami. The franchise was moved to Philadelphia and Parent had problems getting paid, so he walked away. He wanted to return to the NHL but not to Toronto, so the Leafs had little choice but to trade him back to the Flyers in return for goalie Doug Favell and a first-round draft choice, Bob Neely. Leaf fans then had to watch Parent win two Cups in Philadelphia. He was elected to the Hall of Fame in 1984.

Maple Leaf stats:	GP	Wins	Losses	Ties	Shutouts	GAA
regular season	65	25	25	12	3	2.59
playoffs	8	3	5	–	0	2.76

Goalie Bernie Parent makes a save against the St. Louis Blues. Parent was a three-time MVP for the Philadelphia Flyers before he joined the Leafs. (HHOF)

JACQUES PLANTE

IN NOVEMBER 1947, goaltender Jacques Plante was on the negotiation list of the Toronto Maple Leafs, but he wanted to be a Montreal Canadien, so he turned his rights over to the Habs. The Leafs did not protest too loudly and thus lost his services, though they could have used the star goalie in the '50s — while they struggled, Plante took the Canadiens to six Stanley Cups. He wouldn't wear a Leafs uniform until 1970, at age 41. It was worth the wait as Plante was named an NHL all-star for the final time in his illustrious career.

Toronto fans were very familiar with the quirky but innovative goalie who had made face masks a part of every goaltender's equipment. They had seen him beat the Leafs as a Hab, knocking off Toronto in the finals in 1959 and 1960, and witnessed his last game with Montreal in April 1963, when the Leafs clinched a semifinal playoff series with a 5–0 victory.

Plante was traded to the New York Rangers in the summer of '63. He was not the same goalie, though he did manage to stone the Leafs 1–0 on November 7, 1964, by making 27 saves, including a difficult one at the final bell. Leaf fans gave Plante a standing ovation when he was named the first star of the game. The game revived memories of the Plante magic that had seen him win six Vezina trophies.

Plante retired for three years, but returned to play for the St. Louis Blues in 1968 and shared the Vezina Trophy with Glenn Hall. He was as cocky as ever and a goal was rarely his fault. A true student of the game, Plante believed success was 85 percent mental and only 15 percent physical.

The official NHL record book says Toronto acquired Plante in a cash deal with the Blues on May 18, 1970. Other sources indicate that Plante became a Maple Leaf in the deal that saw Tim Horton go to the Rangers on March 3, 1970. Whatever the truth, the Leafs knew why they wanted the veteran goalie: they had a very young defence made up of players like Jim Dorey, Brian Glennie, Rick Ley, Jim McKenny, Mike Pelyk and Brad Selwood, with journeyman Bruce Gamble in net. There was no star player and precious little experience; none had

played more than four years in the league.

Leafs general manager Jim Gregory hoped Plante would teach the youngsters how to help the goalie and play in their own end. He gave Plante a good contract and found him an air-conditioned apartment in the north end of Toronto, so the finicky goalie would not complain about his asthma. The Leafs did everything to make him feel welcome.

It didn't work too well at first, as the Leafs lost often and Plante was not exactly forgiving. He was merciless with any defenceman whose mistake led to a goal — the youngsters would head straight to the bench to avoid being embarrassed on national television by the goalie's gestures. Things started to click when Gregory acquired veteran defenceman (and ex-Leaf) Bob Baun. Plante recorded his first shutout as a Maple Leaf on December 2, 1970, in a 7–0 whitewash of the Los Angeles Kings at the Gardens. The Leafs turned their season around and secured a playoff spot by finishing fourth and Plante posted a 24–11–4 record, with four shutouts and a very impressive 1.88 goals-against average.

His performance earned a spot on the second all-star team, but he had some detractors. Boston goalie Gerry Cheevers thought Plante ducked the hard teams, while a veteran Toronto sports writer dubbed him "the Saturday night goalie" since he always seemed to start at home (where the Leafs invariably played better) before the *Hockey Night in Canada* audience. But there was no doubt the confident goalie gave the Leafs something special in 1970–71.

The playoffs were a different story. Plante started against the Rangers and promptly blew a three-goal lead that ended in a 5–4 loss. The recently acquired Bernie Parent took over and won a couple of games, but Plante was back in the nets at the Gardens for the sixth contest of the series, with the Leafs down 3–2. The game went into overtime with the score tied 1–1, then former Leaf Bob Nevin stepped just over the blue line and beat Plante with a shot he should have stopped (as he admitted afterwards). The Cinderella story of Plante and the Leafs was over and the goalie was never quite the same again.

Jacques Plante prepares to make a save against the New York Rangers' Bruce MacGregor. Plante was the first to write a book about the art of goaltending. [DM]

He played with Toronto for two more seasons but got into only one more playoff game. By the 1972–73 season the Leafs were again in bad shape and saw no need to keep Plante; the Boston Bruins needed a goalie for the playoffs and offered in return veteran netminder Ed Johnston and a number 1 draft choice (the Leafs would select defenceman Ian Turnbull). Gregory completed the deal and was happy to get something back for the ageless goalie. Plante was elected to the Hall of Fame in 1978.

Maple Leaf stats:	GP	Wins	Losses	Ties	Shutouts	GAA
regular season	106	48	38	15	7	2.46
playoffs	4	0	3	–	0	3.71

BORJE SALMING

THE TORONTO MAPLE LEAFS were no longer a top team in the early '70s, but they were the first NHL club to have a European-born player as a bona fide star. Defenceman Borje Salming was spotted by Leafs scout Gerry McNamara while he was watching the Brynäs team play the Barrie Flyers in an exhibition game in Sweden. McNamara was actually interested in Swedish goalie Kurt Larsson, but it was Salming who caught his eye.

Salming was tossed from the game for taking a poke at the referee as the contest took on a North American flavour. McNamara followed him into the dressing room and asked the lanky Swede (6'1", 193 pounds) if he was interested in playing for the Leafs. Salming said yes, so the excited McNamara also approached forward Inge Hammarstrom, who had scored four times in the contest. The Leafs had just finished a horrible year in 1972–73 and they needed some new, skilful players. Both men fit the bill, but Salming would have the greatest impact on the team.

The Leafs signed Salming for $85,000 a year, plus a $50,000 fee to get the Swedish club to release him. It turned out to be a wise invest-ment. He quickly made a name for himself with his superior puck-handling and skating abilities and though he scored only five times in his rookie year, 1974–75, he had 34 assists and helped the Leafs get back into the playoffs. In 1975–76 he established a club record for defencemen, with 57 points, including 41 assists. He then put together season assist totals of 66, 60, 56, 52 and 61 and was named an NHL all-star for six straight seasons from 1975 to 1980, once on the first team.

The Leafs had two of the NHL's best defencemen in Salming and Ian Turnbull, who anchored the points on the Leafs power play while formidable attackers like Darryl Sittler and Lanny McDonald got the goals. Salming adapted quickly to the NHL style of play and showed he would not be run out of the league when he battled Philadelphia tough guy Dave Schultz in his second game. His play made him very popular in Toronto, and he knew he had been accepted in the Leafs dressing room when captain Dave Keon had Salming sit next to him.

At the 1976 Canada Cup tournament, he got the loudest ovation when the Swedes played Canada at the Gardens, much to the displeas-ure of Canadian players like Bobby Clarke, who complained about it to the press. Competitive and tireless in his efforts to win, Salming was the glue that held the shaky Leafs blue line together for many years.

He missed out on the Leafs' greatest playoff moment during his career with Toronto when a stick in the eye sidelined him at the start of a very physical series against the New York Islanders in 1978. After that great run, Toronto was not a contender for the rest of Salming's time there. Poor trades seemed to turn him off the game and he lost his early gusto. Many Leafs stars, including Sittler, McDonald and Turnbull, were traded away and the Swede probably would have fol-lowed because his style did not sit well with the new general manager, Punch Imlach.

Imlach felt Salming went down on the ice far too often when attempting to check the opposition and took himself out of the play. There was some truth to this, but Salming was a fine sweep-checker who blocked a lot of shots; Leafs broadcaster Bill Hewitt once called him the "backup goaltender" after the defenceman had blocked countless Islander shots in a 2–1 Toronto win. Other Salming critics included Don Cherry, who was coaching the Boston Bruins at the time, and star centre Phil Esposito, who had fought a running feud with Salming's brother, Stig, throughout the two exhibition games between Team Canada and Sweden in 1972.

But Salming had a big fan in Leafs owner Harold Ballard. Ballard treated many players shabbily but was good to Salming. He paid the Swede well and overruled Imlach when it came time to offer a new contract, giving his favourite son $350,000 a year for three years and $400,000 for two more years. On January 4, 1988, Ballard gave Salming a Chevy Blazer to celebrate his 1,000th game as a Leaf.

Salming was not a natural leader and turned down the captaincy when Sittler left the club. He did his best to avoid office confronta-tion, especially if it meant challenging management. He had some

Leafs defenceman Borje Salming has Boston's Phil Esposito all tied up. Salming won the Molson Cup (based on three-star selections) four times in Toronto, including the inaugural award in 1973–74. (DM)

bad off-ice habits — he admitted he used drugs on one occasion, and once went skiing on the morning of a game. He was known as a party animal, and his lack of discipline infuriated coach John Brophy who — to put it mildly — did not like Salming. Referees around the NHL also came to dislike his constant harping and regular dives.

Yet when the game was on, Salming was the ultimate warrior and the fans and many in the media loved him for his recklessness. Late in his career his face was cut to shreds when Detroit's Gerard Gallant stepped on him during a game; the gruesome wound needed 300 stitches. Toronto newspapers displayed Salming's battered mug on their front pages, but the scars healed reasonably well after a great stitching job by Dr. John Finley.

Salming had a small rebirth in the 1985-86 season when the team made the playoffs and he had seven points in 10 postseason games. This was his last great moment with the Leafs. After two more unexceptional years in Toronto, he asked for a new $500,000 contract and found himself in Detroit, instead; he played his last season in the NHL there in 1989–90. The Leafs' all-time assist leader with 620, Salming was elected to the Hall of Fame in 1998.

Maple Leaf stats:	GP	G	A	P	PIM
regular season	1,099	148	620	768	1,292
playoffs	81	12	37	49	91

Leaf file:

Borje Salming had many great games in his time with the Leafs, but none is better remembered than the 1976 playoff series against the Philadelphia Flyers. It was a brutally physical series that went seven games as the Leafs tried to prove they could beat the Broad Street Bullies at their own game. The Leafs lost the first two games in Philadelphia and the third, at Maple Leaf Gardens, was one of the most controversial contests in NHL playoffs. It was filled with fights and the Toronto police force had to become involved: Salming was beaten so badly by Mel Bridgeman that the police decided to charge the Philadelphia player with assault, along with two of his teammates who had committed similar infractions. The home crowd was incensed, but the Leafs won the game 5–4.

The next game was fierce but not as brutal and the Leafs won it 4–3, with Salming scoring a spectacular goal against Bernie Parent. He took a pass on the fly near centre and split the Philadelphia defence with a full head of steam before rifling a shot home. The Leaf fans leapt to their feet and exploded with thunderous applause for the Leafs defenceman: Salming had shown the thuggish Flyers how hockey should be played. The Flyers went on to win the series, but the Leafs had softened them up and they had little left in the finals against Montreal.

Borje Salming (#21) looks to get the puck, with teammate Stan Weir (#14) helping out. Salming won three player-of-the-game awards during the 1976 Canada Cup tournament. (DM)

Maybe I could have become a free agent and got more money from another team. But Toronto is a clean city, a safe city. You can walk where you want and there's a lot to do. **The people** have been good to us. If you're ever in any trouble, if you need help, they are always there.

Borje Salming, *Hockey Illustrated*, March 1981

DARRYL SITTLER

THERE WAS VERY little hoopla when Darryl Sittler was drafted eighth overall by the Leafs in 1970. Sittler was not even there — in fact, he was working at his summer job installing swimming pools when he heard the news over the radio. The Leafs never interviewed him, either, but they must have been impressed with the big centre (six feet and a solid 190 pounds) who had graduated from the London Knights of the Ontario Hockey Association. Sittler scored 42 goals and added 48 assists in his last year of junior and went to the Leafs training camp in the fall of 1970 determined to make the team.

Leafs general manager Jim Gregory sensed that Sittler was going to be a special player and at camp gave him sweater number 27. Sittler recognized the importance of the gesture, since he knew Leafs legend Frank Mahovlich had worn that number during his career in Toronto. Sittler had an old-fashioned approach to life that he had learned while growing up in the Mennonite community of St. Jacobs, Ontario. He had once worked as a street cleaner in a town that used horses as the main form of transportation and brought an honest work ethic to his hockey career. He tried to make himself a better player every day and every season. He showed a willingness to battle (breaking teammate Brian Glennie's nose at camp) and worked extra hours with Leafs captain Dave Keon to improve his game. He made the team in his first attempt and never saw the minor leagues on his way to a Hall of Fame career.

Sittler's rookie year did not go well at all, however. He broke his wrist during a game with the Los Angeles Kings, thanks to a body-check dished out by Gilles Marotte, and was restricted to 49 appearances (10 goals, eight assists). More importantly, he was being played out of position at left wing because the Leafs had too many centres. When Jim Harrison jumped to the World Hockey Association, Sittler had the chance he needed to play in the middle and made the most of it.

In 1972–73, he had Leaf fans dreaming that they had found a new leader when he scored 29 goals and 77 points. For the next eight seasons Sittler never scored fewer than 36 goals (reaching a high of 45 in 1977–78) or earned less than 80 points (hitting a then club-record 117 in 1977–78). At age 24, he replaced Keon as captain.

Sittler showed a strong desire to lead his teammates and was not afraid to battle management when necessary, notably when it came to standing up to Harold Ballard. He was the undisputed leader of the team and ran the dressing room through consensus, though he was not afraid to tell a teammate to get his act together, and did so with goalie Wayne Thomas and defenceman Ian Turnbull. The Leafs played some exciting hockey during Sittler's best years but never had enough to challenge for a Stanley Cup, especially when faced with the Montreal Canadiens in the middle of a dynasty.

The sum of Sittler's game was greater than any one part. He was not the fastest skater, yet he was seldom knocked off his feet. His shot was not overpowering, but still very accurate. And while he was not a league heavyweight, Sittler could throw punches with just about anybody and wasn't averse to stirring things up if the Leafs were not playing well. His skill level did not match that of some of the other top players in the NHL, but nobody outworked the fiery Leaf and his touch around the net made him a leading point man year after year; he led the Leafs in points eight times in his career.

There was no better captain in the NHL at the time because Sittler cared about his teammates and wanted to see people treated decently. He was also an unselfish player, who went so far as to pass up an open net so that teammate Lanny McDonald could record a hat trick during a playoff game. Hockey legend Bobby Orr watched that game and called Sittler's wife, Wendy, to say how impressed he was with the selfless gesture.

The year 1976 was a magical one for Sittler. First, he set an NHL record with 10 points — six goals and four assists — in one game, on February 7 in an 11–4 Leafs win against the Boston Bruins at Maple Leaf Gardens. The record is one of the few even the great Wayne Gretzky couldn't match (eight was as close as number 99 got) and still stands today. A few months later, on April 22, Sittler tied a playoff record with five goals in one game, an 8–5 Toronto victory over the Philadelphia Flyers.

He capped off this memorable year by scoring the winning goal in overtime in the very first Canada Cup tournament. Prime Minister Pierre Trudeau was watching from the stands at the Montreal Forum on September 15 as Canada beat Czechoslovakia in the final. Sittler's performance proved he belonged with the game's elite and he was named a tournament all-star, at left wing. It was the best of times for Sittler. The Leafs yearbook boasted he received 3,000 letters a day from across Canada at the height of his popularity.

When Toronto hired Roger Neilson as coach, the players suddenly had a mentor interested in defence. This philosophy worked for the first season, as the Leafs won 41 games and 92 points; Sittler enjoyed his best year as a Leaf with Neilson and the team made it to the semifinals with an upset win over the New York Islanders. When things did not go nearly as well the following year Neilson's job was saved by Sittler and the players, but it was only a reprieve. The coach was gone after the 1979 playoffs and in came Punch Imlach, a man determined to make changes. In his second coming as general manager, Imlach firmly believed the team captain should be part of management. This was contrary to Sittler's beliefs and the two were destined to clash.

The conflict started with Imlach trying to keep Sittler and goalie Mike Palmateer from playing in a skills competition known as *Showdown*, despite the fact that Sittler had done so before. The players won a court battle to participate, but relations with Imlach continued to decline. Soon he was saying that Sittler had lost his speed, and he used this as an excuse to try to trade the longtime captain. Only a promise from Ballard kept Sittler in Toronto.

Sittler was determined to stay with the Leafs and eventually outlasted Imlach, even sending the manager a "get well" card when he suffered a heart attack. But the team was severely damaged from all the poor deals made during Imlach's reign of error. Sittler resigned the captaincy when his best friend Lanny McDonald was traded, a deal from which the Leafs never recovered. Everyone picked sides in the feud between the Leafs' best player and the general manager and many who were loyal to Imlach — media people, for the most part — attacked Sittler's reputation. But Sittler was ultimately vindicated when Imlach's record is taken into account.

By 1981 Sittler was worn down from playing in Toronto and asked to be moved when Ballard refused to meet his contract demands. He was dealt to Philadelphia in another poor deal for the Leafs and had several productive years as a Flyer, but the ruthless Bobby Clarke, who was now the Philadelphia general manager, traded him to Detroit just as Sittler was about to be named captain of the Flyers. He played for one unhappy year in Detroit before trying to re-sign with the Leafs to play for his former juniors teammate Dan Maloney, the new coach. Leafs GM Gerry McNamara and the vindictive Ballard did not approve the move.

Cliff Fletcher brought Sittler back into the Leafs organization in the early '90s and the team has promised to raise his number 27 to the rafters at the Air Canada Centre. When this happens, Darryl Sittler will finally take his rightful place among the Leafs greats.

Maple Leaf stats:	GP	G	A	P	PIM
regular season	844	389	527	916	763
playoffs	64	25	40	65	120

Darryl Sittler in front of the New York Islanders net occupied by goalie Billy Smith. Sittler holds the Leafs' team record for most career hat tricks with 18. He recorded one (and a total seven points) against the Islanders on October 14, 1978, when the Leafs won a 10–7 shootout at Maple Leaf Gardens. (DM)

The Business of the Maple Leafs:

When Darryl Sittler signed his first contract with the Leafs he was given a salary of $15,000 a year, with a $10,000 signing bonus. He was earning $29,000 a year when the Toronto Toros of the World Hockey Association came along and offered him $1 million for a five-year contract. Sittler's agent, Alan Eagleson, also had Toros owner John Bassett Jr. include a $2,000 shopping credit at Eaton's department store, two watches from Peoples Credit jewellers and a deal with McDonald's restaurants (all these companies were partners with Bassett). But Sittler wanted to stay in the best league and turned down the Toros, signing for five years with the Leafs for a total of $750,000.

By 1982 Sittler was approaching 1,000 points and not far from his 1,000th game as a Maple Leaf. He felt it was time owner Harold Ballard upped his $190,000 salary toward the $300,000 given to defenceman Borje Salming. Ballard refused, flat out, after "consulting" the Leafs' board of directors, so Sittler asked to be traded and let the media know that he had a "blockbuster" reason for leaving. As general manager Gerry McNamara dragged his feet on completing a deal, the "blockbuster" angle was dropped and Sittler was vilified for leaving the team while waiting for the trade. For one of their greatest players the Leafs received Rich Costello, Ken Strong and a second-round draft choice, Peter Ihnacak.

Darryl Sittler takes a shot against the Montreal Canadiens. Sittler finished his career as the Leafs' all-time leader in goals (389) and points (916). (DM)

IAN TURNBULL

BEFORE THE 1973 NHL entry draft Ian Turnbull told his juniors teammate Denis Potvin that one of them was going to be the first defenceman selected. The statement was a bit of a shock to Potvin, who had always assumed he was going to be the first selection, but it also showed what a confident young man Turnbull was.

He had every right to be cocky after a fine career with the Montreal Junior Canadiens (playing on the Memorial Cup championship squad in 1970) and the Ottawa 67's, where he teamed up with Potvin. The hard-shooting defenceman scored 65 goals and 163 points in his last two years of junior yet, surprisingly, Turnbull was not taken until the Maple Leafs selected him 15th overall. He was the third defenceman chosen, after Potvin (the top pick overall, selected by the New York Islanders) and Bob Dailey (selected ninth overall by Vancouver).

Turnbull made the Leafs as a 19-year-old, the youngest player in the NHL at the time. The six-foot, 200-pound native of Montreal soon showed he was worthy of a first-round selection, scoring seven goals and totalling 27 assists in 1973–74, when the Leafs climbed back into the playoffs. His game was all about handling the puck and using his powerful skating stride to get the team out of trouble. He had a low, hard shot from the point that earned many points on the power play and he was incredibly strong physically. He was not a fighter, but did not back away from confrontation and was difficult to handle when riled.

His second season was marred by a knee injury caused by a hip check from Bob Plager of St. Louis. Turnbull had played only 20 games, amassing six goals and 13 points. The Leafs missed him badly, but he came back the next season to score 20 goals and 56 points. He was an emerging star on the blue line.

The 1976–77 season was Turnbull's finest as a Maple Leaf: he set a team record for defencemen with 22 goals (later tied by Al Iafrate) and had an impressive 57 assists. Turnbull thrived under coach Red Kelly's wide-open style and loved to attack with the puck, but Kelly was gone after the 1977 playoffs after the Leafs were again knocked out early. Under new, defensive-minded coach Roger Neilson, Turnbull's numbers fell to 14 goals and 61 points but the team did much better in the playoffs, knocking off the New York Islanders.

Turnbull came to the fore with his performance against the Islanders, especially when Borje Salming was hurt in the middle of the series. Turnbull was a workhorse. In the seventh game he scored one goal and got the puck to Lanny McDonald for the 2–1 winner in overtime. In 13 postseason games during the '78 playoffs, Turnbull recorded six goals and 16 points.

Neilson did not see eye to eye with him and wanted the defenceman traded while his value was high, but Leafs owner Harold Ballard refused to get rid of Turnbull, once bellowing that he wouldn't trade him for God. Neilson was stuck with a player he did not want for the 1978–79 season, so when Ballard fired the coach Turnbull was pretty happy.

Unfortunately, Ballard could not find a replacement for Neilson on short notice and when all the players (with the obvious exception of Turnbull) said they wanted the coach back he felt he had no choice but to give the job back to the Leafs' curly haired mentor. Turnbull finished the year with 12 goals and 63 points, both highly respectable numbers, but he was glad to see Neilson gone for good at the end of the season.

Turnbull came to the Leafs' 1979 training camp in a much better mood. He was happy to hear that coach Floyd Smith was offensive-minded, especially as his contract was up for renegotiation in a year. He scored 11 goals and 39 points in 1979–80 but rebounded with 19 goals and 66 points in 1980–81. His good year won Turnbull an excellent contract — $200,000 a year — from new general manager Punch Imlach. However, Imlach never saw Turnbull after the contract was signed and felt he was duped by the friendly defenceman.

Early in the 1981–82 season Turnbull had had enough of the Leafs and basically walked out on the team. Coach Mike Nykoluk

Ian Turnbull (#2) of the Maple Leafs tries to beat Philadelphia's Ross Lonsberry to a loose puck. Turnbull still holds the Leafs' team record for most points in a season with 79, set in 1976–77. (HB)

Leaf file:

Prior to a February 2, 1977, game against the Detroit Red Wings, Leafs defenceman Ian Turnbull had scored only two goals in 37 games. But he was red-hot that night, bagging five goals in a 9–1 slaughter, two on Ed Giacomin and three against Jim Rutherford. Borje Salming, who assisted on three of the goals, set up the fifth by springing Turnbull with a perfect pass at the Detroit blue line. Turnbull went in all alone and fired a low shot past Rutherford. It was 18:30 of the third period and the entire Leafs bench came onto the ice to congratulate Turnbull (at the time there was no penalty given for doing this). The five goals set an NHL record for defencemen that has yet to be broken; Paul Coffey has come closest in recent years, scoring four as an Oiler in a game against Calgary in 1984. Another NHL record holder, captain Darryl Sittler, did not play for the Leafs in this game.

told him to go home and wait for a deal, which was completed on November 11, 1981. Turnbull headed to the Los Angeles Kings in return for Billy Harris and John Gibson (neither had any impact on the Leafs' fortunes). In 42 games for the Kings Turnbull scored 11 goals, including four in one game, and 26 points. He was released as a free agent to Pittsburgh the next season but played only six games as a Penguin before his NHL career was over.

A laid-back character, Turnbull enjoyed Rolls-Royces and fine wines, played the guitar and owned an upscale Toronto restaurant called Grapes. Many feel those outside interests kept him from living up to his potential on the ice.

🍁

Maple Leaf stats:	GP	G	A	P	PIM
regular season	580	112	302	414	651
playoffs	55	13	32	45	94

NORM ULLMAN

NORM ULLMAN sensed a trade was in the works when he left a Detroit Red Wings practice late in the 1967–68 season and told his wife to expect a deal. They both hoped Toronto was a possibility and their wishes were fulfilled on March 3, 1968. The Leafs picked up Ullman, Paul Henderson and Floyd Smith in exchange for Frank Mahovlich, Peter Stemkowski, Garry Unger and the rights to Carl Brewer in one of the biggest trades in NHL history.

Despite his premonitions Ullman was shocked to be leaving the Red Wings, his club since 1955. The centre had led the NHL in goals scored in 1964–65 (42) and scored 20 or more goals 11 times in his career with Detroit. The Leafs were thrilled to acquire such a steady performer.

In 1968–69, his first full year in Toronto, Ullman had 35 goals (his best total since 1964–65) and 42 assists, totalling 77 points to lead the Leafs in all three categories. His play slipped the next season, with only 18 goals, but he rebounded to set a new Leafs record of 85 points (34 goals and 51 assists) in 1970–71, breaking Mahovlich's mark of 84. Ullman played at centre that season between wingers Ron Ellis and Paul Henderson, in a trio that was fast becoming one of the best lines in the NHL and was given the moniker "the Hue Line," based on a combination of their names. Before his career as a Leaf was over, Ullman led the team in points on three occasions and in assists four times. He was one of the most reliable players to wear a Toronto sweater and he and Dave Keon formed a dynamic duo at centre.

Ullman's game was anchored by his great skating abilities. He was dedicated to staying physically fit and kept his legs in shape by running in the off-season; his powerful skating allowed him to be a dogged forechecker. A very focused player, he was efficient rather than flashy, though he had the knack of showing up at just the right moment to set up a teammate or knock in a goal. He was a good goal scorer (490 in 1,410 career games) and a very skilful playmaker (739 career assists). His work in the slot was excellent and he was known for his quick release of a shot or pass.

Ullman might have been overshadowed by more colourful characters, but he was tougher than his 712 career penalty minutes might indicate. While he was a youngster with Detroit, he angered Maurice Richard in a game and the Montreal legend took his stick to Ullman in retaliation. Another time he knocked Leafs defenceman Carl Brewer for a loop with one punch. But most of the time Ullman played a quiet though deadly game with little fanfare. He competed hard every night until he simply couldn't do it any more.

Off the ice, Ullman proved to be a shrewd negotiator and often won himself good contracts. He was earning $57,000 in 1970–71, a very good wage at the time. He was bright and articulate, and when Bob Pulford of the Leafs was forced to give up the presidency of the National Hockey League Players Association Ullman took his place. He was also good to younger players like Dave "Tiger" Williams, who appreciated a veteran like Ullman taking the time to welcome a newcomer like himself. The Leafs tried to send Ullman to the Los Angeles Kings in a proposed exchange for Dan Maloney during the 1973–74 season but he refused to go, showing management he would stand up for his rights as an NHL veteran.

Eleven games into the 1973–74 season, Ullman became the NHL's all-time leading scorer among active point players when former teammate Alex Delvecchio retired. He scored 22 times for the Leafs that year and had 69 points in 78 games played. His next season was his last as a Maple Leaf and in the NHL as he started to show signs of slowing down. He racked up only nine goals and 35 points but managed to play in all 80 games. Let go along with Keon, the native of Provost, Alberta, went home to play for a couple of years with the Edmonton Oilers in the World Hockey Association. He recorded 130 points in 144 games.

Toronto's Norm Ullman (#9) watches teammate Ron Ellis (#6) dig for the puck along the boards against the Pittsburgh Penguins. Ullman played 20 seasons in the NHL but never won the Stanley Cup: the closest he got was game 7 of the finals in 1964 when his Red Wing team lost, ironically, to the Maple Leafs. (DM)

Maple Leaf stats:	GP	G	A	P	PIM
regular season	535	166	305	471	160
playoffs	26	3	6	9	6

DAVE 'TIGER' WILLIAMS

As a former RCMP officer, Leafs scout Torchy Schell knew a genuine tough guy when he spotted one. Schell scoured western Canada for future Maple Leafs and strongly recommended the club select Dave Williams in the 1974 draft. Schell had been watching Williams develop as a player with the Swift Current Broncos, where he scored 96 goals in his last two years of junior hockey while racking up 376 penalty minutes. In high school, Williams wrote across a guidance-counselling form that he would play in the NHL one day. A determined competitor with a fierce pride in doing a job to the best of his ability, the left-winger known as "Tiger" seemed to belong in an earlier era of Leafs players. When Toronto selected him 31st overall in the '74 entry draft, Williams' dreams of an NHL career were about to come true.

At his first training camp with the Leafs he made an impression by taking on Ian Turnbull (a player who would always frustrate Williams) in a scrap, but his camp performance was rather poor overall and he was sent to Oklahoma City for some seasoning. He scored 16 goals in 39 games and piled up 202 penalty minutes. The Leafs were being embarrassed physically during the early part of the 1974–75 season, so Toronto general manager Jim Gregory called up Williams to give the team some punch. From that day until he was traded to the Vancouver Canucks in 1980, Williams was an integral part of the Leafs.

In 42 games in 1974–75 he scored 10 goals and made 19 assists while staying true to form by pounding out 187 penalty minutes, getting into a fight with Gary Howatt of the Islanders in his very first game. The Leafs were not going to be pushed around any more. Williams could score the occasional goal, as well: his first came against the Montreal Canadiens at the Forum on January 18, 1975, tying the game 3–3 and sparking the Leafs to a 5–3 win.

Williams had a tremendous work ethic that was a legacy of his days in the Alberta oil fields. He knew he was not the most skilled player, nor the biggest at 5'11" and 190 pounds, but nobody was going to be tougher. Williams took boxing lessons to prepare himself for the inevitable fights and he was not above being dirty. He used his stick as a weapon when necessary and would fight all comers no matter how big — he often knocked the stuffing out of Philadelphia's Dave Schultz, the NHL heavyweight champion, and fought with other tough guys like Dan Maloney, Terry O'Reilly, Bob Gassoff and Wayne Cashman.

His stickwork got him into trouble a couple of times, notably against Dave Hutchison of the Kings in a playoff game and another time against Denis Owchar of the Penguins, when Williams was charged by the Toronto police. But he generally dropped the gloves. Williams was a good fighter when he could get an opponent in close and pound away; he knew he would not win every fight, but he was going to show up for all of them. Williams enjoyed taking care of teammates like Darryl Sittler, Lanny McDonald and Borje Salming but expected all the Leafs to play as hard as he did. He did not like floaters and would try to keep known party guys in line: George Ferguson and Jim McKenny both felt Tiger's wrath. The Leafs players appreciated the protection Williams provided, but he sometimes went too far and found himself spending too much time in the sin bin. He never recorded fewer than 298 penalty minutes in any full season during his career as a Leaf.

Williams was usually around the 20-goal mark, producing seasons of 21, 18, 19, 19 and 22 goals with the Leafs, and he would have scored more had he shown more discipline on the ice. He was also effective on the power play, keeping the defencemen in front of the net occupied. He loved playing for coach Roger Neilson, whom he backed to the hilt. Neilson did his best to refine Tiger's play and became his greatest fan after the Leafs beat the Islanders in the 1978 playoffs.

When Punch Imlach came back to run the Leafs, Williams became furious when the manager fined him for not wearing a tie at the executive offices. While that was petty behaviour by Imlach, it was nothing compared with the feud he had going with Sittler. Williams backed his captain and railed at the manager.

The Leafs lost something special when they sent Williams (and

Tiger Williams prepares to take on Pierre Plante of the St. Louis Blues in a fight. Williams had 351 penalty minutes in 1977–78, his high mark as a Maple Leaf. (HHOF)

Jerry Butler) to Vancouver. They received Rick Vaive and Bill Derlago in the trade and did well with a couple of highly regarded prospects. but even former Toronto owner Conn Smythe commented that Imlach was foolish to trade away such a loyal and spirited player .

Williams helped the Canucks get to the finals in 1982 and had a career-best 35 goals for Vancouver in 1980–81. He also played for the Detroit Red Wings, the Los Angeles Kings and the Hartford Whalers, finishing with 241 goals and as the all-time NHL penalty minutes leader with 3,966 in 962 games.

The Business of the Maple Leafs:

When Dave Williams was playing junior hockey in Swift Current, Saskatchewan, he refused to sign with agent Richard Sorkin. The team had encouraged him to do so and benched him for one game when he would not cooperate, but Williams spotted the fake the agent proved to be and he threatened to go to the media about the coercion attempt. He signed with Herb Pinder instead.

It was a good choice: Pinder negotiated a three-year Leafs deal that reportedly paid Williams $100,000 in the first year, $110,000 in the second and $115,000 in the final year. He also got a $30,000 signing bonus (his salary in the minors would have been $65,000, a good sum at the time). The $435,000 commitment the Leafs made to Williams proved to be a wise investment.

Why shouldn't I feel a little cocky? It wasn't a half dozen years ago that I was busting my backside as an oil rigger in northern Alberta in the cold. I feel good because I'm doing what I like, the team is looking good and I'm having fun. How many people can say that? Dave "Tiger" Williams, *Hockey Illustrated*, January 1979

Maple Leaf stats:	GP	G	A	P	PIM
regular season	407	109	132	241	1,670
playoffs	44	5	11	16	240

SALMING AND THE EUROPEAN INVASION

by Jim O'Leary

THROUGHOUT HIS CAREER, Borje Salming yearned to blend in. He avoided interviews, shunned endorsements and refused public appearances. So he'd be embarrassed to have anyone suggest his career was revolutionary. But that's what it was, all right, although you could argue the revolution was, like Salming himself, a quiet one.

The Maple Leafs hall of fame defenceman was the standard-bearer for what may be hockey's most significant development of the past quarter century: the European colonization of the NHL. Today, approximately 25 percent of NHL players come from Europe. Thirty years ago, when Leafs scout Gerry McNamara first drooled over Salming, European hockey was barely an afterthought with NHL teams.

In its history, the NHL has spawned only a handful of players who truly changed the game. Jacques Plante introduced the mask to goaltenders. Bobby Orr begat generations of offensive defencemen. Bobby Hull deployed the curved blade and slap shot with panache to embed them into the game. And then there is Salming.

In the face of unparalleled hostility, particularly during a rookie season dripping with malice, he exhibited élan and courage and forced NHL barriers to tumble. Today the NHL is a multinational game because of Salming. Like Plante, Orr and Hull before him, his career forever altered the game.

The year 1972 was a pivotal one for hockey. The World Hockey Association came to life, Canada squeaked by the Soviet Union in the historic Summit Series and, in Philadelphia, Fred Shero was introducing his newest rookie, Bill Barber, to the likes of Dave Schultz and preparing a fist-first pursuit of the Stanley Cup. Although Salming had no inkling at the time, all three events—the birth of the WHA, the aftershock of the Canada-Russia summit and the war-room planning in Philadelphia—became subplots to his own story.

In the five years that followed the Leafs' Stanley Cup victory in 1967, the NHL expanded from six to 16 teams and, when the WHA launched with 12 teams, a mad scramble ensued to fill the new clubs. WHA raids thinned out most NHL rosters, with the Leafs enduring several key hits.

Meantime, Salming had begun to contemplate an NHL career. Prior to the Moscow leg of the Summit Series, Canada played two exhibitions against the Swedish national team, which included Salming. Canada won the first 4–1, but needed a final-minute goal to tie the second game 4–4. For Salming those games, coupled with the scare the Soviets were giving Team Canada, signalled that there might be room for a Swede in the NHL.

As these events unfolded, Shero was finalizing his battle plan in Philadelphia. A smart coach, he recognized that the dilution of the NHL talent pool meant every team was stuck with several unskilled players, so he unveiled a plan to put those "cement hands" to good use. The Broad Sreet Bullies were born.

This was the NHL that awaited Salming. NHL-calibre talent was so scarce that the Leafs, having lost defencemen Brad Selwood and Rick Ley to the WHA, were forced to gamble on a Swede. To keep his job — and open doors for other Europeans — Salming had to endure the NHL's most violent era.

His rookie year became a hallmark in NHL history. All rookies are tested, but Salming was not just a rookie: he was a foreigner who had arrived at a time when Canadian pride was smarting after the Summit Series and the Flyers were polishing their brass knuckles. He was no fighter, but he was tough and fearless. He lacked the language skills to trade insults with league goons, but was fluent in the universal hockey language of a slash across the ankle or a spear to the gut.

His second NHL game was in Philadelphia. The Flyers welcomed him with the taunt, "You're dead meat, Chicken Swede!" Early in the game he was speared by defenceman Ed Van Impe. Minutes later, Schultz slashed him; when Salming slashed back, Schultz dropped his gloves and they fought to a draw. The rest of the season played out much the same: Salming was challenged in every rink and in every rink he gave back as much as he got.

More than tough and fearless, Salming was skilled. He was a six-time league all-star (on one first team) from 1975 to 1980, and finished his career as the Leafs' all-time leader in assists and third

Borje Salming showed the NHL that Europeans could play solid defence and play a physical game. Here Salming (#21) dives to block a Philadelphia scoring chance with help from Errol Thompson and goalie Wayne Thomas. (DM)

overall in points. It was that combination of mettle and moxie that caused NHL scouts to scurry off to Europe.

Prior to Salming, only one European had been drafted by the NHL. In the six years following Salming's arrival, NHL clubs selected 46 Europeans. In the 1980s the number swelled to 199 and it hit 613 in the 1990s. Included in that group, circa class of '89, was Mats Sundin, the first European to be selected first overall.

Today, the WHA is long gone and the Summit Series and Broad Street Bullies are distant memories. But Salming's contribution to the game lives on.

the '80s

f the '70s were difficult for Maple Leafs fans to take, the '80s were much worse. This was easily the worst decade in team history, largely thanks to general manager George "Punch" Imlach, an irony considering he had given the Leafs so many great moments in the '60s. Imlach might never have had the opportunity to cause such an upheaval if Scotty Bowman or Don Cherry had taken owner Harold Ballard's offer to join the team in 1979, but Bowman refused because he knew Ballard would interfere too much and Cherry was already committed to the Colorado Rockies. With nowhere else to turn, Ballard put his faith in an old friend and Francis "King" Clancy (then Ballard's assistant) talked Imlach into returning to Toronto. As the team nosedived Ballard realized his mistake but made it worse by then hiring other general managers who were overwhelmed by the pressure.

Facing page: *Toronto captain Rick Vaive becomes the first Maple Leaf to score 50 goals in one season when he beats Mike Liut of the St. Louis Blues on March 24, 1982, in a 4–3 Leafs win.* [GA]

Rob Ramage (#8) was named captain of the Leafs before he had played a game for them in 1989. He was a top defenceman on the team and over two seasons finished with 18 goals and 66 assists in 160 games. He also had 375 penalty minutes. [Dennis Miles]

By the end of the decade Ballard was sick and dying and the Leafs' future was the hottest topic of conversation around Toronto. Except for the last season (when even then they were only a .500 team at 38–38–4) the club was awful for most of the '80s, with an occasional playoff upset thrown in to make people think they were going somewhere. Here is why they were so awful for an entire decade.

Management and Coaching

Imlach loyalist Floyd Smith was given the coaching duties when the general manager returned to the Leafs. Smith did not last a season, due to a car accident, and Imlach was forced to name himself coach for a brief period. The 1980–81 season saw Joe Crozier (another man beholden to Imlach) named head coach but he was quickly replaced by Mike Nykoluk, a radio colour man who had hinted he wanted the job from the broadcast booth. A heart attack gave Ballard all the reason he needed to replace Imlach; Gerry McNamara, a longtime scout, was given his job as general manager.

McNamara set about trying to build the Leafs through the draft but forgot that they needed to put a competitive team on the ice. He seemed more interested in pleasing his boss than in making the right moves. Both he and Nykoluk went to war with the local media, an unwise move. Nykoluk was gone by 1985 (with a 89–144–47 record) and his assistant, Dan Maloney, was put in charge. Just as the young coach was improving, Ballard refused to give him a decent contract and forced him to leave for Winnipeg.

The new coach, career minor-leaguer John Brophy, had a hard time relating to the modern player. The Leafs were back in the lower echelons of the NHL, which cost McNamara his job; he complained bitterly that he had not been given the opportunity to select his own coach, but he didn't say so until after he was dismissed. Ballard turned to a young man who had been in the organization for a number of years, but at age 30 Gord Stellick was not ready for the position of general manager. He thought he could get through to Ballard, but some vicious attacks in the newspapers from the boss made him realize things were never going to change and he resigned after one season. The Leafs owner then turned to Smith,

but the former scout was not skilled enough to handle a complex job in a major hockey city. Former Leaf George Armstrong coached the team briefly in 1988–89, then Doug Carpenter was hired by Smith for the 1989–90 season.

Best Trades and Acquisitions

Imlach made one very good deal when he got two young players from Vancouver. Bill Derlago and Rick Vaive were excellent acquisitions even if they cost the Leafs the services of warrior Dave Williams. Imlach also picked up a decent goalie, but Michel "Bunny" Larocque did not last long behind a porous Leafs defence. McNamara made good deals to land Dan Daoust, Tom Fergus, Mark Osborne and Ed Olczyk, and Smith acquired Rob Ramage, a top Leafs defenceman and team captain.

The Leafs were so bad during the '80s that they were often drafting in the top 10. They made the most of their position by selecting Craig Muni, Bob McGill, Stuart Gavin, Al Iafrate, Gary Leeman, Russ Courtnall, Todd Gill, Wendel Clark, Vincent Damphousse, Darryl Shannon, Daniel Marois, Mike Eastwood, Damien Rhodes and Scott Thornton. Defenceman Luke Richardson was also a passable first-round selection, although the club could have selected Joe Sakic instead. The Leafs should have been able to win with this group of players by around 1990, but very bad management and coaching squandered an excellent opportunity.

Notable Events

The best thing to happen to the Leafs in the early part of the decade was winger Rick Vaive's 50 or more goals for three straight seasons. The drafting of Clark was a turning point for the team as it selected first overall for the only time in team history; he turned the city back on to hockey after four or five years of terrible performances. Leeman scored 51 times in 1989–90 but could not do so on a consistent basis.

Leeman was just one of many young players that Leafs fans watched develop very slowly (and sometimes very painfully). Some were very skilled and their consistent underachievement was a mystery. The Leafs did not win a major award, though Clark came second in the Calder Trophy voting in 1986; nor was there a single all-star on the club. The decade was notable for the constant losing and also for the failing health of owner Harold Ballard. As the '80s drew to a close, he was no longer seen in his bunker at one end of Maple Leaf Gardens and his children battled to make certain the ownership of the Leafs was protected from unscrupulous hands. Ballard passed away in April 1990, setting off a battle for ownership of the Leafs and the Gardens.

Worst of the decade

There were so many bad moments in the '80s that a whole chapter could be devoted to the issue. It started with Imlach feuding with captain Darryl Sittler. Ballard took the manager's side, but Sittler was determined to outlast Imlach in Toronto — which he did. The damage the general manager inflicted on the Leafs with his constant trading was severe. Sittler was never the same in Toronto after his battle with Imlach and eventually asked for a trade, which netted the Leafs nothing more than a second-round draft choice used to select Peter Ihnacak.

Dealing away Lanny McDonald was supposed to be Imlach's signature mark on the team but the main player the Leafs received in return, Wilf Paiement, was traded by McNamara for Miroslav Frycer in a terrible deal in 1982. McNamara also gave away Laurie Boschman and John Anderson for very little, while he sent two draft choices to Detroit for Jim Korn. Al Secord was a complete bust in Toronto, but the worst two deals of the decade were made by Stellick (sending Courtnall to Montreal for enforcer John Kordic) and Smith (sending a number 1 draft choice to New Jersey for defenceman Tom Kurvers).

Both Kordic and Kurvers could have been useful additions to the team, but the trades to acquire them were very inequitable. The deal that saw the pick go to New Jersey hung over the Leafs for two full seasons. It nearly turned out to be the first pick overall, which Quebec used in 1991 to select Eric Lindros, so if the Leafs had hung onto it team history might have been very different. The Leafs also drafted their share of duds in the eighties, such as Gary Nylund (who did have one good year as a Leaf), Ken Spengler, Scott Pearson (injuries ruined his career), Steve Bancroft and Rob Pearson.

Bottom-line results

The bottom line from 1980–81 to 1989–90 was a horrible 266–441–96 record. For eight straight seasons the Leafs lost 40 or more games and they suffered a club-record 52 defeats in 1984–85 in an 80-game schedule. They failed to make the playoffs on four occasions and did not win a playoff series until 1986, when they beat Chicago in three straight games. In 1987 they won a seven-game series against St. Louis, but surrendered a 3–1 series lead to Detroit in the next round. They lost another series to the Red Wings in 1988 and another to the Blues in 1990. A decent 1989–90 season fed optimism that the team was finally on the way up, but that quickly dissipated early in the next season. Coach Carpenter, hailed as something of a hero just a year earlier, was replaced by Tom Watt.

Best Leafs of the decade

IN GOAL: Ken Wregget and Allan Bester (there is really no one else to choose).

ON DEFENCE: Al Iafrate and Todd Gill (who was much better in the next decade).

AT FORWARD: Rick Vaive, John Anderson, Gary Leeman, Ed Olczyk, Tom Fergus, Dan Daoust, Vincent Damphousse and Mark Osborne (who also had good years in a checking role in the '90s).

HAROLD BALLARD

FORMER LEAFS OWNER and founder Conn Smythe admitted he had a certain admiration for Harold Ballard's guile. But he did not care for his style at all and went so far as to call Ballard a "buccaneer." If Smythe had known that Ballard was involved in the ownership group put together by his son Stafford (John Bassett was the third partner), he might never have completed the deal to sell the franchise. But he found out too late and Ballard rode on the coattails of his good friend Stafford Smythe to find himself in prime position to take control of the Leafs.

The three new owners agreed to sell to each other first in the event of death or if they ever wanted to get out, which moved Ballard even closer to the ultimate position of authority. It would take some time for him to get there, but the seeds of a takeover were planted back in November 1961 when Conn Smythe decided to sell his stake in the team and the arena.

In the early years Ballard left the running of the team to Stafford and gave his full attention to maximizing revenues at Maple Leaf Gardens. In a few years he had turned the building into "the cashbox on Carlton Street." Ballard had new seats added and started booking all manner of shows into the building.

The '60s and '70s were great times to own and run an arena. With the baby-boomer generation growing up, rock concerts became huge earners and the Gardens was the only venue in Toronto that could handle big crowds year-round. Ballard even managed to sign up the Beatles, booking two shows without telling the group's manager and forcing them to play not once but twice. He even turned off the water fountains so he would sell more drinks at the concession stands, which only offered large-size cups. Ballard once told religious leader Billy Graham that he couldn't believe what a scam he was running — then added that he was happy to host the evangelist's events. He brought in advertising revenue by letting companies put up signs in the previously pristine Gardens. Political rallies, circuses, the Ice Capades, wrestling and hockey meant the arena was never dark, and the debt incurred by the new owners was soon wiped out.

With Ballard little more than a hanger-on, the Leafs won four Stanley Cups in the 1960s while the junior Marlboros took two Memorial Cups. But he and Smythe tried to take further advantage of the team's prosperity by charging personal items to the Gardens and an inside source told Revenue Canada of these irregularities: the tax authorities laid charges. The two Leafs owners were facing jail time for their thievery, but the Gardens' board of directors did not oust them from their positions.

When Bassett could not muster enough support to take over as owner, he sold out to Ballard. Smythe died before coming to trial and Ballard succeeded in buying his shares at market value. Now he was king of the palace. Ballard was convicted in 1972 and went to prison for one year, then returned as if nothing had happened and began a long reign of error that would ruin one of hockey's greatest franchises. The NHL watched but could or would do nothing to stop him.

It has been said that Ballard was never the same after the death from cancer of his wife Dorothy in 1969. She was a refined lady, quite unlike her husband, and had a way of keeping him in line. But with her gone and the Smythe family out of the way (he shunned them all once the will was executed), Ballard could run the team as he saw fit.

Unfortunately, he had no idea how to run a successful hockey club. He inherited general manager Jim Gregory, but could never give a good hockey man the support and funds he needed to run the team properly and the Leafs soon lost a number of players to the rival World Hockey Association for small amounts of money. Ballard then dismissed Gregory and in 1979 brought back his old friend Punch Imlach to run the Leafs, as he had in the 1960s. That disastrous decision set the Leafs back for many years. Both Scotty Bowman (as coach and general manager) and Don Cherry (as coach) turned Ballard down in 1979 before he turned to Imlach.

The Leafs turned into a laughingstock in the '80s as one bad season followed another. Ballard hired poor managers in Gerry McNamara and Floyd Smith, who were both better suited to scout-

Harold Ballard began to turn Maple Leaf Gardens into the "Cashbox on Carlton Street" as soon as the deal to sell the building to him and his partners was completed. (The Globe and Mail)

Harold Ballard (seated on right) and partner Stafford Smythe (also seated) sign to complete their purchase of the Maple Leafs in 1961. Standing in the middle is future Leafs president Don Giffen. (York University Archives — Toronto Telegram collection)

ing, and they in turn appointed mediocre coaches such as Mike Nykoluk (a complete bust) and John Brophy (never more than a competent minor league instructor).

As the team floundered on the ice, Ballard shred the organization of any tradition and history. He even trashed Foster Hewitt's famous Gondola when it was found in the Gardens basement. His abominable treatment of loyal employees like publicity manager Stan Obodiac (whose wife was forced to return the car the Gardens had given him one day after his funeral) and coach Roger Neilson (fired on television) are legendary for their callousness. He dismissed long-term Gardens' employees and ex-Leafs such as Ace Bailey, Bob Davidson and George Armstrong by letter or simply by stopping their pay cheques. He conveniently forgot that it was another former Leaf player and coach, Hap Day, who had helped to keep him around the team when he had been at loose ends. Ballard showed no such compassion, even shunning Day when the Smythe family cut him loose.

The gregarious Ballard thrived on keeping his name in the newspapers and always had time for interviews, especially with his favourite writer, *Toronto Star* columnist Milt Dunnell. He loved to tease the media and was rarely challenged directly, although he had his share of personal feuds. He bought the Hamilton Tiger-Cats of the Canadian Football League, but in general he was tight with money and gave it only to those he liked, such as Leaf defenceman Borje Salming and longtime friend and travelling companion King Clancy. Ballard could be good and bad to the same people and got even more unpredictable as he got older.

His supporters argue that Ballard was a generous man who gave a great deal to various charities, including many of them in his will. To those he treated well — a small but loyal group — he was something of a hero. At the end of his life, his personal relationship with a woman kept everyone interested. As he had predicted, when he died on April 11, 1990, there was a huge fight over the details of his will. Ballard would not have wanted it any other way.

🍁

VINCENT DAMPHOUSSE

THE TORONTO MAPLE LEAFS had their sights set on Vincent Damphousse as their first choice in the 1986 NHL entry draft, but didn't think they had much chance of landing the high-scoring graduate of the Quebec Major Junior Hockey League. Damphousse had been a scoring machine for the Laval Voisins, recording 155 points (45 goals, 110 assists) in 69 games in his final season. He was named to the QMJHL's second all-star team in 1985–86 and was expected to be a high selection.

As anticipated, Joe Murphy was selected first overall by Detroit and the Los Angeles Kings selected centre Jimmy Carson second. New Jersey then pulled a surprise by taking Neil Brady (who turned out to be a complete flop) third. Defencemen Zarley Zalapaski and Shawn Anderson went next, and suddenly the Leafs had their man. They happily took Damphousse sixth overall.

Damphousse and Carson were the only first-round picks to play in the NHL the next season. The Leafs saw no need to send Damphousse back to the Quebec league, so he joined the team for the 1986–87 season and scored 21 goals as a rookie. Knowing he was not a strong skater, they moved the excellent playmaker to the left wing so he would have less ice to cover. He scored his first goal against Minnesota on November 6, 1986, in a 4–1 road loss. He added 25 assists to his impressive rookie numbers and showed remarkable poise. A highly skilled player, Damphousse could leave his mark on any game with his superior passing and ability to see the entire ice surface. He was never a physical presence, but his puck control more than made up for his defensive deficiencies.

His second year with the Leafs was not as smooth as the first (12 goals and 36 assists), but he rebounded the next year with 26 goals and 42 helpers for a team that did not make the playoffs. In 1989–90, the Leafs saw Damphousse team very well with right-winger and fellow Quebecer Daniel Marois. The pair seemed to be able to score at will, combining to bag 64 goals (33 from Damphousse) as the team made it to the .500 level. An early playoff exit was hastened by a lack of defence, but Toronto's future looked brighter than it had in a long time.

The next season quickly fell apart under coach Doug Carpenter. Under his replacement, Tom Watt, Marois soon found himself out of the picture, but Damphousse still managed 73 points (26 goals and 47 assists). The awful season led to further changes in the front office and a new general manager, Cliff Fletcher, who was intent on making more moves.

Fletcher traded Damphousse to Edmonton in a multi-player deal that brought Grant Fuhr and Glenn Anderson to Toronto. After one year as an Oiler Damphousse was sent to the Montreal Canadiens, where he shed his losing playoff image by helping the Habs to a surprise Stanley Cup victory in 1993. Once again, Leaf fans had to watch a young player who had been drafted in Toronto succeed elsewhere. He was dealt to San Jose in 1999 and was still a productive player for the Sharks in the 2001–2 season.

Maple Leaf stats:	GP	G	A	P	PIM
regular season	394	118	211	329	262
playoffs	23	1	8	9	20

Vincent Damphousse (#10) set a team record for left-wingers in 1989–90 with 94 points (33 goals, 61 assists), passing the previous mark set by Frank Mahovlich with 84 in 1960–61. (DM)

TODD GILL

DEFENCEMAN TODD GILL had a very good junior career with the Windsor Spitfires of the OHA and hoped he would be selected in the first round of the 1984 NHL entry draft. He had put up good numbers for a blueliner, including 57 points in 1983–84, and had been named a second-team all-star and co-captain of the Spitfires. Windsor coach Wayne Maxner, a former NHL player, had worked with Gill to make him a better defender and it paid off when he was selected by the Toronto Maple Leafs in the second round, 25th overall. The Leafs had also selected defenceman Al Iafrate out of Belleville, fourth overall, and hoped their never-ending search for young blueliners was finally over.

Gill played one more year in Windsor (1984–85, in which he also participated in 10 games for Toronto) before going to St. Catharines to play for the Leafs' farm club under coach John Brophy. He played most of the 1985–86 season in St. Catherines and had 33 points in 68 games, also scoring one goal and two assists in 15 games with the Leafs. He then played in 67 games for the Leafs in 1986–87, his first of many full seasons with the big club.

Gill suffered many ups and downs during his years with the Maple Leafs and was even moved out of position to the wing when he couldn't get into the lineup on defence. He had a hard time when Doug Carpenter took over as coach and relegated him to the press box for several months in favour of defencemen like Brian Curran (who was then benched after one playoff game). Gill asked for a trade during this dark period, but luckily his request was not met. When Tom Watt was named coach early in the 1990–91 season, Gill was back on the Leafs blue line. He would soon enjoy his best years.

The strength of Gill's game was his puck handling. When things were going well, Gill would handle the disc with great confidence and make an important contribution to the offense. But when things went badly his elaborate stickhandling got him in trouble, as on one night in Chicago when the Leafs lost the final game of the season and a playoff spot after Troy Murray stripped Gill of the puck and scored an overtime winning goal. Such noticeable gaffes got him in trouble with the fans and media and hurt the competitive defenceman's confidence. Still, Gill's other strengths included excellent skating and a willingness to battle all opponents (he was very tough and a very good fighter). When his whole game was working, the fans finally saw why the club had drafted him so high in 1984.

Gill's best years coincided with the arrival of coach Pat Burns. Gill seemed to thrive under the demanding Burns, and playing alongside the highly skilled Dave Ellett helped his game enormously. No longer everyone's favourite whipping boy, he scored 11 goals and produced a career-best 43 points in 1992–93. He scored a memorable goal in a game at the Montreal Forum when Burns returned to face his old club: Gill jumped out of the penalty box and sped by defenceman Patrice Brisebois before putting a shot past Patrick Roy. The Leafs won 5–4 and went on to get within one game of the finals with an exciting playoff run (Gill had 11 points in 21 postseason games).

He played three more seasons for the Leafs before he was dealt away to San Jose. Gill also played for Detroit, St. Louis, Phoenix and Colorado before the Avalanche released him in the 2001–2 season.

Maple Leaf stats:	GP	G	A	P	PIM
regular season	639	59	210	269	922
playoffs	77	5	26	31	171

The biggest goal Todd Gill ever scored as a Maple Leaf was an overtime winner in the 1994 playoffs,
when he beat Chicago's Ed Belfour to give the Leafs a 1–0 victory. (DM)

AL IAFRATE

Whenever a large (6'3", 235 pounds) mobile defenceman who can skate is selected in the first round of the NHL entry draft, huge expectations are placed upon his broad shoulders. Such was the case when the Leafs selected Al Iafrate fourth overall in 1984, making the native of Dearborn, Michigan, the first American-born player the club had ever selected in the first round of the draft. Given his natural skills, Iafrate looked like a sure-fire superstar. He smiled with his mother, Alice, after he was selected and the two posed with Toronto owner Harold Ballard and Iafrate's first Leafs sweater. It looked like a perfect fit, but time would prove otherwise.

Iafrate was raised in an extended Italian family and his parents knew nothing about hockey. Young Al was a good all-round athlete who excelled at soccer, football and track and field before turning to hockey. His mother quickly became a "hockey mom" but his father, Albert, wanted his son to continue with his schooling.

Iafrate progressed through the local hockey system and won a title with a well-known midget hockey team, Detroit Compuware, scoring 30 goals and 75 points in 66 games in 1982–83. He was then selected by the Belleville Bulls of the OHA but decided to play for the United States Olympic team for one season. He didn't see much action during the 1984 Olympic games in Sarajevo (now in Bosnia, then part of Yugoslavia) but joined Belleville for 10 games toward the end of the season, recording six points. He was drafted by the Leafs that summer and was given a job with the struggling team to start the 1984–85 season.

It was clear that Iafrate was not yet ready for the NHL, but the Leafs kept him on the team. He managed five goals and 21 points in 68 games yet his immaturity was evident to everyone except the Leafs, who were very low on talent at the time and in no position to challenge in the NHL. Iafrate reported to his second camp 25 pounds overweight and was turned over to assistant coach John Brophy, the so-called "Grey Ghost," who scared Iafrate so much that he went home (Leaf coach Dan Maloney had to go and retrieve the upset defender). Iafrate scored eight goals (with 25 assists) in his second year as the Leafs crawled into the playoffs, mostly because they were in such a poor division. In his fourth season, Iafrate scored 22 goals, tying a club record for defencemen, and had 52 points in 77 games. It looked like he had turned a corner and finally got his career on track.

As skilled and as strong as Iafrate was, he lacked direction. Blessed with great speed and a terrific shot from the point, he wasn't very useful in his own end. He was very sensitive about what others thought and said about him and this affected his play.

Iafrate somehow managed a great year in 1989–90, producing 21 goals and 63 points before a knee injury derailed him (and the Leafs) in the playoffs. After 42 games of the 1990–91 season, the Leafs had seen enough and traded him to Washington for two good if less talented players, Bob Rouse and Peter Zezel. Another player of great potential had been lost by Toronto.

Iafrate had some success with the Capitals and was named to the NHL's second all-star team in 1993 despite recurring knee problems. He played for Boston and San Jose and finished with 463 points (152 goals, 311 assists) in 799 career games.

Maple Leaf stats:	GP	G	A	P	PIM
regular season	472	81	169	250	546
playoffs	429	4	10	14	21

Al Iafrate was the Leafs representative at the NHL all-star game in 1988 and 1990. In 1990 he won the hardest-shot competition and almost won the fastest-skater award. (DM)

GARY LEEMAN

TORONTO NATIVE Gary Leeman left the city to attend the famed Notre Dame College in Wilcox, Saskatchewan, where he could get twice as much ice time as he could at home. Small in stature at 5'11" and 175 pounds, he was a very talented athlete who caught the attention of junior scouts when he racked up 38 points in 24 games for the Notre Dame Hounds. He was invited to play for the Niagara Falls team in the OHA but instead chose to go to Regina and play for the Pats, who had shown more interest in him. He excelled with the Pats and was named a Western Hockey League all-star. He had 60 points in 72 games in 1981–82 and the Maple Leafs selected him 24th overall in the 1982 entry draft. They made a big deal about their first-round selection that year — defenceman Gary Nylund, chosen third overall — but there was no fanfare for Leeman.

Leeman played one more year for the Pats in 1982–83 and scored 24 goals and added 62 assists. He was named the WHL's top defenceman and the Leafs were so impressed that they called him up for a couple of playoff games in 1983. For the next two years he bounced around from the minors to the Leafs, but still managed nine goals and 33 points for Toronto. Leeman started the 1985–86 season with St. Catharines and scored 15 goals and 29 points in just 25 games. His fine play earned him a promotion to the Leafs and he got into 53 games, scoring nine goals and recording 32 points. By that point Leeman had been switched to the right wing position and put on a line with fellow Notre Dame Hounds graduates Russ Courtnall and Wendel Clark. The "Hound Line" was especially effective in the playoffs as the Leafs knocked of Chicago in three

straight games and took St. Louis to a seventh game before losing.

In the next season Leeman finally became a regular member of the Leafs. He scored 21 goals and proved that was no fluke by following it up with seasons of 30 and 32 goals. The feisty right-winger could switch back to defence in a pinch and showed finesse to go with his scoring touch. He had a good shot which he released very quickly and was willing to take a lot of punishment in front of the net to get a goal. His speed allowed him to get into open holes with some momentum and his determination did the rest. He was a surprisingly good fighter for a player of his size: he held his own against the much larger Trevor Linden of Vancouver and battled Dave Manson of Chicago during a wild brawl at the Gardens in 1989. Leeman put together a great year in 1989–90 when he scored 51 goals and had 44 assists. There were few better wingers in the NHL that year.

His star rapidly descended in the next season when he injured a shoulder badly just as turmoil was striking Toronto. He scored only 17 times in 52 games and was accused, perhaps unfairly, of not being a team player; he and good friend Ed Olczyk were somewhat isolated from the rest of the Leafs and this seemed to cause resentment. As the club struggled and changed coaches once again, Leeman found himself out the door in the deal that brought Doug Gilmour to the Leafs. Gilmour's fortunes soared in Toronto while Leeman's plummeted in Calgary. During the 1992–93 season he was dealt to the Montreal Canadiens and contributed to their Stanley Cup win in '93, but his career never reached the heights it had with the Leafs.

Maple Leaf stats:	GP	G	A	P	PIM
regular season	545	176	231	407	463
playoffs	24	7	14	21	36

Gary Leeman scoring against the Washington Capitals. Leeman got his 50th goal of the year during the 1989–90 season on March 28, 1990 against the New York Islanders, when he took a pass from Mark Osborne in the slot and rifled a shot home over Mark Fitzpatrick. (DM)

ED OLCZYK

THE TORONTO MAPLE LEAFS had been chasing Ed Olczyk for quite a while when they finally landed the Chicago native in a major deal with the Blackhawks in September 1987. The trade cost Toronto the services of Rick Vaive, Steve Thomas and Bob McGill, so it was clear the Leafs placed a high value on landing the 6'1", 207-pound centre (they also received a worn-out Al Secord).

Olczyk was no stranger to Ontario since he had played junior "B" hockey in Stratford. He had come there as a 16-year-old to play against better opposition and thrived, leading the junior loop in goals (50), assists (92) and points (142) in just 42 games. He went on to play for the United States national team as that squad prepared for the 1984 Olympics. He was selected third overall by the Black Hawks in 1984 and put in three good years in Chicago before they decided to trade him.

Olczyk was cut up about leaving Chicago, as he had always dreamed of starring in his hometown, but being wanted in Toronto eased the transition and he knew the Leafs were a special team. In his first year he scored 42 goals and 75 points for a bad team that made the playoffs despite winning only 21 games. His most important goals came in the 1988 playoffs, when the Leafs won 6–5 in Detroit to extend the series to six games. The Leafs had been humiliated 8–0 at home and the fans had showed their displeasure by showering the ice with debris, including team sweaters. Olczyk scored three goals in the next game, including the overtime winner,

and helped salvage some sort of respect for a troubled organization.

Toronto was out of the playoffs the following season when Olczyk recorded a career-high 90 points, but the Leafs were a much better team in 1989–90 and finished with a 38–38–4 record. Olczyk played with wingers Gary Leeman and Mark Osborne and had 88 points (32 goals, 56 assists), producing a point in 18 consecutive games to tie a team record set by Leaf legend Darryl Sittler; Olczyk was thrilled to get a phone call from the former Leafs captain after the 18th game.

But just when the Leafs thought they had righted a sinking ship, leaks started to show again. Major changes followed, including a number of trades. Olczyk was dealt to the Winnipeg Jets for defenceman Dave Ellett as the Leafs tried to get some help on the blue line. It was a good deal for Toronto, but they had no centre to take Olczyk's place.

Olczyk had a couple of good years with the Jets but was never as good as he had been in Toronto. He was dealt to the New York Rangers and shared in their 1994 Stanley Cup championship — his name was put on the trophy, though he had not played in the finals or 40 regular-season games, after the Rangers lobbied on his behalf. By this point in his career Olczyk was a much better team player, which is why the Rangers insisted his name go on the Cup.

He went on to play for Los Angeles and Pittsburgh and returned to Winnipeg and Chicago before retiring. He finished his career with 342 goals and 794 points in 1,031 career games.

Maple Leaf stats:	GP	G	A	P	PIM
regular season	257	116	151	267	221
playoffs	11	6	6	12	16

Ed Olczyk tries to score against the Quebec Nordiques. Olczyk was not a speedy skater, but was a very skilled passer with a decent touch around the net. (DM)

MARK OSBORNE

LEFT-WINGER MARK OSBORNE was one of those players who seem to thrive playing in their hometown. Born in Toronto on August 13, 1961, he joined the Leafs in a trade with the New York Rangers near the end of the 1986–87 season and showed he could take the pressure by recording 15 points in 16 games.

It was actually the young player's second move in his short NHL career. An original draft choice of the Detroit Red Wings in 1980 (46th overall), he scored 26 goals and 67 points as a rookie but was sent to the Rangers two years later. He scored 23 times for the Blueshirts in 1983–84 but struggled the following year, and Ranger general manager Phil Esposito felt it was in Osborne's best interests to go home. He proved to be right.

Before leaving to play junior hockey in Niagara Falls, Osborne scored 20 goals and 48 points in 58 games with the Toronto Young Nationals in 1977–78. He was a solid if unspectacular junior, but had a great final year in 1980–81 when he scored 39 goals and 80 points in just 54 games. He only played briefly in the minors for the Detroit organization before making it to the big team.

He was a swift skater in his early years in the NHL and was always a superbly conditioned athlete. He took pride in being in top shape and worked just as hard off the ice as on. Osborne was not an overtly physical player, but was willing to use his size (6'2", 205 pounds) when he had to win a battle along the boards and recorded over 100 penalty minutes three times as a Leaf. He also had good hands in the first half of his career and scored a fair few goals.

His best year with the Leafs was 1989–90, when he scored 23 goals and a career-high 73 points playing on a line with Ed Olczyk and Gary Leeman. The trio was the top Toronto line that year and it looked like they might stay together for a while, but the Leafs started very badly the next year and Osborne found himself on the move. He was sent to Winnipeg with Olczyk for Dave Ellett and Paul Fenton and while the Leafs got a quality defenceman in Ellett, they missed Osborne's enthusiasm. Fenton could not replace him and left the team after just 30 games. It took some time but wrong was righted when the Leafs re-acquired Osborne from the Jets in 1992 in exchange for Lucien DeBlois.

The 1992–93 season was a special one for the Leafs as they regained respectability under general manager Cliff Fletcher and coach Pat Burns. Although he had 12 goals and 26 points that year, Osborne's offensive game was on the decline and he was given a checking job on a line with Peter Zezel and Bill Berg that played a key role in getting the team to the final four and almost to the Stanley Cup finals.

In the 1994 playoffs Osborne scored a couple of short-handed goals in the Leafs seven-game series victory over San Jose. After a second consecutive appearance in the final four the team was changed again and Osborne went back to the Rangers as a free agent. He played a couple of years in the minors for Cleveland before retiring and trying his hand at coaching junior hockey.

Maple Leaf stats:	GP	G	A	P	PIM
regular season	426	94	160	254	563
playoffs	57	9	12	21	102

Mark Osborne was a good checker and penalty killer in two different stints with the Maple Leafs. (DM)

RICK VAIVE

RICK VAIVE had just completed his first season of professional hockey with the Birmingham Bulls of the World Hockey Association when the WHA and the National Hockey League decided to merge. As an 18-year-old he was then made eligible for the NHL draft that summer. Vaive was expected to go high since he had just scored 26 goals and 59 points for the "Baby Bulls" (so called because they had so many young players on the team) and his size (6'1", 198 pounds) made scouts drool.

Vaive used a big stick, the heavy lumber helping him to unleash a fast, powerful shot. Born in Ottawa, he developed his shooting by driving a puck against a barn door in Prince Edward Island, where he was raised. He had been a good scorer at the junior level with Sherbrooke of the Quebec junior league (127 goals in two seasons of play) and had proved a very competent pro with the Bulls despite his youth.

As the '79 draft opened, Vaive's Birmingham teammate Rob Ramage was elected first overall by Colorado, Perry Turnbull went to St. Louis next and Mike Foligno went third to Detroit. Another Bull, Mike Gartner, was selected fourth by Washington before Vancouver chose Vaive fifth overall. This was the best first round of the entry draft since its inception in 1969, as Vaive and his fellow draftees would prove. Other notable selections included Ray Bourque (Boston), Michel Goulet (Quebec), Kevin Lowe (Edmonton) and Brian Propp (Philadelphia). The Leafs selected Laurie Boschman ninth overall.

Vaive was with the Vancouver Canucks for less than a year when he suddenly found himself on the move. The Maple Leafs and the Canucks pulled off a four-player deal that saw him and Vancouver's 1978 first-round draft choice, Bill Derlago, go to Toronto for Dave Williams and Jerry Butler. The Leafs were looking for youth and the Canucks for veteran leadership, and both got what they wanted. Williams and Butler helped the Canucks reach the 1982 Stanley Cup finals while Vaive and Derlago started racking up points for Toronto.

Vaive scored in his first game as a Leaf, a 6–4 win over the New York Islanders on February 19, 1980, and didn't stop until the day he was traded. He joined the team at a time of great turmoil and always seemed to be involved in some sort of controversy, but there is no doubt that Vaive and his goal-scoring abilities were all the Leafs had going for them between 1980 and 1985. Good-looking and charismatic, his personality made him a star in Toronto.

Playing on a line with Derlago and John Anderson in his early seasons, Vaive became the first Maple Leaf to record 50 goals in a season. In fact, he scored 50 or more for three years in a row, an amazing accomplishment considering the mediocre teammates supporting him. He could take the puck as he was breaking down the wing and hammer a shot on goal, much as Lanny McDonald had done earlier. From the top of the faceoff circle Vaive would terrorize netminders and pot a lot of goals. Only Mike Bossy and Wayne Gretzky scored more goals than Vaive during his 50-goal seasons.

Vaive was not afraid to go into the corners and battle for the puck and willingly took a lot of punishment in front of the net to score goals, especially on the power play. He was often tackled, tripped, held and cross-checked from behind but was very adept at drawing penalties. He also had a bit of a temper and would drop the gloves when provoked, which often landed him in the sin bin unnecessarily, but this was all a part of the passionate play that made him a feared and respected opponent. He was one of the few Leafs to play with emotion during some terrible seasons.

Vaive's problems as a Maple Leaf started when he was named captain of the team at the tender age of 22. When previous captain Darryl Sittler was traded away and veteran Borje Salming refused the "C," there was no obvious candidate for the captaincy other than Vaive, the best player on the team. But he did not really understand the role that well and had no opportunity to mature into the leadership as Sittler had years earlier. Vaive also found himself without a support system to share the burden of leading the team.

Eventually, his shortcomings got him into trouble and he fell into disfavour with various Leaf coaches. Dan Maloney benched him for an entire game against Philadelphia on March 16, 1985,

Rick Vaive tries to find the puck against the Los Angeles Kings. Vaive's best year
as a Maple Leaf came in 1983–84, when he scored 52 times and added 41 assists. (DM)

Rick Vaive fights for position with Paul Coffey of the Edmonton Oilers. Vaive won the Molson Cup three times in his career as a Leaf, in 1983, 1984 and 1987. (DM)

Right: Rick Vaive (#22) pumps his arms after scoring another goal for the Leafs. His 299 regular-season goals rank him fourth on the Leafs' all-time list. (DM)

give him a second chance as captain and it would be three seasons before another was named.

On the ice, Vaive's last three years as a Maple Leaf were still fairly productive. He did not score 50 again but did total 35, 33 and 32 goals and the Leafs made some playoff appearances. Regrettably, Vaive could not play in two game sevens, in the 1986 and 1987 playoffs. He had played well in both postseasons but a bad back cost him one game versus St. Louis (he did not even dress) and a hand injury limited his ice time against Detroit in 1987. The Leafs had gone up 3–1 in the series but the Red Wings won the next three, including an easy 3–0 victory in game seven.

By this point Leafs management was looking to move Vaive. After agreeing to pay him $300,000 a year in a new deal, they sent him off to Chicago with Steve Thomas and got Al Secord from the Blackhawks. If Secord was expected to replace Vaive, he failed — Vaive scored 43 goals for Chicago in 1987–88 while all Secord could muster was 15 for the Leafs. Secord left Toronto soon after and Vaive went on to play five more seasons, including almost four years as a Buffalo Sabre. He finished his career with 441 goals and 788 points in 876 games. After a brief spell in the American Hockey League he retired and turned to coaching, with some success.

Vaive returned to the Toronto area and is often seen on television as a commentator and analyst. At age 42 he is in such good physical condition that he was still playing competitive hockey in the 2001–2 season with a senior team in Dundas, Ontario. He hoped the squad would compete for and win the Allan Cup so that he could share in a championship like so many other great Maple Leafs have done over the years.

making him sit on the bench in full uniform as the Leafs lost 6–1 on home ice. Vaive got into shouting matches with John Brophy, a great admirer of his style of play, but was very productive under coach Mike Nykoluk from 1980 to 1984 because he concentrated on his own game during those years.

The Leafs captain wasn't always as disciplined as he should have been and enjoyed the nightlife. When he overslept and missed a practice one morning in Minnesota the Leafs overreacted and took away the captaincy. Vaive's pride was deeply hurt. This happened during the 1985–86 season when a Leafs rookie named Wendel Clark was suddenly the most popular player on the ice and Vaive had to share the spotlight for the first time. The Leafs didn't

Maple Leaf stats:	GP	G	A	P	PIM
regular season	534	299	238	537	940
playoffs	32	14	9	23	53

A LEAF FOR LIFE

by Gare Joyce

WENDEL CLARK's first season with the Maple Leafs happened to be King Clancy's last.

Like everybody else in Toronto, I knew all about Clark's arrival on the scene when I sat down for lunch with the 19-year-old in the Hot Stove Lounge at Maple Leaf Gardens on a spring afternoon in 1986. Leaf fans everywhere could have told you the story — the farm boy from Melville, Saskatchewan, whose father Les thought his son was a better defenceman than a winger, the kid with the moustache and the cannon-like wrist shot, a first trip through the league marked with spectacular goals and epic brawls. And like everybody else in Toronto, I presumed that King Clancy was always going to be kicking around the Gardens. After all, the 84-year-old was a couple of years into a 10-year contract and he was ever on Leafs owner Harold Ballard's good side, a lightly-populated hemisphere. With Clark sitting beside him in the Hot Stove Lounge, Clancy put his arm around the rookie's shoulder and said that he was "looking forward to seeing this young man for years to come."

As it turned out, Clancy would never get to see Clark play again. King died before the next season began.

There are a few things I treasure from my time in sport, but as a lifelong Torontonian who saw dozens of Leafs games at the Gardens as a fan and hundreds more from the press box, I put this lunch at the very top of the list.

Never had the hockey life stood in starker contrast. It wasn't just that one player was seeing everything for the first time, the other for the last time. One was squinting uncomfortably in the spotlight as it shone on him for the first time and the other was enjoying his last turn in it. Since coming over from the original Ottawa Senators and with time off for trips to the racetrack, Clancy had reported to work at the Gardens, first as a player, later as a coach and finally as a house icon and Ballard sidekick, for going on six decades, something beyond the ken of any 19-year-old, even one whose heroics played out every night on the ice, on television and in the next morning's headlines.

Clancy was a Leaf For Life. He wasn't the only one. George Armstrong, captain of the team when it last won the Stanley Cup and the man who scored the Cup-clinching goal in that 1967 game, was still working for the Leafs back then and still is today. There have been a few less-famous others who considered it high praise to be described as fixtures at the Gardens: ushers who worked the same aisles for 30 or even 40 years, staffers at the turnstiles and ticket windows and even the waiters who brought Clark his club sandwich and Clancy his soup.

Clancy was in good spirits but not great health and our lunch had been cancelled several times because he wasn't feeling up to it. It came together on the last possible day that spring — that night, Clark was driving back home with his cousin, Kelly Chase, to work on his father's farm.

It's not surprising that Clancy had a lot more to say than Clark that day. King had a gift for the blarney and a file full of stories, while Clark was shy and painfully soft-spoken.

When Clark mentioned that he had spent the season billeted with the parents of Philadelphia forward Peter Zezel, Clancy took over. "I remember my first year with the Leafs, we used to stay at the Royal York Hotel and it cost us 99 cents a night," he said. "We had the time of our lives, always did things together, card games, going out, things like that. I really don't know if the players have fun like we did in those days."

Nothing Clark said dispelled that notion. He said that all the attention was "taking a bit to get used to." Being a star in Toronto was, he admitted, "a bit different than it was in Saskatoon."

One of the beauties of the "original six" teams is their connection to the past. In Boston, Milt Schmidt and Johnny Bucyk are around the arenas on game days. In Montreal, you're sure to find Jean Beliveau and other Hall of Famers on hand. Some lend a hand in the operation of the hockey club and others are called goodwill ambassadors or designated for "community service." And among that number today is someone whom that 19-year-old at lunch could never have imagined filling that role, namely Wendel Clark himself.

Clark didn't have a career quite like Clancy's. He bounced around a bit, doing stints with the Nordiques, the Islanders, Tampa

King Clancy (left) and Punch Imlach climb into a car that will take them on the parade route to celebrate the Leafs 1967 Stanley Cup victory. (York University Archives)

Bay, Detroit and Chicago. But those are just footnotes to his career. He had three stints as a Leaf and finished his career playing for the club in its 2000 playoff run. That spring, with his best days and a lot of hard miles behind him, Clark still had enough to be called out as one of the three stars and the crowd at the Air Canada Centre roared, sensing this was both hail and farewell.

When he announced his retirement, I asked Clark about that lunch with King Clancy all those years ago. He seemed to have only a vague recollection, remembering a photo of them together more than any of the conversation. "I can understand why someone like King would want to stay around the game and at the arena," he said. "It keeps you young and there are a lot of good memories."

I'm sure there are a lot of good memories, but when you think of how long ago it was that Clark was knocking down Bob Probert, letting that wrist shot fly and listening to King Clancy spin a yarn, it makes you feel a little old, too.

🍁

The '90s produced some of the most exciting times in Toronto since the glory days of the '60s, alongside some of the worst hockey Leafs fans have ever seen. For a while the team was superbly managed by Cliff Fletcher, lured to Toronto from Calgary, but he lost his edge and resigned to get away from the pressure cooker. The Leafs then turned to hockey legend Ken Dryden, hoping the former goaltender who had won six Stanley Cups with the Montreal Canadiens would lead them back to respectability. Dryden started out slowly and methodically, but by 2002, he had put the pieces in place to make the Leafs a competitive club year after year. He took on the general manager's title initially, but hired good hockey people to assist him. The Leafs' management structure had evolved over the last few years but the team has remained quite successful on and off the ice. There were significant changes since Harold Ballard's death, but the Leafs continued to thrive in the big-money era. Here is a look at how they did it.

Doug Gilmour (#93) scores an overtime winner against Curtis Joseph of St. Louis during the first game of the 1993 playoff series between the Leafs and Blues. The Leafs won the game 2–1 after 23:16 of extra time. (GA)

Goalie Grant Fuhr (#31) became a Maple Leaf after a trade with Edmonton in 1991. He posted a 38–49–9 record with Toronto, with three shutouts. He won 25 games in 1991–92 and was 13–9–4 when he was sent to Buffalo in a deal that saw Dave Andreychuk move to the Leafs. (DM)

Management and Coaching

Steve Stavro was well-positioned to take over the Leafs after Ballard's death — he had first right to buy the team, after lending Ballard money — but it was not an easy process. He was forced to pay a much higher price for the Ballard estate and the outstanding shares in Maple Leaf Gardens Limited than he had intended. Ballard's will called for the value of his estate to be given to charities and Stavro was in a strange position, considering he was both the executor of the will and the purchaser of the estate, which was not in good financial condition. Shareholders demanded to be heard and the Public Trustee of Ontario listened, ruling that Stavro was not paying proper market value for the team and building.

Stavro eventually took in partners and turned the company into a private enterprise. As ownership was being settled in the boardrooms, Cliff Fletcher was running the Leafs. He replaced coach Tom Watt (52–80–17) with Pat Burns in 1992. Burns was one of the most successful coaches in Leafs history but even he could not last more than three and a half seasons. Former assistant coach Mike Murphy (60–87–17) became head man, but the team did not respond. Fletcher was gone after the Leafs missed the playoffs in 1996–97 and Murphy was let go one year later. Dryden replaced Fletcher and hired former Winnipeg Jets general manager Mike Smith to handle the team on a day-by-day basis; Smith hired former Leafs defenceman Pat Quinn as head coach and the team was back in the playoffs by 1999.

Best Trades and Acquisitions

Most of the major trading in the decade was handled by Fletcher and for a period of time he could do no wrong. Doug Gilmour, Jamie Macoun, Glenn Anderson and Grant Fuhr were all winning Fletcher acquisitions. He also picked up welcomed additions in Sylvain Lefebvre and Bill Berg without giving up anything from his roster. He got a great scorer in Dave Andreychuk, a smart enforcer in Ken Baumgartner and a good checker in Mark Osborne. These trades in the early days of Fletcher's reign got the Leafs all the way to the confer-ence final in two straight years, but they fell short of the Stanley Cup. He then went wild and started making a trade almost every day. The team began to flounder, though Fletcher did secure Mats Sundin, Dmitry Yushkevich, Kirk Muller, Jason Smith, Steve Sullivan and Alyn McCauley (all still active in the NHL in 2001–2).

When Smith took over the team he acquired a solid veteran in defenceman Sylvain Cote and traded the ineffective and enigmatic Mattieu Schneider to the New York Rangers for Alexander Karpovtsev. The Leafs performance at the draft table was uneven but did produce some gems. Felix Potvin, Yanic Perreault, Nik Borschevsky, Fredrik Modin, Sergei Berezin, Danny Markov and Tomas Kaberle all contributed to the Leafs in the '90s. Grant Marshall was also a good first-round choice, but he was traded before putting on a Leafs uniform.

Notable Events

The 1993 postseason was a fantastic time to be a Leafs fan again. The team pulled off an upset against the Detroit Red Wings in the first round before knocking off St. Louis in the next series. A loss to the Los Angeles Kings spoiled the party, but the city was Leafs crazy for two months after 21 games in 42 days.

The closing of Maple Leaf Gardens on February 13, 1999, was also a very significant event. The Leafs lost 6–2 to Chicago that night, but fans saw many of the Leafs alumni together for the first time. One week later, the team played the first NHL game at the newly built Air Canada Centre and beat Montreal 3–2 in overtime. The beautiful arena became the Leafs' new home when Stavro and his partners purchased the National Basketball Association team the Toronto Raptors, fusing them with the Leafs organization to form a new company called Maple Leaf Sports and Entertainment.

Many faces were added and subtracted from the Maple Leafs organization during the decade. A notable loss was Mike Smith, who could not see eye to eye with Dryden. Quinn soon accepted the coach and general manager positions, making him the only man in the NHL to hold both jobs at once. He was aided primarily by former player agent Bill Watters, with the Leafs since 1991.

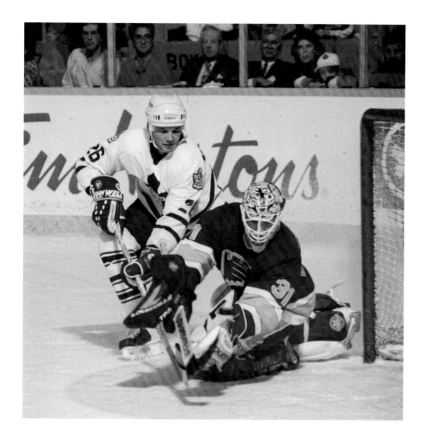

Mike Krushelnyski tries to put one past Curtis Joseph in the St. Louis net. Krushelnyski played in 269 games as a Leaf and scored 50 goals and 113 points. He had his best year with Toronto in 1992–93, with 19 goals and 39 points. The Leafs sent John McIntyre to Los Angeles to acquire the big centre in 1990. (DM)

Free Agents

The '90s saw the NHL become a league dominated by unrestricted free agency, which was available only to players 31 or older. The Leafs dabbled in this market, coming up with Glenn Healy, Derek King, Kris King and Kevyn Adams in their first foray. They had a little more success with the signings of Igor Korolev, Garry Valk, Jonas Hoglund, Steve Thomas and Curtis Joseph as the decade came to a close, but foolishly passed on a great opportunity to add Wayne Gretzky via free agency in 1996. Gretzky would have been a great addition to the team and the perfect second centre behind Mats Sundin.

Worst of the Decade

Fletcher made many great moves as Leafs general manager but also had more than his share of poor deals. The Leafs lost a quality forward in Vincent Damphousse (sacrificed to Edmonton) and John Cullen was never the centre the Leafs hoped for when they acquired him from Hartford. Fletcher tried to replace defenceman Sylvain Lefebvre (traded) and Bob Rouse (lost as a free agent) with Larry Murphy but that failed badly. He traded away Wendel Clark and then did all he could to get him back at great cost (the deal included a number 1 draft choice and defenceman Kenny Jonsson).

Sergio Momesso and Mike Craig (signed as a restricted free agent) were awful players for the Leafs, as was Jamie Baker (the Leafs gave up

Todd Gill to San Jose to get him). Smith traded away Jason Smith (a quality defenceman) for nothing but a draft choice, while Quinn lost Sullivan on waivers. Quinn closed the decade by trading for Dmitri Khristich, a talented but overpaid player who was a failure in Toronto.

Poor draft choices included Drake Berehowsky, Brandon Convery, Landon Wilson, Eric Fichaud, Jeff Ware and Marek Posmyk (only Posmyk was selected lower than 19th overall). A horrible eye injury to Bryan Berard, who had been acquired in a deal for Felix Potvin, was another low point for the club but the Leafs did all they could to help him return to the NHL; Berard, who had never lived up to his potential, repaid the team and the fans who had wished him well by signing as a free agent with the New York Rangers. Still, fans were happy to see him playing again in 2001–2.

Bottom-line Results

The Leafs' overall record from 1990–91 to 1999–2000 is a little above the .500 mark at 349–340–94. The team won over 40 games on four occasions (44 in 1992–93, 43 in 1993–94, 45 in 1998–99 and 1999–2000). The Leafs made it to the final four on three occasions (1993, 1994 and 1999) and the Stanley Cup was tantalizingly close at least once (1993). They won seven playoff series, all seven-game matchups, while losing six. On the down side they failed to make the playoffs four times (1990–91, 1991–92, 1996–97 and 1997–98) and were a terrible club to watch when Mike Murphy was coach. If the decade proved anything, it was that excellent coaches like Burns and Quinn and general managers like Fletcher are essential ingredients to a successful team.

Best Leafs of the Decade

IN GOAL: Felix Potvin.

ON DEFENCE: Dave Ellett and Jamie Macoun (with honourable mention to Bob Rouse and Sylvain Lefebvre).

AT FORWARD: Doug Gilmour, Wendel Clark, Glenn Anderson, Peter Zezel, Steve Thomas and Sergei Berezin. (Other Leafs worthy of mention in the '90s include Sundin, Joseph and Yushkevich.)

GLENN ANDERSON

WHEN CLIFF FLETCHER took over as general manager of the Toronto Maple Leafs he quickly moved to change the face of a losing team by going after some established veterans with winning records. Fletcher found a willing trading partner in Edmonton Oilers general manager Glen Sather, who was looking to move players who were pricing themselves out of "small market" cities. It took a while for the two managers to put a deal together, but at the end of the process the Leafs had a quality goaltender in Grant Fuhr and one of the best left-wingers in hockey in the person of Glenn Anderson (they also acquired tough guy Craig Berube). The move cost the team the services of Vincent Damphousse, Luke Richardson, Scott Thornton and young goaltender Peter Ing, but Fletcher had put his stamp on the Leafs and it would pay off handsomely, at least for a while.

Anderson's game can be best summarized with two words: speed and scoring. He could fly down the wing and take the puck to the net in an absolutely fearless manner. Many players could skate as well, but few had the courage to go to the net on such a steady basis. Once Anderson got there, he had a nice touch and hard shot that scored many goals. With the Oilers between 1980 and 1991, the Vancouver native had seasons of 30, 38, 48, 54, 42, 54, 35, 38 and 34 goals and helped Edmonton to five Stanley Cup titles. He was even better in the playoffs.

At 6'1" and 190 pounds Anderson was not the biggest player in the NHL, but he played bigger by wanting the puck and being willing to dig it out. Like all good goal scorers, Anderson was adept at taking punishment in front of the net, using his stick to get some room and keep the opposition leery of the lumber. He managed to avoid serious injury through most of his career.

After his arrival in Toronto at the start of the 1991–92 season, Anderson had a hard time getting going. The team was dreadful, but began to improve after a flurry of trades and Anderson started to play more like his old self, finishing the year with 24 goals and 57 points in 72 games. He scored only 22 times the following season but managed 65 points in 76 contests, including his 1,000th career point in an 8–1 Leafs win over Vancouver on February 22, 1993.

In the Leafs' surprising '93 playoff run, Anderson again showed he was a clutch player, with 18 points in 21 games. He scored a key goal against Detroit in the seventh game of the series and an overtime winner versus Los Angeles in the fifth game of the Campbell Conference final. Anderson was called for boarding late in the sixth game against the Kings and Wayne Gretzky scored the overtime winner, costing the Leafs a chance to make it to the finals; it was a borderline call not usually made with so much at stake — the game was tied at 4–4 and about to go into overtime. Anderson scored in the next game but the Leafs lost the series with a 5–4 defeat.

Toronto was still a pretty good club in the next season and began with a 10-game winning streak, an NHL record. But by the end of the 1993–94 campaign the team was playing only at a .500 level and Fletcher was desperate to make changes. He started with a curious deal in which Anderson, soon to be an unrestricted free agent, went to the New York Rangers for Mike Gartner. Leafs coach Pat Burns called the trade "four quarters for a dollar," but Anderson won another Stanley Cup with the Rangers while Gartner did not help the Leafs advance any farther than they had in 1993.

He finished his career with 498 goals and 1,099 points in 1,129 games.

Glenn Anderson tries to score on the Los Angeles Kings during the 1993 playoffs. Anderson played on the 1980 Canadian Olympic team after a college career at the University of Denver and proved to be a prolific goal scorer at every level. (HHOF)

Maple Leaf stats:	GP	G	A	P	PIM
regular season	221	63	94	157	267
playoffs	21	7	11	18	31

DAVE ANDREYCHUK

THE MAPLE LEAFS were putting together an unexpectedly good year in 1992–93, but it was still obvious that they lacked a proven goal scorer to play alongside centre Doug Gilmour. Though Gilmour was playing with just about everybody on the team, general manager Cliff Fletcher knew he needed a finisher on the wing to make the Leafs a serious contender. The rise of Felix Potvin in the Leafs goal meant Fletcher was free to trade netminder Grant Fuhr for a quality winger.

As it happened, left-winger Dave Andreychuk was languishing on the Buffalo Sabres bench despite a 29-goal season. The big forward (6'4", 220 pounds) had fallen into disfavour with Sabres coach John Muckler, who did not like his slow skating style. The Leafs saw his potential and Fletcher arranged a deal in which they received Andreychuk, goalie Darren Puppa and a first-round draft pick (used to select defenceman Kenny Jonsson) for Fuhr. Gilmour finally had a winger on the first line and the Leafs were on their way to becoming a strong playoff contender.

Andreychuk was very good at using his size and strength. He was selected by the Sabres under the direction of Scotty Bowman in the first round in 1982 and quickly proved he could score in the big league. He was usually around the 30-goal mark and had his best year with the Sabres in 1991–92, when he scored 41 times; he had 40 in 1989–90. Andreychuk was excellent on the power play and difficult to move from in front of the net with his imposing body. He had a quick release and worked hard at scooping up rebounds around the net. His long reach helped him to pick off stray passes and he often stole the puck on the forecheck. Andreychuk was not a gifted skater or playmaker, but his goal-scoring skills rank him among the best forwards in NHL history.

Coming to the Leafs seemed to re-energize Andreychuk and he finished the 1992–93 season with 25 goals, bringing his combined total to 54. His tally of 32 power-play goals was the highest in the NHL and he worked so well with Gilmour that it looked as if they had played together for years. Coach Pat Burns played him in all sit-

uations, even in penalty-killing, and he responded well to the increased ice time. In the '93 playoffs Andreychuk helped to shed a bad image by scoring 12 goals (a new mark for Leafs right-wingers in the postseason) and 19 points in 21 games. Though he worked hard, he could not a score a goal in the series against the Los Angeles Kings and the Leafs failed to advance to the finals for the first time since 1967.

In 1993–94 Andreychuk kept up his stellar performance, scoring 53 goals — only the third Leaf to break the 50-goal barrier — and 99 points. His name was often mentioned as an MVP candidate early in the year, but as the Leafs faded late in the season that talk also faded, although linemate Gilmour finished second to Detroit's Sergei Fedorov in the Hart Trophy race. Andreychuk was now a force at both ends of the ice and one of the Leafs' steadiest players. Toronto made the final four again in the '94 playoffs, but his postseason numbers were down to five goals and 10 points in 21 games. The loss to Vancouver in the Western Conference final precipitated changes but Andreychuk was still considered untouchable.

The lockout-shortened 1994–95 season left Andreychuk with 22 goals and 38 points in the 48-game schedule. The Leafs blew a 2–0 series lead to Chicago in the playoffs and lost in seven games. By 1995–96 they were not the happy crew they had been, and the newspapers were full of stories about Andreychuk not getting along with his teammates, Gilmour in particular. Apparently some players thought Andreychuk was interested only in getting goals. After 61 games in which he could muster only 20 goals the high-scoring winger, now armed with a big contract was moved to the New Jersey Devils. The Leafs were trying to balance their budget after some acquisitions and Andreychuk was told the news moments after a 3–3 tie with Winnipeg on March 13, 1996, in which he had scored a goal. He went back into the Leafs' dressing room and announced, "Hey, guys! I've been traded to the Devils!"

Since then Andreychuk has bounced around the NHL and played for a variety of teams including Boston, Colorado and

Buffalo (for a second time); he ended the 2001–2 season with the Tampa Bay Lightning. In New Jersey, Andreychuk found himself alongside Gilmour again and, while they did not rediscover the magic they once had in Toronto, both put up good numbers playing in the Meadowlands Arena. According to some media reports, Gilmour tried to talk Andreychuk into joining him on the Montreal Canadiens during the 2001–2 season, so perhaps there was never a rift between the two. Going into the 2002–3 season, Andreychuk had tallied 593 goals and 1,247 points in 1,443 games.

Dave Andreychuk bags another goal. Andreychuk scored his 50th of the season for the second time in his career on March 24, 1994, in a 2–1 Leafs loss to San Jose, beating Arturs Irbe for the milestone goal. [DM]

Maple Leaf stats:	GP	G	A	P	PIM
regular season	223	120	99	219	194
playoffs	46	20	14	34	76

Wendel Clark (#17) leaps into the air to score against the Chicago Blackhawks. He had 34 goals as a rookie in 1985–86,
more than any other first-year player that season. (DM)

WENDEL CLARK

"THE TORONTO MAPLE LEAFS are very happy to select Wendel Clark from Saskatoon." With that statement the Leafs made a burly left-winger-defenceman the first player chosen in the 1985 NHL entry draft. The club had the right to select first after a horrendous 1984–85 season, its worst in the modern era, with a paltry 20 wins against 52 losses. Management did not want to make a mistake with this precious choice and for once in the wretched '80s, they hit a home run.

Before the draft, held in Toronto, there was heated debate on whether the club should choose Clark or Craig Simpson of Michigan State (Dana Murzyn, Craig Wolanin and Jim Sandlak were also considered). Simpson expressed some initial reservations about playing for such a poor organization, though later he said he'd be pleased to go to Toronto, while Clark was just happy to be drafted into the NHL. The Leafs decided Clark was their man, and they would never regret this selection.

At 5'11" and 194 pounds, he was not the biggest player in the draft or the most obviously talented, but he was an impressive all-round package. He was certainly the most aggressive player available (473 penalty minutes in his last two years of junior) and could unleash a wicked shot from anywhere on the ice; he had 55 goals in his final two seasons in Saskatoon, impressive for a defenceman. A first-team Western Hockey League all-star in 1985, Clark was also a strong skater and difficult to knock off his feet. Clark delivered crushing bodychecks and, to put it simply, he liked to fight.

When he joined the Leafs for the start of the 1985–86 season few knew what to expect from Clark, but he soon took a wrecking ball approach to introduce himself to the NHL. He scored a club record 34 goals as a rookie and finished second to Gary Suter of Calgary in the voting for the Calder Trophy. A few more assists (he only had 11) might have earned Clark the Calder but few would argue he had the most impact of any first-year player. The Leafs made him a left-winger and Clark became a typical power forward, even if he did not have the size normally associated with that role.

Clark did not pick his spots, either. He took on tough opponents like Rick Tocchett and Behn Wilson and didn't mind steamrolling star players such as Dino Ciccarelli and Mark Howe if they happened to get in his way. Clark was developing quite a reputation for fighting and scoring, often in the same game, netting 37 goals in his second year while racking up 271 penalty minutes.

He was the Leafs new star and Toronto fell in love with his style, as Clark single-handedly revitalized the Leafs and helped them win three playoff series over his first two years. But just when the future was looking bright, he injured his back at the 1987 Team Canada training camp. Suddenly, the seemingly indestructible Clark was rarely in the lineup and the Leafs were on the ropes.

Over the next three seasons Clark played in only 81 games (scoring 37 goals) while nursing assorted injuries and the nagging back problem that would not go away. Things finally improved when newspaper mogul Lord Thomson offered to send him to a back specialist in England and the Leafs hired a very bright athletic therapist in Chris Broadhurst. They nearly dealt Clark to Montreal for Shayne Corson and Claude Lemieux, but held on to him in the hope his back woes would one day end.

In the 1990–91 season, Clark managed to play in 63 games and score 18 goals, but the next year he appeared in only 43 and scored 19. The Leafs clearly needed him in the lineup and were a different team when he couldn't play. In 1992–93, Pat Burns took over as coach and reduced the dependency on Clark by putting him on the second line with John Cullen and Rob Pearson. Clark scored 17 goals in 66 games and was ready to rumble as well, taking on Detroit's Bob Probert, who had given him a beating years earlier, and pounding out a win. Clark and Toronto seemed to be back on track.

The Leafs met the Red Wings in the first round of the '93 playoffs and Clark was outstanding as he and Doug Gilmour led the Leafs past the more talented Detroit club. Clark was ripped in the newspapers after the Leafs lost the first two games of the series, but

When Wendel Clark was named Toronto captain on August 8, 1991, Darryl Sittler presented him with the captain's sweater. (DM)

The disappointment of losing to the Kings didn't seem to bother Clark, who started the next season scoring at a great pace until an ankle injury set him back once again. He finished with 46 goals in just 64 games, but was never healthy in the postseason. Clark's hit on Chicago defenceman Chris Chelios put the exclamation mark on a six-game series win for the Leafs. He gutted out a top performance against the San Jose Sharks, but like the team he had nothing left for Vancouver in the conference final.

The Leafs wanted to make changes and it was no secret that Burns sought a player he could count on night after night. On June 28, 1994, Clark was dealt to the Quebec Nordiques in a multi-player swap. It took the Leafs several years to recover from losing such leadership.

The normally stoic Clark cried the day he met the media to discuss the trade, and as soon as he was gone the Leafs seemed to be plotting ways to bring him back. They eventually did so (at a high price) and he made a somewhat successful return in the 1995–96 season. He left the team again as a free agent, only to be brought back one more time for 1999–2000. His last memorable moment as a Leaf came on a solo rush against the New Jersey Devils in the playoffs at Air Canada Centre. He didn't score — his shot hit the post — but the crowd stood and applauded, not so much for the one nice effort as for a thank you for giving so much of himself as a Maple Leaf.

Clark, who always claimed to be a simple farm boy, retired after that season was over. He cried again at the announcement, but no one seemed to mind.

he would not respond except to lead the team on the ice. He was strong in the next series against St. Louis, especially in the seventh game at the Gardens, and even better when the Leafs went up against the Los Angeles Kings in the Campbell Conference final. His three-goal performance in the sixth game of the series was probably his greatest as a Maple Leaf and if he could have hit the ice in overtime, Clark might have shot the team into the finals.

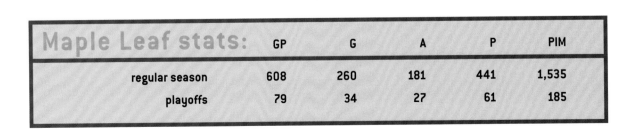

Maple Leaf stats:	GP	G	A	P	PIM
regular season	608	260	181	441	1,535
playoffs	79	34	27	61	185

Wendel Clark (#17) fights for position in front of the Minnesota net. He is the Maple Leafs' all-time leader in goals scored in the playoffs, with 34, followed by Dave Keon with 32. (Dennis Miles)

It was special when the Maple Leafs had the **confidence in me to be the captain.** I was able to play with a lot of players who helped me a lot when I was captain. Guys like Doug Gilmour, Todd Gill, Dave Ellett and Bob Rouse, guys who were leaders on the team they played for before coming to Toronto.

Wendel Clark, Leafs program, 1994–95 season

Leaf file:

As captain from 1991 to 1994, Wendel Clark was a team player and Toronto fans always appreciated the way he stood up for his teammates. There was no greater example of this than during the first game of the Campbell Conference final in 1993 against the Los Angeles Kings: The Leafs had the game well in hand and were on a power play when Kings defenceman Marty McSorley delivered a high hit to the head of Toronto star Doug Gilmour. Clark saw Gilmour go down and immediately challenged McSorley, nailing the bigger opponent with a few great punches and showing the Kings that the Leafs would not be intimidated.

Above: *Wendel Clark (#17) gets in front of St. Louis netminder Curtis Joseph during the 1993 playoffs. In the seventh game of the series between the Leafs and Blues, Clark scored two goals in a 6–0 Toronto win. It was the first time Maple Leaf Gardens had hosted a deciding playoff game since 1964. (HHOF)*

DAVE ELLETT

IT'S NOT OFTEN that a player comments on a trade made by a team other than his own, but when Wayne Gretzky speaks, everybody listens. Gretzky was with the Los Angeles Kings when the Leafs acquired defenceman Dave Ellett from the Winnipeg Jets and he knew a lot about Ellett, since they had been Smythe Division rivals for many years when Gretzky was an Edmonton Oiler. He said Toronto had made a great move in obtaining the 6'2", 205-pound Ellett in a deal that sent Ed Olczyk and Mark Osborne to the Jets in November 1991. The "Great One" proved to be right again.

Ellett's arrival meant the Leafs had finally found a smooth-skating defender who was not afraid to handle the puck. He would be a big part of the team in the '90s and helped it some of its greatest successes since 1967.

Born in Cleveland, Ohio, Ellett was the son of longtime minor-league player Bob Ellett, who skated in many cities while carving out a living in pro hockey. Young Dave landed a hockey scholarship to Bowling Green University after playing some junior hockey in the Ottawa area and there he enjoyed a great season in 1983–84, with 15 goals and 54 points in 43 games.

He had already been selected in the 1982 entry draft, 75th overall by the Jets, and made the Winnipeg club in his first attempt. In his rookie year in the NHL, Ellett produced 11 goals and 38 points in 80 games. He went on to have points seasons of 44, 46, 58, 56 and 46 with Winnipeg before he was dealt to Toronto for Ed Olczyk. It was strange that the Jets would give up the high-calibre defenceman and general manager Mike Smith later would express regret about doing so, but the Leafs were quick to spot a good opportunity to upgrade their blue line.

They hoped Ellett could run the power play from the point and unleash his blistering shot, which was hard, accurate and usually on net. He had set up many goals from his perch on the point and his ability to read the game made him an effective playmaker. He was a natural athlete and rarely lost his cool. Ellett scored eight goals and had 38 points in 60 games after the deal, then in 1991–92, his first full year as a Maple Leaf, he scored 18 times and earned 51 points in 79 games.

The next season Pat Burns arrived as Leafs head coach and Ellett's style changed. Burns got his defencemen to support the rush rather than lead it and Ellett's points production was never as high again, though as he took care of his own end the team was much more successful and there was no reason to question the strategy. During the 1992–93 season, Ellett scored only six goals, but managed 40 points in 70 games. He lost part of his season to a shoulder injury inflicted by notorious cheap-shot artist Dale Hunter of the Washington Capitals on March 9, 1993 (Burns was furious at Hunter). Ellett recovered in time to deliver a superb playoff performance, with 12 points in 21 games and show he could play well when it mattered most.

Ellett had 43 points in 68 games for the Leafs in 1993–94 and again was at his best in the postseason, when he racked up 18 points (including 15 assists) in 18 games. Leaf fans often expressed frustration with his style, as they had hoped he would attack more, but Ellett was quite effective in his withdrawn role, especially under Burns' system. He also helped make partner Todd Gill a better defenceman. Ellett focused on getting the puck out of danger and moving it up to the forwards.

With age, injuries slowed Ellett and he seemed to lose interest in attacking, though he still got into 80 games in the 1995–96 season and recorded 22 points. The Leafs started to decline after Burns was let go and Ellett soon followed, in a deal struck with New Jersey in February 1997.

Always quick with a quip, Ellett commented that he was glad to see Doug Gilmour had been "thrown into the deal" that made him a Devil (the Leafs got Steve Sullivan, Jason Smith and Alyn McCauley in return). He played only 20 games for New Jersey before going to Boston as a free agent. He joined St. Louis before retiring, finishing his career with 568 points in 1,129 games.

Dave Ellett was nicknamed 'Roy,' for Roy Hobbs, the main character in the baseball movie The Natural. *(DM)*

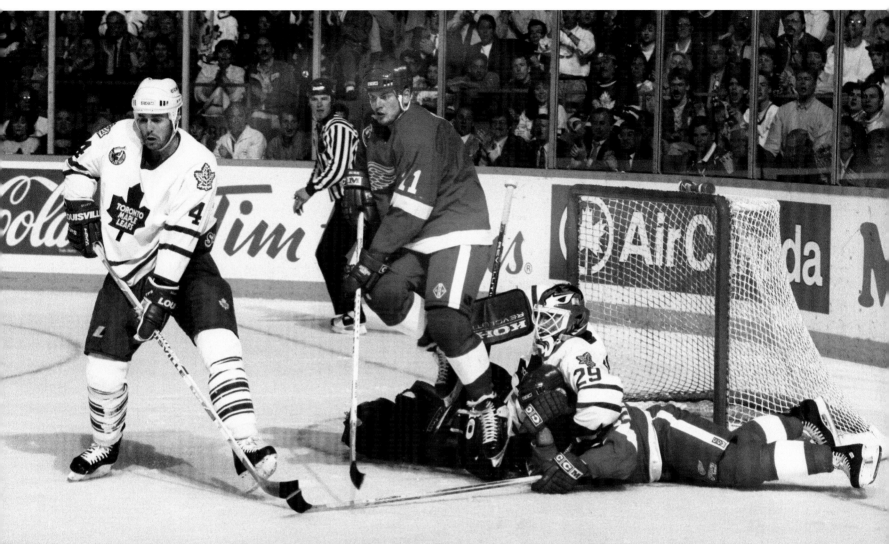

Dave Ellett (#4) gets ready to block a Detroit drive while Leafs goalie Felix Potvin (#29) has his hands full. Ellett holds the Leafs playoff record for most assists by a Toronto defenceman in one playoff year — 15, in 1994. (DM)

Leaf file:

In the 1999 playoffs, the Leafs and the Los Angeles Kings staged a memorable seven–game series that was ultimately decided by one goal. The Kings had tied the series by winning the sixth game but the Leafs were at home for the seventh game. The Kings jumped out to a 2–0 lead. Toronto tied the game, only to see Wayne Gretzky score again to make it 3–2. Wendel Clark tied the contest early in the third, but the Kings got the go-ahead goal with just under four minutes to play. Gretzky then banked in a shot off Dave Ellett's skate from behind the Leafs net to give the Kings a 5–3 lead. Ellett scored at the other end with just over a minute to play and gave the Leafs some hope, but the valiant effort came up short. It was the third time the Leafs had gone to a seventh game in the '93 playoffs.

Maple Leaf stats:	GP	G	A	P	PIM
regular season	446	51	172	223	371
playoffs	52	7	25	32	43

211

DOUG GILMOUR

TORONTO MAPLE LEAFS general manager Cliff Fletcher knew he had to reshape the team midway through the 1991–92 season. Toronto was pounded 12–1 by the Pittsburgh Penguins on December 26 and lost the next two games to Detroit and Quebec. The situation looked hopeless as the club floundered with only 10 wins. Then, at the start of 1992, Fletcher pulled off a miracle trade that would completely transform the team.

Centre Doug Gilmour had walked out on the Calgary Flames after a bitter contract dispute (he wanted $1.2 million and the Flames offered $500,000; an arbitrator settled the issue at $750,000). Fletcher moved quickly to land the pivot, as he had years earlier when he brought Gilmour to the Flames and watched him help his new team win the Stanley Cup in 1989 by scoring the winning goal at the Montreal Forum. Now, in acquiring Gilmour as part of a 10-player swap, Fletcher completed the largest regular-season deal in NHL history — and one of the most one-sided.

Because of his small size, 5'11" and 175 pounds, Gilmour had always been an underdog. But he had made the most of his opportunities and the St. Louis Blues saw enough in him to select him 134th overall in 1982. He started out as a defensive player and slowly started to add offence to his game, scoring 42 goals and totalling 105 points by his fourth season in St. Louis. After another good season there, personal problems forced a move.

Fletcher was managing the Flames at the time and took Gilmour's rights as part of a trade. Gilmour scored 26 goals and 85 points in his first year in Calgary, then added 20 points in 20 postseason games as Calgary won its first Stanley Cup. By the 1991–92 season he was not seeing eye to eye with Flames general manager and former teammate Doug Risebrough. The Flames executive gave up four other players who had helped the Flames win the Cup (and one prospect in Kent Manderville) and all he got in return was Gary Leeman, Michel Petit, Jeff Reese, Alexander Godynyuk and Craig Berube. But it was Gilmour's performance as a Leaf that turned the trade heavily in Toronto's favour.

His game was all about heart and determination and he would not hesitate to carve his initials into an opponent. His use of the stick kept other players wary and he would go a little "crazy" every now and then when the team needed a spark. He was too small to be a fighter but would always defend a teammate, taking on the much larger Brett Lindros one night after Lindros had crushed Todd Gill into the boards. Gilmour was a gifted playmaker with a deft passing touch and he scored just enough goals to be a threat. Give him some wingers to work with — as the Leafs did with Glenn Anderson, Wendel Clark, Nik Borschevsky and Dave Andreychuk — and Gilmour could make anyone with a little talent look like a star. Unlike many attackers, he paid attention to defence, and he was the best two-way player on the team.

Gilmour gave a hint of things to come in his first game as a Maple Leaf on January 3, 1992, with a goal and an assist in a 6–4 loss to Detroit. His 49 points in 40 games after his arrival almost single-handedly lifted the Leafs to a 20–18–2 record and they nearly caught a playoff position. The next season was even better as the team amassed 99 points and Gilmour set a club record with 127 points (32 goals and 95 assists); the highlight was his six assists effort at the Gardens against the Minnesota North Stars on January 13, 1993, but he was a star in almost every game he played that year. He appreciated the support fans gave the team and promised them that the Leafs would "do something for you."

He kept his word. In the '93 playoffs, Gilmour produced 35 points in 21 games but the Leafs were stopped just short of the finals. He was an incredible warrior and his face often showed the tremendous beating he was taking to get the Leafs past Detroit and St. Louis and almost by Los Angeles. Gilmour was the king of Toronto and the Leaf fans had a legitimate superstar for the first time since the days of Darryl Sittler and Lanny McDonald. Gilmour found the attention suffocating at times, though he handled it well enough and kept performing his magic on the ice. He finished second to Pittsburgh's Mario Lemieux in the voting for the Hart

Doug Gilmour recorded his 1,000th career point in a 6–1 win against the Edmonton Oilers on December 23, 1995. The point was an assist on a goal scored by Mats Sundin. (DM)

You can just tell that the fans are all excited. It's kind of a thrill to see that — to see the reaction when Pat Burns was signed and to see such a good crowd when we had the unveiling of the new uniforms. Doug Gilmour, Leafs program, October 6, 1992

Left: *Doug Gilmour (#93) was not a large player but that never stopped him from taking on bigger men like Eric Lindros (#88) of Philadelphia. Gilmour's 25 assists in the 1993 playoffs were the most by any player in postseason play, a record shared with Wayne Gretzky.* (Dennis Miles)

Right: *Doug Gilmour holds the puck along the boards as St. Louis forward Brett Hull moves in to check him. Gilmour is the Leafs' all-time playoff points leader with 77; Dave Keon is second, with 67.* (Dennis Miles)

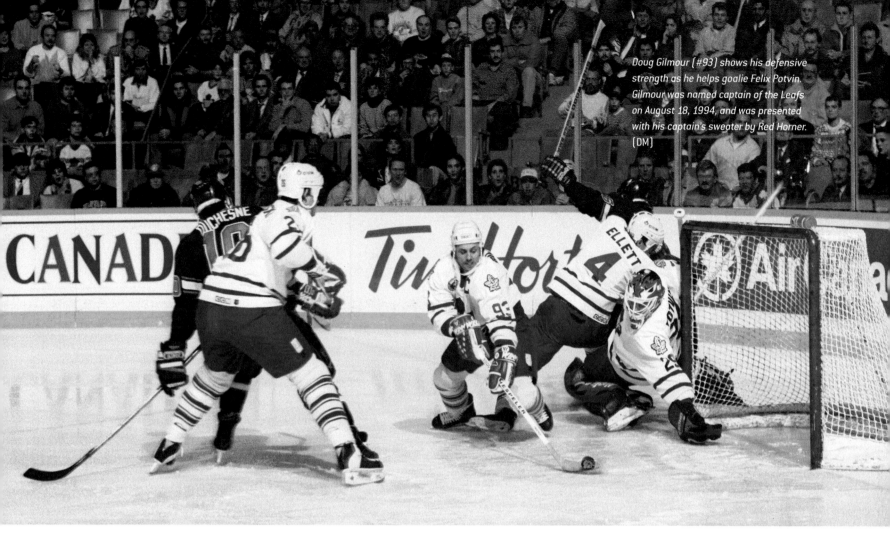

Doug Gilmour (#93) shows his defensive strength as he helps goalie Felix Potvin. Gilmour was named captain of the Leafs on August 18, 1994, and was presented with his captain's sweater by Red Horner. (DM)

Trophy as the NHL's best player, but was named winner of the Selke Trophy as the top defensive forward.

In 1993–94 he continued his fine play and recorded 111 points (27 goals and 84 assists). He was superb again in the playoffs (28 points in 18 games) despite an injury that forced him to take a needle before every game. Gilmour even skated double shifts, but the Leafs could advance no farther than they had in 1993. Looking back at his two 100-point seasons it is hard to imagine a more valuable player than Gilmour was to the Leafs, yet he was never named a league all-star and never won the Hart Trophy.

It was never the same for Gilmour after the '94 playoffs. His good friend Wendel Clark was dealt away and the Leafs defence was suddenly springing leaks with the new personnel. His gritty application of the previous two-and-a-half years disappeared and he struggled with a variety of nagging injuries and an operation on his feet. He did not click with the newly acquired Mats Sundin, though the pair produced some good offence together when they were on the same line.

Gilmour earned a decent 33 points in 44 games in the shortened 1994–95 season and 72 points in 80 games in the next season, but as he got older, Gilmour grew tired of playing for a team that at best could be said to be "rebuilding." He wanted to get out and asked his friend Fletcher to deal him away; he got his wish 61 games into the 1996–97 season (after producing 15 goals and 60 points for Toronto) when he was moved to New Jersey.

After failing to regain the Cup with the Devils as hoped, Gilmour began moving around the NHL. He signed as a free agent with Chicago and eventually was dealt to Buffalo. Not wanting to retire, he tried to return to the Leafs for the 2001–2 season but was rebuffed. He signed with Montreal, where he was still very productive once he was again skating well.

No matter where or when Gilmour ends his career, he will always have a special place in the hearts of all Toronto fans.

Maple Leaf stats:	GP	G	A	P	PIM
regular season	392	131	321	452	386
playoffs	52	17	60	77	90

SYLVAIN LEFEBVRE

WHEN LEAF FANS talk about the deal that saw Wendel Clark go to the Quebec Nordiques, defenceman Sylvain Lefebvre is not always mentioned. Yet the big blueliner's loss might have been even more important to the Leafs than that of the hugely popular Clark.

The deletion of Lefebvre and Bob Rouse from two very good Leafs teams (1992–93 and 1993–94) meant the Toronto defence had to be rebuilt, a feat general manager Cliff Fletcher could not pull off with the likes of youngster Kenny Jonsson and veteran Larry Murphy. As a result the Leafs began a steady decline that eventually saw them miss the playoffs and cost Fletcher his job. It was no accident that both Lefebvre (Colorado) and Rouse (Detroit) won Stanley Cups while the Leafs were wondering what had gone wrong.

Lefebvre arrived in Toronto to little fanfare. He was acquired in 1992 for a third-round draft choice from the Montreal Canadiens, where he had played three seasons. New Leafs coach Pat Burns was familiar with Lefebvre from his time as Habs mentor and knew the team could use his talents on their always-thin blue line.

Lefebvre, a very smart player, understood his limitations on the ice. He was not fast, but could angle off opposing skaters perfectly until they had no place to go. With great reach at 6'2" and 205 pounds he used his size as needed but rarely fought, though in one memorable scrap at Maple Leaf Gardens he punched out the lights of Rob Brown of the Chicago Blackhawks. As a Maple Leaf, Lefebvre and his partner Jamie Macoun always made the safe play;

it was strictly defence first. Burns used the duo in all important situations and the Leafs could count on them to get the puck out of their end. Lefebvre's offensive skills were limited, but he chipped in the odd goal or made a nice play to keep the puck in the other team's zone on occasion.

During the 1993 playoffs former Leafs coach Dan Maloney, at the time a scout for another organization, said in a radio interview that the trade the Leafs had made to get Lefebvre was "the steal of the century." Getting a quality defender for a third-round pick was indeed a rarity and it looked as if Lefebvre could be a Leaf for the next 10 years. He was outstanding during the 1993 playoffs, scoring three goals and making three assists in 21 games. He scored a big goal against the Los Angeles Kings during the fifth game of the Campbell Conference final which sent the game to overtime; the Leafs went on to win, putting themselves within one game of the finals. The following season Lefebvre continued his consistent play on defence but a second loss in the conference final spelled the end of a brief stay at the top of the NHL for the Leafs.

Lefebvre had probably his greatest moment in hockey when the Colorado Avalanche won the Stanley Cup during the 1995–96 season. He had scored a career-high five goals that year and assisted on 11 others, and again was one of the team's best defenders. By the end of the 2001–2 season he had played for three years with the New York Rangers, who signed him as a free agent in 1999.

Maple Leaf stats:	GP	G	A	P	PIM
regular season	165	4	21	25	169
playoffs	39	3	6	9	36

Sylvain Lefebvre playing the Chicago Blackhawks. Lefebvre developed his skills by playing two seasons with the Sherbrooke Canadiens in the American Hockey League. (DM)

JAMIE MACOUN

WHEN THE MAPLE LEAFS acquired a pair of defencemen in the trade that landed them Doug Gilmour, few realized the impact Jamie Macoun and Ric Nattress would have on the team. But when you consider that the gutsy performers replaced two underachievers in Michel Petit and Alexander Godynyuk, it's little wonder the Leafs suddenly started to improve. Nattress was lost to free agency (signed by Philadelphia) but Macoun stayed a Maple Leaf and became a steady fixture on the blue line. When he was teamed with Sylvain Lefebvre, the pairing gave the Leafs the best defensive combination they had seen in years.

A native of Newmarket, Ontario, Macoun didn't plan a professional hockey career. While attending Ohio State University he played three seasons of varsity hockey, thinking it was a great opportunity to get an education while having fun. He was not drafted, but the Calgary Flames offered him a contract and he joined them for the last part of the 1982–83 season. He did not play a game in the minors and quickly established himself on the Flames blue line.

Macoun knew his role was primarily to keep the puck out of his own end but he showed some flair for offence, with 19 goals and 76 points in his first three years. He was a good size at 6'2" and 200 pounds and was not afraid to use his body or his stick to stop an opponent. In the early years of his career, Macoun was a very good skater and never afraid to handle the puck. Away from the ice he was known as a guy who marched to the beat of his own drummer, but he showed up ready to play every game no matter how banged up he might be.

Macoun missed the entire 1987–88 season after he was injured in a car accident that nearly took his life, returning to help the Flames win the 1989 Stanley Cup after recording a career-high 35 points during the regular season. But when players like Gilmour and Macoun started to demand more money, the Flames felt they had to move them out. Leafs general manager Cliff Fletcher added Macoun to the package of players he wanted in the 10-player swap.

Macoun's point totals dipped somewhat with the Leafs, although he earned 30 in 1993–94, but all the Toronto coaches he played for wanted him to be tough in defence and not worry about scoring. As he slowed a little, Macoun started taking too many penalties and he never found a partner to replace Lefebvre when the latter was traded away. But even as he struggled, Macoun rarely missed a game. He played in his 1,000th career contest as a Leaf and his consistency was appreciated by a coach like Mike Murphy, who often defended the blueliner when Leaf fans began to complain about him.

During the 1997–98 season there was clearly no reason to keep Macoun on a losing Leafs team and Fletcher did him a big favour, sending the defenceman to Detroit. Macoun won a second Stanley Cup with the Red Wings in 1998; interviewed on *Hockey Night in Canada* just after that victory he said it was too bad he could not have been a Cup winner with Toronto.

Macoun played one more year in Detroit before retiring and moving back to Calgary. He played in 1,128 career games, recording 358 points and 1,208 penalty minutes.

Maple Leaf stats:	GP	G	A	P	PIM
regular season	466	13	88	101	506
playoffs	52	2	11	13	64

Jamie Macoun (#34) tries to track down the puck during a game against the St. Louis Blues. There was a time (prior to the start of the shortened 1994–95 season) when the Leafs had a record of 32–5–5 when Macoun recorded a point a game. (DM)

FELIX POTVIN

WHEN STARTING GOALTENDER Grant Fuhr was injured early in the 1992–93 season, the Maple Leafs put out a call to their St. John's farm club and promoted Felix Potvin to the big team. He played so well that when Fuhr was ready to return to the lineup, the team was faced with a difficult decision.

General manager Cliff Fletcher discussed the situation with coach Pat Burns and they agreed that Potvin, only 21 at the time, was ready for the NHL on a full-time basis. They also agreed that there was no point in keeping two number 1 goalies when one could be traded for a much-needed forward. The starting job went to Potvin and Fletcher found a willing taker for Fuhr in the Buffalo Sabres (netting the Leafs left-winger Dave Andreychuk, backup goalie Darren Puppa and a first-round draft choice). Dealing Fuhr was a bold move by Leafs management but they were proved right when Potvin delivered for the team.

The Leafs had been anticipating Potvin's arrival for some time after selecting the 6'1", 190-pound netminder 31st overall in the 1990 entry draft. A native of Anjou, Quebec, he had enjoyed an all-star junior career with the Chicoutimi Saguenéens of the Quebec Major Junior Hockey League. He took his club to the Memorial Cup finals in 1991 and though it did not win, Potvin was named top goaltender in the tournament. The Leafs assigned him to the St. John's Maple Leafs of the American Hockey League, where he won the rookie-of-the-year award by posting an 18–10–6 record, with two shutouts. He was great in the playoffs as the baby Leafs went all the way to the Calder Cup finals, only to lose in seven hard-fought games to the Adirondack Red Wings. Potvin also gave fans a glimpse of the future by playing in three games for the Leafs that year (0–2–1). He was the first goalie the Leafs had developed in their own system since Mike Palmateer in the '70s.

Potvin made the most of his opportunity with a league-low 2.50 goals-against average in 48 games and a 25–15–5 record in '92–'93. He allowed just 116 goals and had two shutouts while showing remarkable poise for such an inexperienced netminder. Potvin's

greatest attributes were his quickness (he was nicknamed "Cat") and his competitive nature. He was a cool customer and could put a bad moment behind him quickly. Like many other goalies trained in the Quebec junior circuit, Potvin wanted to take the bottom of the net away from a shooter and force him to go high. A quick glove hand would capture many of the shots aimed at the top shelf, and keeping the paddle of his stick down on the ice helped him to control rebounds and block low drives. As well as going down early, he played back in his net, which was fast becoming the new style of play for goaltenders as they adjusted to more across-ice passing in the NHL.

Potvin quickly became a hero in Toronto. He took the Leafs to the Campbell Conference final in the 1993 playoffs, winning two of three game 7 showdowns along the way. He faltered in the last two games of the series against the Los Angeles Kings, allowing a total of 10 goals, but stayed composed throughout a gruelling schedule as the Leafs played 21 games in 42 days in that magical spring of 1993.

In 1993–94, his first full year as a Leaf, Potvin played in 66 games and won 34. Once again he got the Leafs as far as the Western Conference final before an overtime goal in Vancouver finished them off. He recorded three shutouts in the first round of the '94 postseason, blanking Chicago 1–0 each time. In the 1995 playoffs Potvin nearly got the Leafs past the Blackhawks again, but a much weaker Toronto club wilted in seven games after winning the first two in Chicago. He was never the same for the Leafs after that painful loss.

In the early years Potvin was helped by coach Burns' sound defensive system and a team of solid, experienced defencemen. With Burns gone and most of the defence traded or aging fast, Potvin was often left on his own. Larry Murphy, Garth Butcher, Grant Jennings, Drake Berehowsky, Kenny Jonsson and Dmitri Mironov all failed to make their mark as Leafs defencemen during this time and Potvin seemed to sink deeper and deeper into his net. While NHL shooters were adjusting to him, he refused to change

Felix Potvin (#29) stops Montreal's Vince Damphousse in close. Potvin earned his first career shutout on January 23, 1993, at Maple Leaf Gardens in a 4–0 win over the Canadiens. (DM)

Left: Felix Potvin (#29) played his first game as a Leaf on November 14, 1991, a 3–0 loss to Chicago. Two nights later he earned a 2–2 tie against the Blackhawks. His performance in both games showed he could be an NHL goaltender. (DM)

his game. In his last three seasons with the Leafs, his win totals were 30, 27 and 26, but his last two years also featured 36 and 33 losses. The worst came one night at home against St. Louis, when defenceman Al MacInnis bounced a long shot in from centre ice at 19:58 in the third period to beat Potvin and give the Blues a shocking 3-2 win. It was a shot the goalie should have had and it shattered everyone's confidence in him.

During the off-season prior to the start of the 1998–99 campaign, the Leafs signed free-agent goalie Curtis Joseph. It was the end of Potvin's time in Toronto and he waited to be traded (he played in five games, going 3–2). When the deal did not happen fast enough, a sulking Potvin left the team. He was eventually sent to the New York Islanders for defenceman Bryan Berard, a former rookie of the year, and spent a year there before being dealt to Vancouver. The Canucks couldn't wait for Potvin to find his game and packed him off to Los Angeles, where he started to show some of the form that had made him the darling of Toronto just a few years earlier.

Leaf file:

Felix Potvin was known for his coolness under fire but he displayed a temper at times. During the 1993 playoffs, the Leafs opened with a couple of embarrassing losses to the Detroit Red Wings and Potvin let it be known that he did not like having red sweaters in his crease by tangling with Dino Ciccarelli and Bob Probert. Potvin was told to tone it down and the Leafs came back to win the series in seven games behind his stellar goaltending.

In Philadelphia on the night of November 10, 1996, the Leafs net-minder showed his fighting days were not over. Potvin and the Leafs were beaten 3–1, but a brawl broke out at the end of the contest after Potvin took a slash at one of the Flyers. That brought hot-head Flyers goalie Ron Hextall down to the Leafs end, where he went after Potvin. It was a bad move as Potvin gave him a severe beating, cutting open his forehead. Hextall had always thought of himself as the fighting champion among goalies but he was stripped of his "title" that night.

Maple Leaf stats:	GP	Wins	Losses	Ties	Shutouts	GAA
regular season	369	160	149	49	12	2.87
playoffs	52	25	27	–	5	2.75

BOB ROUSE

DURING HIS TERM as general manager Floyd Smith made a number of moves to make the Maple Leafs a veteran-laden team. He felt that someone used to playing in the NHL would be best able to handle the pressures of performing in Toronto. His more notable acquisitions included Mike Krushelnyski, Mike Foligno, Michel Petit, Lucien DeBlois, Aaron Broten, Mark Laforest and Tom Kurvers. Some of these players performed well for the Leafs, while others moved out quickly, but the best trade Smith pulled off had to be the acquisition of centre Peter Zezel and defenceman Bob Rouse. The deal cost the Leafs a potential star, defenceman Al Iafrate, but he was not doing much for the team. The two players who came in from the Washington Capitals became very productive members of the Leafs and were a major part of Toronto's resurgence in the early '90s.

A native of Surrey, British Columbia, Rouse was drafted by the Minnesota North Stars in 1982 (80th overall) after a junior career in Lethbridge, Alberta. He was a North Star for the next five seasons before being dealt to the Capitals in 1989; he stayed there for two seasons before the Leafs acquired the 6'2", 215-pound defenceman in 1991. Rouse immediately gave the struggling Leafs some stability and much-needed toughness on defence.

His game was designed around his defensive abilities, especially in clearing the front of the net. His offence was very limited: five was his highest goal total and he never recorded more than 26 points in a season. He could handle the puck and was good enough to play the point on the power play at times, but he was always more interested in taking care of his own end first. Rouse was a very good fighter (he beat Wendel Clark in a fight during Clark's rookie year with the Leafs) but had to be very upset to actually drop the gloves and go, though he did record over 100 penalty minutes eight times in his career. He was not fleet of foot, but was strong on his skates and hard to knock around. Rouse could also be counted upon to lead —he was one of three captains on the North Stars during the 1988–89 season and was given an "A" on his sweater while with Toronto.

Leaf fans remember Rouse best for his performance in the 1993 playoffs, when he had 11 points in 21 games. He was outstanding in the 4–3 overtime win in the seventh game of the series against the Detroit Red Wings, coming in from the blue line to score a goal to tie the game 2–2 and then taking the shot that Nik Borschevsky tipped into the net to win the game. Rouse hugged little Borschevsky and let out a holler as the Leafs poured over the boards in celebration. It was a moment no fan will forget. The Leafs had not been expected to beat the Red Wings but the Herculean efforts of players like Rouse proved they were a resilient bunch.

The Leafs foolishly let Rouse get away as an unrestricted free agent after the 1993–94 season. They could have signed him during the year, but felt he was asking too much and was curious about being free to go to another team. The Red Wings offered a suitable contract and he made three trips to the finals with Detroit, winning the Stanley Cup in 1997 and 1998. He was signed as a free agent by San Jose after the '98 Cup win and played a couple of years for the Sharks before retiring. He played in 1,061 career games.

Maple Leaf stats:	GP	G	A	P	PIM
regular season	237	13	45	58	338
playoffs	39	3	11	14	58

Leafs defenceman Bob Rouse (#3) has his hands full with Calgary Flames Gary Roberts (#10), Gary Leeman (#11) and Joe Nieuwendyk (#25), battling in front of his net. Rouse had 22 points in his best season for the Leafs, in 1991–92. (DM)

PETER ZEZEL

THE TRADE that brought centre Peter Zezel to the Maple Leafs was a homecoming for the Toronto native. Born on April 22, 1965, he played in the Metropolitan Toronto Hockey League in 1981–82 for the Don Mills Flyers. He then moved to the Toronto Marlboros, where he scored 82 goals and totalled 207 points in two seasons. Toronto scouts could watch him every time he played for the Marlies at Maple Leaf Gardens, but despite the impressive numbers the Leafs did not select him in the 1983 entry draft. Instead the Philadelphia Flyers chose him 41st overall (the Leafs took Russ Courtnall sixth and Jeff Jackson 28th in the same draft) and he made the big team without spending any time in the minors. Zezel scored 15 goals and had 46 assists as a rookie and proved to be a very pleasant surprise to the Flyers.

He stayed in Philadelphia for the next few seasons, going to the Stanley Cup finals in 1985 and 1987 before being dealt to the St. Louis Blues in 1988. With the Blues he played at centre on a line with high-scoring winger Brett Hull and recorded a career-best 72 points, including 47 assists. He was moved to the Washington Capitals in 1990 but partway through the 1990–91 season he was acquired by the Leafs with Bob Rouse. He finished the season with 28 points (including 14 goals) in 32 games and seemed to be at home in Toronto. The next season he racked up 49 points (16 goals, 33 assists) in 64 games.

Leaf fans certainly liked Zezel's approach to the game. Not tall at 5'11" but extremely sturdy at 220 pounds, he was difficult to knock down. He used his stocky body to push opponents off the puck and could make dangerous passes once he got hold of it. He was more a playmaker than a goal scorer and was never afraid to battle for a loose puck.

His creativity kept him in the NHL for his first few years, but as he got older, Zezel changed his game to become more of a checker and top face-off man. When Pat Burns became Leafs coach in 1992, he found an excellent role for Zezel by putting him in the middle of his checking line. Mark Osborne flanked him on one side and Bill Berg eventually joined the team to play on the other wing. The line clicked and was soon getting plenty of ice time, often against the best opposing line. In 1992–93 Zezel scored 12 goals with 23 assists, very respectable numbers considering his role on the team.

In the 1993 playoffs, his work in the face-off circle was nothing short of spectacular and his ability to tie up an opposing centre was a work of art. His soccer background made him one of the few players in the league who could control the puck with his feet, a skill especially useful in the face-off circle. Leaf fans were comforted to know they had Zezel to take all the face offs during the playoffs. In the 1994 conference final series against Vancouver, Zezel scored the winning goal in overtime in the first game of the series. It turned out to be his last marker as a Maple Leaf.

The Leafs decided to make some major changes after the '94 playoffs. They felt Zezel was injury-prone and included him in their compensation offer to the Dallas Stars when they signed Mike Craig. Zezel bounced around after leaving the Leafs, playing with St. Louis for a second time, New Jersey and Vancouver. He finished with 608 points in 878 career games.

Maple Leaf stats:	GP	G	A	P	PIM
regular season	207	50	78	128	73
playoffs	38	4	5	9	14

The Toronto Maple Leafs were Zezel's favourite team as a youngster but he was drafted in 1983 by his second-favourite team, the Philadelphia Flyers. (DM)

TWO HOMES: THE GARDENS AND THE AIR CANADA CENTRE

by Frank Orr

IN THE WORST OF times and the best of times in the last century, the Maple Leafs moved into posh new homes, buildings that set standards for their eras, constructed under conditions and at costs that were poles apart.

That Maple Leaf Gardens was built at all was a miracle, opening at Church and Carlton Streets in 1931, when the world was in the depths of the Great Depression. Conn Smythe's finding the $1.5 million in those dreadful economic times remains a great business feat. By contrast, when it opened in 1999, the Air Canada Centre was a symbol of an economic boom, a luxuriously-appointed arena loaded with the corporate boxes, fine restaurants and padded-seat amenities that the sports fan of the New Millenium demanded.

The Gardens completed Smythe's vision of the Maple Leafs as the major entertainment draw in Toronto, a site and a team to be regarded the way European cities view their opera houses, with patrons who dressed accordingly. The $300-million ACC was an economic necessity for Maple Leaf Sports and Entertainment Ltd to upgrade its income to remain competitive in the "new" sports marketplace: income in Canadian dollars and many expenses, i.e. players' salaries, in U.S. funds. The Leafs owners purchased a basketball team, the Toronto Raptors, to gain control of the arena site and improve their cash flow.

Had Smythe not been fired after assembling the roster for the first New York Rangers NHL team in 1926, Toronto hockey history would have followed a much different plot. When the Rangers dumped him, Smythe vowed revenge on the ice and used his severance pay as down payment on the St. Patrick's, the city's NHL team based in a dumpy old duck blind, the Mutual Street Arena.

Smythe and his assistant Frank Selke Sr., immediately changed the team name to the Maple Leafs and its colours to blue and white and began to build a strong hockey club that would create a demand for a proper stage on which to perform.

Smythe loved his image as a great gambler and his stories about parlaying a few bucks into working capital by winning bets on sports events changed often in his frequent re-telling. But his firm belief in what he wanted to accomplish helped to sell investors on his projects, notably the Bickell mining family and a storekeeping Eaton or two.

In a strange way the "hard times" worked in Smythe's favour. The brilliant little Selke, a former union official, was the pitchman in convincing the trade unions to accept stock in MLG in lieu of as much as 40 per cent of their salaries. Those who took the stock never regretted the move.

The Gardens was built in little more than six months and opened in November, 1931. With Foster Hewitt broadcasting nationally from the Gondola in the rafters, the building quickly took on its aura of a hockey shrine. Smythe was adamant that those in the best seats should dress as if they were attending high-tone entertainment, not a blood-and-guts hockey game.

When Smythe sold the building and the franchise in 1961 to a group headed by his son Stafford and Stafford's pal Harold Ballard, the building changed. The Queen's picture and the big pipe organ were replaced by seats, mostly crowded-in small pews at high prices. "You have to be a rich fat banker to afford them and a starving kid to fit into them," Conn Smythe said when he saw the changed building.

The Gardens made huge sums of money through Ballard's ownership in the '70s and '80s but became more of a joke than a shrine because of his money-grubbing and weak hockey teams.

When a new ownership group headed by grocer Steve Stavro took control of MLG and the Leafs in the early '90s, the building was doomed, like a beloved old aunt whose clothing is three decades out of date. When the basketball Raptors arrived, playing in the gigantic Skydome, it appeared for a couple of years that Toronto would have two new arenas.

The Raptors made the first move, taking over Toronto's historic post office property at Bay and Lakeshore and launching construction of a house built for basketball. The Leafs talked of their own building — Stavro liked the Bloor Street location of old Varsity Stadium — but in the end the pucksters bought the ball bouncers and took over their embyro playground in time to change the design into a two-sport facility.

The Maple Leafs began the new millennium by having to qualify for the playoffs on the last night of the 2000–2001 campaign. They made up for an average season with a decent postseason, a 4–0 sweep of Ottawa before a seven-game loss to New Jersey but knew they had to make changes. After some significant additions they put together a 100-point season in 2001–2, with the third-best record in the NHL, 43–25–10 with four overtime losses. The injury-riddled team did remarkably well in the playoffs, knocking off the New York Islanders and Ottawa Senators before losing to the Carolina Hurricanes in the Eastern Conference finals. As gritty as the Leafs were in the 2002 postseason, they were still well short of the Stanley Cup. Here is a look at why the Leafs are still searching for their first championship since 1967.

Left: *A wide view of the Maple Leafs' new home, Air Canada Centre.* (DM).

Corey Schwab (#35) jumped in to the number 1 role when regular goalie Curtis Joseph was injured. Schwab ended the 2001–2 season with a 12-10-5 record. (DM)

Management and Coaching

This discussion begins and ends with Pat Quinn. Firmly ensconced as coach and general manager, Quinn had complete control over the hockey operation as the century began. He had certainly done well as coach since he joined the club, also finding time to take Canada to its first Olympic gold medal in 50 years, but his performance as general manager was average at best into 2002. Due to health issues that developed during the 2002 playoffs, Quinn might be forced to give up one of his titles eventually.

Upper management was happy as long as Quinn kept the Leafs in the playoff hunt and the profitable postseason home dates kept the team in the black. But in 2002 no one above Quinn was push-

Travis Green (#39) was acquired in a deal that sent Danny Markov to Phoenix. Green was very good in a defensive role during the 2002 playoffs and great in the faceoff circle, where he won many key draws. (DM)

ing him to get the players the team needed to win a Cup, and as long as ownership took that approach a championship for Toronto fans would remain a fantasy.

Best Trades and Acquisitions

Quinn's trading record was uneven overall — he generally preferred to make one-for-one trades and shunned blockbusters — but he had pulled off a few gems. Picking up defenceman Bryan McCabe from Chicago for Alexander Karpovtsev was simply a steal. Getting Darcy Tucker from Tampa Bay was another excellent deal, as the feisty winger brought a tremendous determination to the team. Defenceman Aki Berg was a very good acquisition for essentially a fourth-line player (Adam Mair) and he has the potential to improve in the years to come. Mikael Renberg was a nice addition, especially as the Leafs had to give up only Sergei Berezin, a once-useful player, in return. Renberg fitted nicely on Mats Sundin's wing but his injury woes were a major concern, as was his lack of goals. Wade Belak, Jyrki Lumme and Tom Barrasso were also decent acquisitions, though the last two might only be short-term. In 2002 the team had high hopes for recent choices centre Brad Boyes and defencemen Carlo Colaiacovo, Jay Harrison and Karel Pilar (who had already played for Toronto).

Notable Events

The most notable event in the first two years of the century was the Leafs' 2002 playoff run. Depleted by injury and faced with an ailing head coach and some very questionable officiating they managed to get to the Eastern Conference final, showing great heart, determination and a never-say-die attitude. Few teams in Toronto history have shown such a scrappy approach and few other NHL clubs would have survived with so many injuries. Leafs fans were enthralled with the 2002 playoff squad and let down when the Carolina Hurricanes beat Toronto in six games to end their Cup hopes. The Leafs were smothered by a stifling Hurricane defence and their best scorers could not find the net more than six times all series long. They lost three contests in overtime.

Alyn MacCauley had a terrific playoff for the Leafs in 2002 with 15 points, after recording 16 during the entire regular season. (DM).

Free Agents

The Leafs kept adding players through free agency and did well by it. Alex Mogilny gave them a genuine game breaker while Shayne Corson and Gary Roberts provided veteran leadership and toughness. On the flip side defenceman Anders Eriksson was a flop in the 2001–2 season and rebounded only slightly in the playoffs, still coughing up the puck at key moments, while blueliner Dave Manson faded badly and was sent to Dallas in a trade for Lumme. Another free-agent blueliner, Gerald Diduck, was so bad he was simply given to Dallas.

Worst of the Decade

During the 2000–2001 season two players not even on the team loomed large in Leafs rebuilding plans that didn't materialize. Superstar Eric Lindros let it be known that his greatest desire was to play for the Leafs, but he could not force the Philadelphia Flyers to complete a deal. Quinn thought he had a trade worked out, but Flyers manager Bob Clarke reneged at the last moment. The story dragged on all year and ended with Leafs fans watching Lindros end up in New York with the Rangers. A chance to acquire one of the best players in the game was lost.

Toronto also wanted to land defenceman Rob Blake from the Los Angeles Kings and media reports indicated a trade was worked out, but the Leafs could not get the all-star blueliner to agree to a new contract. They could have gambled and completed the deal, but the conservative Leafs management would not let that happen. The Leafs badly needed a player like Blake to help them get into the finals during the 2001 postseason. Instead, he won the Stanley Cup in Colorado.

The Leafs made no moves to acquire top players such as Jaromir Jagr, Pavel Buré, Doug Weight, Jason Allison or Jeremy Roenick, all of whom changed uniforms in this period. They traded a quality young defenceman in Danny Markov to Phoenix for pivot Robert Reichel, a poor choice to play second-line centre as his performance in the 2002 playoffs confirmed (no goals, three assists). Quinn was not able to add any defencemen to the team either, despite a serious injury that kept Dmitry Yushkevich out of the 2000 playoffs.

Bottom-line Results

For the two seasons beginning in 2000–2001, the Leafs posted a respectable 80–54–21 record, with nine overtime losses. The team won three seven-game series (two against Ottawa, one versus the New York Islanders) and lost two (to New Jersey and Carolina). They did make it the final four again for the fourth time in 10 years, but could not get past the Eastern Conference final. The Leafs had the best chance of getting to the final since 1993 but the goal-scoring dried up — they were the highest scoring team in the East with 249 goals during the season — and they lost three games at home and three games in overtime while scoring only six goals against the Hurricanes.

Best Leafs of the Decade So Far

IN GOAL: Curtis Joseph.

ON DEFENCE: Tomas Kaberle, Bryan McCabe and Dmitry Yushkevich

AT FORWARD: Mats Sundin, Gary Roberts and Alex Mogilny (honourable mention to Shayne Corson and Darcy Tucker).

SHAYNE CORSON

WHEN SHAYNE CORSON put on his Leafs sweater for the first time at a press conference on July 4, 1999, it was a dream come true for the native of Barrie, Ontario. The Leafs were his favourite team when he was a youngster and the only thing he regretted was that his father, Paul, was not around to share the moment. Corson had been very close to his dad and was devastated when his mentor passed away a few years earlier.

Corson turned down more money from the likes of the Philadelphia Flyers just to play for his childhood heroes. For the Leafs, it was a great opportunity to add a gritty forward to a group of skilled players with the hope of giving the team the right balance. Corson is much more than a grinder — he has 261 career goals — but it is his heart and determination that make him so valuable.

Corson's career began with the Montreal Canadiens after they drafted the 6'1", 202-pound center-winger eighth overall in 1984. He impressed by playing an aggressive brand of hockey and made the Habs in 1986–87 without going to the minors. By his third season in the NHL, Corson had established himself as a power forward, with 26 goals and 193 penalty minutes. In 1989–90, he scored a career-high 31 goals and 75 points. He was with Montreal for two more years before going to Edmonton. The feisty Corson scored 25 times for the Oilers in 1993–94 but signed as a free agent with the St. Louis Blues in July 1995. After a little more than one season in St. Louis he was dealt back to his original team and played for four more years in Montreal before becoming an unrestricted free agent and signing on with the Maple Leafs.

Corson's game was centred on his willingness to use his body and take on any foe who got in his way, but he could get into unnecessary trouble at times and was at his best when he played with more discipline. Corson also showed strong leadership abilitiesand led by example. As his scoring touch declined, he proved an effective checker who could set up goals and pot the odd one himself. He showed great courage in dealing with colitis, a digestive disorder, and often worried about his health in light of his father's premature death. During the 2000–2001 season, Corson suffered from panic attacks, but was steadied by the support of brother-in-law and Leafs teammate Darcy Tucker.

After picking up a bad virus at his first training camp with the Leafs Corson did not get off to a great start, though he finished the season with eight goals and 26 points. He was superb in the playoffs, helping to shut down Alexei Yashin of the Ottawa Senators as the Leafs salvaged a somewhat disappointing season with a first-round playoff win. Corson was much healthier in 2001–2 and upped his goal total to 12, with 21 assists. His anxiety attacks were no longer an issue and his strong play helped the Leafs get back to the 100-point level.

Corson played a significant role in helping the Leafs get to the Eastern Conference final during the 2002 playoffs despite a slew of team injuries during the postseason. He was at his feisty best for the first two rounds, even getting suspended for one game for trying to kick an opponent, but injuries kept him from contributing more in the series against Carolina. He is likely to focus on checking duties for as long as he remains with the Maple Leafs.

Maple Leaf stats:	GP	G	A	P	PIM
regular season	151	20	39	59	309
playoffs	30	2	7	9	47

Shayne Corson was given sweater number 27 when he joined the Maple Leafs. (DM)

KEN DRYDEN

AT THE END of the 1996–97 season the Maple Leafs had posted a record of 30–44–8 for total of 68 points. Not only were they last in the Central Division of the Western Conference, their points total was better than only three other NHL teams. Naturally the organization was not happy with the results and set out to make changes at the top. When Cliff Fletcher decided to resign as team president and general manager rather than implement the changes proposed by the owners, the Leafs approached hockey legend Ken Dryden with the challenge of turning the team back into a contender.

A success at everything he had tried beforehand, Dryden was intrigued by the possibility of making hockey's most famous franchise a winner again. The former all-star goaltender knows what the Maple Leafs meant to Toronto in particular and to hockey fans in general, while the Leaf fans knew they had a very respected man in a key position and anxiously awaited his first moves.

Dryden's playing career began at Cornell University, where he posted a remarkable record of 76–4–1 in three seasons. He made an even greater impression when he joined the Montreal Canadiens late in the 1970–71 season and took the Habs all the way to a Stanley Cup win, earning the Conn Smythe Trophy as the best player in the playoffs. In the next season he won the Calder Trophy as the NHL's best rookie and he went on to win five more Cups and five Vezina Trophies.

While still at the top of his game, Dryden decided to retire from hockey after the Canadiens' Stanley Cup win in 1979. He did a variety of things after leaving the limelight, including becoming a best-selling author: Dryden's *The Game* is one of the greatest hockey books ever

written. He was Ontario's youth commissioner between 1984 and 1986, but it seemed inevitable that he would return to hockey and when the Leafs came calling he was ready for the challenge.

As new team president, Dryden tried to recruit former Montreal teammate Bob Gainey as new general manager, but the offer came at a bad time for the retired winger. After some hesitation Dryden took on the general manager's role himself and hired former Winnipeg Jets general manager Mike Smith to assist him. Smith initially made some good moves, bringing in a top goalie in Curtis Joseph and a quality coach in Pat Quinn. But a power struggle forced Dryden to dismiss Smith and he decided to hand the general manager's job to Quinn.

Dryden then immersed himself in a variety of projects. Early in his tenure he succeeded in getting the Leafs back into the Eastern Conference in the same division as the Montreal Canadiens, a move that delighted Leaf fans. Toronto hosted the NHL All-Star game and the entry draft in 2002.

Dryden was often the face and voice of upper management to the media, a role he handled well. He developed his sense of humour, and his thoughtful answers to questions provided insight rare among former NHL players. His methodical approach was too slow for some, but Dryden was dedicated to making the right choices for the right reasons and held his ground while understanding that issues and people change. Now he faces the great challenge of making a competitive Leafs team champions once again.

Maple Leaf stats:	Games	Wins	Losses	Ties
As General Manager: regular season	164	75	73	16
playoffs	18	9	8	–

Ken Dryden at a press conference to announce the signing of Mats Sundin to a new contract. (GA)

CURTIS JOSEPH

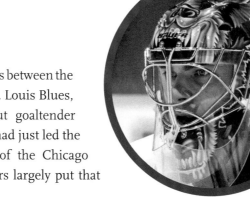

BEFORE THE 1993 playoff series between the Toronto Maple Leafs and the St. Louis Blues, few people knew much about goaltender Curtis Joseph. The netminder had just led the Blues to a four-game sweep of the Chicago Blackhawks, but most onlookers largely put that down to luck.

Leaf fans found out that Joseph had had a lot to do with the Blues' success when he made 62 saves during the first game of the next series. The Leafs should have won easily, but spectacular goaltending forced overtime and only a great goal by Doug Gilmour in the second extra session won the contest for Toronto. Two nights later Joseph made 57 stops as the Blues won in double overtime. The Leafs went on to win the series in seven games, but Joseph had made lasting impression.

Joseph became a goaltender for an old-fashioned reason — he couldn't skate very well. Rather than wobble about on the ice, he stayed put in the net and flopped down to stop the puck. He was successful and before he knew it, Joseph was stuck in goal. By the time he reached 18 it was too late to change positions, so he stayed with goaltending.

Joseph never developed a definitive style of play but relied on his quick reflexes. He was ultracompetitive and never gave up on a shot, no matter where he was around the net. His approach made him look like a flopper but he could be a stand-up goalie when required. At 5'11" and 190 pounds he was not one of the bigger goalies in the NHL, but he had a way of getting into the right spot to make a save. Joseph has never patterned himself after another goaltender and believes in doing whatever works best. It is a philosophy that seems to work.

Joseph grew up in Sharon, Ontario, and played all his minor hockey in the area. He attended high school in Newmarket while playing junior hockey for Richmond Hill of the Ontario Provincial Hockey League. His good play there was noticed and he was offered a position with the famed Notre Dame College in Wilcox, Saskatchewan. He played one year at Notre Dame (posting a 25–4–7 record) before attending the University of Wisconsin on a scholarship for the

1988–89 season, going 21–11–5.

The NHL had never drafted him but scouts had the young netminder under observation. As a free agent Joseph could sign wherever he pleased and the Blues gave him a good enough contract to leave school. He played in 15 games for St. Louis in 1989–90, winning nine, and also played in Peoria of the International Hockey League that season for 23 games. He went 16–10–2 in 30 appearances the next season and the Blues had found themselves a quality netminder: he played for five years in St. Louis and won 137 games there.

Joseph was traded to the Edmonton Oilers in August 1995 and eventually signed a deal (he was a holdout) with the team that had him play in 34 games and win 15. The Oilers did not make the playoffs that year, but Joseph played in 72 games in 1996–97 and posted a 32–29–9 record. In the '97 playoffs, he stole a series for the Oilers when they knocked off the Dallas Stars in seven games: Edmonton fans still talk about his glove save on Joe Nieuwendyk in overtime in game 7 — the Oilers soon scored the winner shortly afterwards. It was the big save at the right moment, a Joseph trademark.

He played in 71 games for the Oilers in the next season, but a new contract was out of the question in "small market" Edmonton. Joseph was once again a free agent and seemed destined to sign with Philadelphia, which was looking for a goalie, but the Flyers decided to sign John Vanbiesbrouck instead and the Maple Leafs pounced on Joseph.

The Leafs had finished the 1997–98 season with only 30 wins and were spectators when the playoffs began. Toronto management decided to make changes that included a new coach in Pat Quinn. They had a good goalie in Felix Potvin, but when Leafs general manager Ken Dryden ran into agent Don Meehan at a local store he inquired about the status of Joseph and learned he was still available. The Leafs signed Joseph on July 15, 1998, in the hope that he would improve on Potvin's performance; they also hoped to make a good trade for their incumbent netminder and eventually got defenceman Bryan Berard in return.

Joseph won his first game as a Maple Leaf, a 2–1 victory over the

Curtis Joseph was signed as a free agent by the Leafs in 1998 after he left the Edmonton Oilers. [DM]

Left: Curtis Joseph helped the Leafs win six playoff series. [DM]

Detroit Red Wings, and went on to win 35 games for the club in 1998–99. In the playoffs he practically won the Leafs' opening-round series against Philadelphia on his own, with two shutouts and three games in which he gave up just one goal. The Leafs got by the Pittsburgh Penguins in the next round before losing to Buffalo in the Eastern Conference final. Joseph looked tired by the end of the playoffs and gave up a few goals that normally he would have stopped, but Leaf fans welcomed the new hero with open arms.

For the next two seasons Joseph won 69 games and was the best Leaf on a nightly basis. He shone again in the playoffs, taking the team past the Ottawa Senators in two straight years. But two consecutive losses to the New Jersey Devils kept the Leafs from advancing; Joseph performed well, but the team faltered at key moments.

The start of the 2001–2 season brought new talk about a contract and Joseph's role on the Canadian Olympic team to be coached by Quinn. Joseph's play in the season leading up to the Salt Lake City Olympic games was good, but below his usual high standard. He was selected for the Olympic squad but was not effective in an opening loss to Sweden and was replaced by Martin Brodeur, who did not lose a game and gave Quinn no reason to replace him, though Joseph wanted to play again.

In his first game back with the Leafs, Joseph broke a bone in his hand and played only in one game (a win over Pittsburgh) from late February to the second week of April. The playoffs were to be his redemption and a possible springboard to a new contract with the Leafs or another NHL club.

Joseph did not get off to a great start in the 2002 playoffs — rust and his hand injury were factors — but he gradually got back into top form. He won two game sevens, against the New York Islanders and the Ottawa Senators, and was outstanding in the Eastern Conference final against the Carolina Hurricanes. His performance against the 'Canes gave his team a chance to win the series but the Leafs attackers were not up to the task, scoring only six times in the six-game series.

In June 2002, "Cujo" turned down a generous offer from the Leafs to sign with Detroit, a team he believes has a better chance of winning a Stanley Cup in the near future.

Growing up north of Toronto, I idolized most of the players who played on the Maple Leafs. To actually put the sweater on and be a part of the Maple Leafs team is extremely exciting. Curtis Joseph, Leafs program, December 12, 1998

Maple Leaf stats:	GP	Wins	Losses	Ties	Shutouts	GAA
As General Manager: regular season	249	133	88	27	17	2.42
playoffs	60	32	28	–	8	2.44

TOMAS KABERLE

WHEN A PLAYER is selected 204th overall, he is not expected to have a big impact on his new club. Few knew much about defenceman Tomas Kaberle when the Leafs drafted him in 1996 and he was still an unknown quantity when he made the team to start the 1998–99 season. But Kaberle quickly proved that he belonged in the lineup.

The Leafs wanted to implement a puck movement system and Kaberle showed tremendous poise with the puck, which made the young blueliner a perfect fit for the new-look Toronto squad. In his first game in a Leafs uniform, he played for 29 minutes—more than any other player—in a 2–1 win over the Stanley Cup champion Detroit Red Wings on the opening night of the season. It looked as if the Leafs had found a diamond in the rough.

Kaberle began playing hockey at age five. He had a leg up on the competition: his father, Frantisek, was an international player for Czechoslovakia and his older brother, also Frantisek, was destined to join Tomas in the NHL. Young Tomas rose through the ranks in the Czech Republic without overwhelming anyone with his numbers, averaging about 20 points a season.

The Leafs saw enough in him to take a chance on the baby-faced defenceman. They felt he needed some time in St. John's with their farm club, but Kaberle played only two games there before finding himself in the NHL. Like all young defenders he had some difficulty adjusting to the pace, but he got into 57 games in 1998–99 and recorded 22 points. Two of his four goals were game winners, including an overtime marker against the Montreal Canadiens on December 5, 1998.

In 1999–2000 Kaberle played in all 82 games, scoring seven goals and notching up 33 assists. His puck-handling skills continued to improve and his skating stride was as smooth as ever; Kaberle's main strength was getting the puck out of the Leafs' end with pinpoint passing and then joining the rush. He had a good shot from the point and his vision was excellent. He had a sharp sense of anticipation that told him when to attack and when to hang back.

Kaberle was not very physical and had only 62 penalty minutes in four seasons with the Leafs but at 6'2" and 190 pounds he could handle the rough stuff. He sometimes got into trouble when he hung onto the puck too long, but had nonetheless set up 119 goals in his career as a Leaf through 2001–2. During the 2000–2001 season, Kaberle recorded 45 points, but that year is best remembered for a trade that never happened: the Leafs refused to give up Kaberle for the Philadelphia Flyers superstar Eric Lindros. Only time will tell if they made the right decision.

Before the 2001–2 season Kaberle had a contract dispute with the Leafs (he had been making $250,000), but he finally signed a new deal and played in 69 games. He came back strongly by putting up 39 points (10 goals and 29 assists) and had only one minor penalty all year long. Kaberle was good in the 2002 postseason, but did not excel. His offensive skills continued to shine and some of his passes were works of art, but his rather weak defensive work cost the team dearly at times. Still, the Leafs are counting on Kaberle, Bryan McCabe and Aki Berg to serve as the nucleus of their defence for years to come.

Maple Leaf stats:	GP	G	A	P	PIM
regular season	290	27	119	146	62
playoffs	57	4	18	22	18

Tomas Kaberle had a career-high 45 points during the 2000–2001 season. (DM)

BRYAN McCABE

FOR A YOUNG PLAYER just 26 in 2002, Bryan McCabe had moved around a lot in his brief NHL career. He was drafted 40th overall by the New York Islanders in 1993 after a junior career in the Western Hockey League with Medicine Hat, Spokane and Brandon. The 6'1", 201-pound swift-skating defenceman was also a member of Canada's gold medal-winning junior world championship squads in 1994 and 1995. He made the Islanders in 1995–96 and never played a game in the minors.

McCabe was with the Islanders for three seasons, but the club was constantly shifting players and McCabe found himself in Vancouver by the end of the 1997–98 season (after being named Islander captain at the start of the year at age 22). One season as a Canuck was all he saw of the west coast before he was shipped to Chicago.

McCabe spent the 1999–2000 campaign in the Windy City and recorded 25 points (six goals, 19 assists) before being traded again, this time to the Maple Leafs. Toronto did not want to give defenceman Alexander Karpovtsev the contract he was looking for and saw an opportunity to pick up a young blueliner. Former Leafs employee Mike Smith was now in charge of the Blackhawks and he could not resist adding Karpovtsev to his new club. The Leafs gladly accepted McCabe in the swap and have never looked back.

In Toronto, McCabe improved steadily and became the top defenceman on the team. His fine all-round play in 2000–2001 and 2001–2 indicated he would be a major part of the Maple Leafs for years to come.

In his first year with the Leafs, McCabe scored five goals and had 24 assists for a club that made the playoffs only on the last night of the season before nearly knocking off the New Jersey Devils in the second round. It was during the series against the Devils that McCabe started to show how well he could play in big games. He was given a new contract by the Leafs in the summer and produced a great campaign in 2001–2 with 17 goals and 43 points. In a game against the Phoenix Coyotes on December 11, 2001, McCabe had two goals and four points and set the team alight. He scored one goal by knocking in a Mats Sundin rebound and got another by taking a centering pass from Darcy Tucker and drilling a shot home. Bryan McCabe had arrived as a big-time player.

McCabe as a confident defender now knew how to use his talent and strength to great effect. The native of St. Catherines, Ontario, was still a strong physical presence and added a great deal of punch to the Leafs attack. Besides learning to play under control, McCabe developed a low, hard shot from the point that was starting to gain respect from opposing goalies.

McCabe was outstanding in the 2002 playoffs and had plenty of ice time. He responded to the challenge with some spectacular efforts and provided most of the offense mustered by Leafs defenders. He managed five goals in the postseason and became the undisputed leader of the Leafs blue line. McCabe looks to be a future captain and it seems the team would be wise to sign him to a long-term deal.

Maple Leaf stats:	GP	G	A	P	PIM
regular season	164	22	50	72	252
playoffs	31	7	8	15	46

Bryan McCabe's 17 goals tied him for second among all NHL defencemen in 2001–2. (DM)

233

ALEX MOGILNY

THE MAPLE LEAFS were very familiar with Alex Mogilny before they signed him as a free agent in the summer of 2001. He had just helped the New Jersey Devils knock Toronto out of the 2001 postseason, in part with a four-point effort in one game. The year before that, the Devils had eliminated the Leafs in the playoffs on the way to a Stanley Cup win and so, to match the competition, the Leafs thought they should take away an important part of New Jersey's roster. Mogilny wanted to stay in New Jersey, but when a good contract offer was not forthcoming from the Devils he was happy to sign with another Cup-contender.

Born in Khabarovk, Russia, Mogilny came to North America as a defector from the former Soviet Union in 1989. The Buffalo Sabres had drafted the talented winger 89th overall at the 1988 entry draft, but were not sure when he would play in the NHL. Mogilny took matters into his own hands and played for the Sabres as a 20-year-old in 1989–90. He scored 15 goals with 28 assists as a rookie and raised his goal-scoring totals to 30 and 39 over the next two seasons.

Mogilny was spectacular in 1992–93, scoring 76 goals and 127 points. He was in Buffalo for two more years but decided to move on when the Sabres refused to offer him a big contract; general manager John Muckler sent Mogilny to Vancouver in a deal that gave Buffalo centre Michael Peca. As a Canuck Mogilny had a great year in 1995–96, when he scored 55 times and earned 107 points. But he was considered a disappointment overall because of the high expectations of Vancouver management.

The Canucks were rather pleased to send Mogilny to New Jersey for Brendan Morrison and Denis Pederson, but the speedy skater improved his all-round game (as the Devils demand of all their players) and made an impact. He helped the Devils win their second Cup in 2000 and then scored 43 times in the 2000–2001 season. The Devils made it to the finals again, though they were beaten out by the Colorado Avalanche in seven games. Given his fine play, it was logical to assume Mogilny would get a decent contract offer, but the Devils were tight with a dollar (and deep in player development) so they decided to let him go as a free agent. The Leafs agreed to pay him $5.2 million a year and were glad to steal a star from one of their main competitors in the NHL's Eastern Conference.

Apart from an injury in early February, Mogilny was everything the Leafs had hoped for: he had 24 goals and 57 points in 66 games and made the Leafs second line very dangerous. Mogilny's superb passing skills were very evident on the power play and he appeared to have lost none of his speed. He remained one of the most skilled players in the NHL (420 career goals and 898 points in 846 games). He spoke to the media in a matter-of-fact style and knew that all teams are judged by what happens in the playoffs.

Mogilny responded to his first playoff as a Maple Leaf in 2002 with some clutch performances, first by scoring twice in game 7 against the New York Islanders, then with key goals in the last two games against the Ottawa Senators. He played hard against Carolina but could not deliver the heroics the Leafs required to reach the Stanley Cup finals for the first time since 1967.

Maple Leaf stats:	GP	G	A	P	PIM
regular season	66	24	33	57	8
playoffs	20	8	3	11	8

Alexander Mogilny led the team with eight goals during the 2002 playoffs. (DM)

PAT QUINN

WHEN PAT QUINN was let go as general manager of the Vancouver Canucks during the 1997–98 season he thought he was probably done with the NHL. He had managed or coached the Canucks since 1987 and enjoyed some success, including a Stanley Cup finals appearance in 1994. But when new owners took over the struggling club, the writing was on the wall for Quinn.

While he was contemplating his future, his friend Mike Smith was helping to manage the Maple Leafs. Smith knew the Leafs needed a coaching change and wondered if Quinn would consider going back behind the bench for the team he had played for between 1968 and 1970. Quinn would. Since his arrival in Toronto, the Leafs have been one of the most exciting teams in the NHL and have posted one of the best records, with 170 victories over four seasons.

Quinn's playing career was not stellar but he was a stay-at-home defenceman who was appreciated for his toughness and leadership. He was captain of the Atlanta Flames and played in 606 games and racked up 950 penalty minutes while producing 18 goals and 113 assists. He began his coaching career with Philadelphia and led the Flyers to the finals in 1980. He then went to the Los Angeles Kings for three seasons before moving to Vancouver.

Quinn wanted to bring some excitement to Toronto. He sought to implement a puck movement system and brought in players who were good at getting the puck up the ice quickly. In his first season with the team the Leafs scored 268 goals, the most in the league, and went all the way to the Eastern Conference final before a surging Buffalo team knocked them out.

Smith was let go by the Leafs at the end of the 1999 playoffs and Quinn was forced to add the general manager's duties to his job. He did not relish the idea of doing both, but he had capable assistants in Bill Watters and Mike Penny, who was hired away from the Canucks.

Quinn tried to retool the Leafs on at least three occasions in his search for the right balance. He was a conservative trader but dabbled extensively in the free-agent market for medium-range players. Quinn was intent on building Leafs player development and recruiting so that the team was not too dependent on making blockbuster deals or signing big-money free agents.

In 2001–2 Quinn coached Team Canada to victory at the Olympic Games in Salt Lake City. The country was ecstatic. Coaching a team heavy with superstars was not easy and every move was scrutinized by the media, but Quinn stayed the course. His next objective was to do the same for the Maple Leafs.

The Maple Leafs suffered an extraordinary number of injuries as the 2002 playoffs began and Quinn had to juggle his lineup constantly just to ice a team; at one point eight regulars were out. Somehow Toronto survived to win two rounds but as the club got healthier the team sputtered, losing the Eastern Conference final to the Carolina Hurricanes and missing out on their first Stanley Cup finals since 1967. Quinn experienced health problems of his own (an irregular heart beat), missing two playoff games behind the bench. At his season-ending press conference, he maintained he would keep both his titles despite health issues. Time will tell if this is best for Quinn and the Maple Leafs.

Maple Leaf stats:	Games	Wins	Losses	Ties
As Coach: regular season	328	170	122	35
playoffs	60	32	28	—

By the end of 2001–2, Pat Quinn had won 328 games in four seasons behind the Leafs bench. (DM)

GARY ROBERTS

DARRYL SITTLER made his share of great plays as captain of the Maple Leafs. In retirement he made another for the team, albeit inadvertently. He was in the audience when Calgary Flames left-winger Gary Roberts was receiving the Bill Masterton Trophy. Despite producing 22 goals and 24 assists in 1995–96, the bruising winger was about to announce his retirement due to severe neck and spinal injuries. Roberts was very touched when he noticed that Sittler was the first person to stand to give him an ovation as he accepted the Professional Hockey Writers Association award for perseverance and dedication. Although he missed the entire 1996–97 season, Roberts vowed to give it all he had to get back into the NHL and used Sittler's admiration as a motivating force. He also wanted to return and play for his daughter, Jordan.

Ironically, the problems that plagued Roberts had begun in Toronto when he was cross-checked by Leafs defenceman Bob Rouse during a game on November 9, 1991, at Maple Leaf Gardens. The hit from behind, one of the worst of many the winger had taken over a number of years, sent Roberts into the boards. That's the price power forwards like Roberts often pay.

Roberts combined physical play (over 200 penalty minutes, five times) with a deft touch around the goal and played with great energy, a style that allowed him to score 257 goals as a Flame. He was drafted 12th overall in 1984 and helped make the Calgary club one of the best teams in the NHL during the late '80s and early '90s. He scored 53 goals in 1991–92 and was on the Flames' Stanley Cup-winning team in 1989.

Tired of all the travelling involved in playing for a team in the West, Roberts felt it was best to resume his career in the East. He asked for a trade and the Flames sent him to the Carolina Hurricanes, where he played for three seasons. He scored 20 goals in 61 games in his first year back in the NHL and 23 in the 1999–2000 season, his last in Carolina. As an unrestricted free agent, the native of Whitby, Ontario wanted to go home to finish his career and he happily signed with the Maple Leafs.

Roberts is the type of player who enjoys the pressure of playing in Toronto. He adapted to his new team in no time and scored 29 times to lead it in goals in 2000–2001. In the 2001 playoffs, Roberts had 11 points in 11 games before the Leafs were stopped short by the New Jersey Devils. He had lost none of his enthusiasm for the game and soon became a great leader for the Leafs both on and off the ice.

As the 2001–2 season began Roberts was not pleased to be taken off the first line centred by Mats Sundin, but the consummate pro kept working hard and produced 21 goals and 48 points in 69 games played. He recorded his first hat trick as a Leaf on December 6, 2001, against the New York Rangers at Madison Square Garden. All three goals were typical of the way Roberts scored: one was on a tip-in; the next followed a Roberts barrage through the Ranger defence and flew between the pads of goalie Mike Richter; the third was a backhand shot scored after taking a pass while coming across the goal crease. One of the hardest-working players in the NHL, Roberts was missed whenever he was not able to play and injuries were the only thing that could stop him.

In the 2002 playoffs, Roberts became the Leafs leader, with superb performances as the team passed the New York Islanders and the Ottawa Senators. He threw his weight about recklessly and scored key goals in the first two rounds. The pounding he put his body through in the early going slowed him for the third round, against Carolina, and his goal-scoring touch was no longer evident. But no one could question Roberts' great heart and determination in nearly leading the team to its first Stanley Cup finals appearance since 1967.

Gary Roberts (#7) scored an overtime winner against Ottawa in the second round of the 2002 playoffs that ended the third-longest game in Leafs history. (DM)

Maple Leaf stats:	GP	G	A	P	PIM
regular season	151	50	51	101	172
playoffs	30	9	21	30	56

MATS SUNDIN

ON THE PLANE RIDE home from Vancouver, where the Maple Leafs had lost the Western Conference final for the second year in a row, the Leafs' coach and general manager decided changes were needed if the team was to keep challenging for the Stanley Cup. The players knew manager Cliff Fletcher would not stand still and that coach Pat Burns would be pressing for new talent. Most in Toronto could sense that something dramatic was going to happen, but few were ready for the announcement that was made at the NHL entry draft in Hartford on June 28, 1994.

The Leafs sent Wendel Clark, captain and heart and soul of the team, and stalwart defender Sylvain Lefebvre to the Quebec Nordiques for Mats Sundin. Fletcher was never afraid to pull the trigger on a deal, but this was big even for him. Clark's departure was never going to be a popular move in Toronto, but Fletcher and Burns knew whom they wanted. It is ironic that they would be long gone from Toronto before Sundin saw his best days in a Leafs uniform.

Toronto had had its eye on the 6'4", 220-pound Swedish-born Sundin for some time and his name had circulated in trade rumours during the 1993–94 season. The Leafs were waiting for Quebec to make him available and quickly moved in with their offer. The Leafs also got forward Todd Warriner (a disappointment) and defenceman Garth Butcher (a bust) in the deal, but Sundin was their main target.

Sundin had gone to the Nordiques as the first player chosen overall in the 1989 entry draft. His first NHL season was 1990–91 and he proved that Quebec had made a good choice, with 23 goals and 59 points. In his third year in the league, Sundin produced a career-high 47 goals and 114 points, but the Nordiques were dismissed in six games by the Montreal Canadiens in the playoffs. After they missed the playoffs in 1993–94, the Nordiques were anxious to make moves and willing to sacrifice their big center-right-winger for a leader in Clark and a sound defenceman in Lefebvre.

When he arrived in Toronto, Sundin made it clear that he could not duplicate Clark's game. Sundin is all finesse, and most effective when he uses his superior skating skills and hard shot. He sees the ice very well and his backhand drive — he is one of the few players in the NHL to still use this shot — is the best in the game. He can score from just about anywhere on the ice and would probably produce many more goals if he shot more instead of looking to pass.

Sundin has never produced fewer than 70 points as a Maple Leaf and by 2001–2 had accumulated 608 points with Toronto. He led the team in points for a club-record eight straight years (from 1994–95 to 2001–2) and had been the best player on the team since the day of his arrival. Although Sundin put up good numbers, the team had started to decline just as he began his career as a Leaf and the fans did not forgive any deficiencies in his game as a result.

Many players and coaches had come and gone in Toronto during the eight seasons Sundin had played there and was the one constant throughout the turmoil. He learned to live with the pressures of playing in a hockey-obsessed city and seemed eventually to seek the limelight much more than when he first arrived. He accepted the captaincy — the first non-Canadian to do so — and became comfortable with the responsibilities of the job. Well-spoken in his media interviews, he was rarely upset when challenged about his performance.

Sundin has the respect of his teammates and they are usually the first to defend their captain against unfair criticism; nobody can question Sundin's immense talents but there was doubt that he had what it takes to lead a team deep into the playoffs. He silenced many critics with a 2001 playoff performance that included 11 points in 13 games (the sweep of Ottawa was initiated by a Sundin overtime goal in the first game of the series). More importantly, Sundin showed a willingness to lead physically, a quality not always evident before. After the arrival of Pat Quinn as Leafs coach in 1998, Sundin thrived in the offensive system the bench boss liked to employ. Effective on the attack, he could lead a rush or finish a play with equal ability.

In the 2001–2 season Sundin continued his strong performance with 80 points, fourth overall in the NHL. He scored 41 goals

Mats Sundin finished tied for second (with Glen Murray and Bill Guerin of Boston) in goals scored with 41 during the 2001–2 season. (DM)

Mats Sundin (#13) continued a running feud with Ray Bourque of Boston (#77) whenever the two met on the ice. (DM)

To win a Stanley Cup in Toronto would

beat anything else that you could do as a hockey player.

Mats Sundin, *Leafs Insider*, 2001–2.

for the second time in his career as a Leaf and was the best player on the team most nights. Sundin was playing a more aggressive game. The large Swede had many opportunities to flash the big smile he often showed after scoring a goal or making a nice pass to set up a teammate. Leaf fans were looking forward to seeing Sundin perform some playoff magic.

It was not to be in 2002. He broke a bone in his wrist in the first game of the playoffs and did not return until the third round against Carolina, but the Leafs ran out of time before he could find his range. Sundin managed one goal against the Hurricanes but it was not nearly enough to get the Leafs to the finals. He was named to the second all-star team at the end of the season.

Maple Leaf stats:	GP	G	A	P	PIM
regular season	606	262	346	608	442
playoffs	61	27	30	57	52

DARCY TUCKER

A NATIVE OF CASTOR, Alberta, Darcy Tucker was standing on skates at the age of two. He was playing organized hockey by age four and started to show a competitive edge that would take him all the way to the NHL. He played junior hockey with the Kamloops Blazers of the Western Hockey League for four seasons and won the Memorial Cup three times, in 1992, 1994 and 1995. He was a good goal scorer for the Blazers with 116 goals and 277 points over his last two years and was drafted 151st overall by the Montreal Canadiens in 1993. The only reason he didn't go higher in the entry draft was concern about his size, listed at 5'11", 185 pounds. The scouts didn't measure the largeness of his heart.

Tucker made the Canadiens in 1996–97 after spending a year with the Habs American Hockey League farm club in Fredericton, where he scored 29 goals and added 64 assists. He played in 73 games for Montreal that year and scored seven goals and 20 points. Midway through the next season he was sent to the Tampa Bay Lightning in a trade and had more chances to play. He scored 22 goals for Tampa in his only full season there, but the Lightning decided to move the feisty winger the next year. The Leafs offered winger Mike Johnson and defence prospect Marek Posmyk and that clinched the deal on February 9, 2000. About the only thing Leaf fans knew about Tucker was that he feuded with Toronto winger Steve Thomas; soon they would be cheering him for his reckless style and the grit he added to the club.

In his first 27 games as a Leaf, Tucker closed out the 1999–2000 season with seven goals and 10 assists before adding six points in 12 postseason games. He scored 16 times in 2000–2001, but was getting into far too much trouble with the referees and racked up 141 penalty minutes, many of them needless. To be fair, Tucker was concerned with protecting his teammate and brother-in-law Shayne Corson on the ice and at times he seriously lacked discipline. He was strong in the playoffs in a checking role and helped the Leafs nearly get past the New Jersey Devils.

Tucker returned to Toronto for the 2001–2 season with a new approach. Gone was the mouthing-off to officials and the overreactions on the ice. He still used his body as much as ever, but he realized he could be more effective if he stayed out of the penalty box and his total fell to 92 minutes. He scored a career-high 24 goals and 59 points (second most on the team), and displayed a touch around goal few had expected. He also led the team with a plus 24 rating, 14th best in the NHL.

Tucker's intensity was as high as ever and he still lost control on occasion — like the time a high hit on Washington defenceman Sergei Gonchar cost him a two-game suspension — but for the most part he stuck to hockey. He was at his most intense in the 2002 playoffs, fighting like a tiger though a hit from behind by Daniel Alfredsson of Ottawa severely injured Tucker's shoulder so that he missed three games and played hurt when he returned. A more mature Tucker had now become a very valuable member of the Toronto Maple Leafs.

Maple Leaf stats:	GP	G	A	P	PIM
regular season	186	47	66	113	228
playoffs	40	8	8	16	99

Darcy Tucker had his best season in 2001–2 when he scored 24 goals and 59 points, both good for second on the team. (DM)

DMITRY YUSHKEVICH

DMITRY YUSHKEVICH made quite an impression when he joined the NHL for the 1992–93 season as a member of the Philadelphia Flyers, who had drafted the 5'11", 208-pound defenceman 122nd overall in 1991. He scored five times and added 27 assists in his rookie year. He looked strong on the point and was not afraid to handle the puck. In his second year he scored 30 points, and he was an important part of the Flyers team that nearly got to the finals in 1995.

His good performance warranted a good contract but his agent, Mark Gandler, and Flyers management represented by general manager Bobby Clarke did not see eye to eye. Clarke knew Toronto wanted to add an experienced defenceman who was not too old, so he called Leafs general manager Cliff Fletcher and was offered a couple of high draft choices, including a first-rounder.

The Leafs hoped Yushkevich could help rebuild their defence and just as he had in Philadelphia, Yushkevich made quite an initial impression. Coach Pat Burns compared him to former Leafs hard rock Bob Baun, since both could dish out punishing bodychecks. But as the 1995–96 season wore on Yushkevich's play declined. Burns was gone before the season was over and knee woes kept Yushkevich out of the lineup: the knee problem was described as "chronic," but Fletcher claimed that he had known about it prior to the deal and insisted everything would be fine. The next two seasons were not great ones for the team or Yushkevich, who seemed to be uncomfortable as a Leaf and was prone to chasing the puck in his own end. His offence virtually vanished.

The arrival of Pat Quinn as coach saved Yushkevich's career in Toronto. Quinn upgraded the talent on the blue line, adding capable youngsters like Danny Markov and Tomas Kaberle and good veterans like Alexander Karpovtsev and Sylvain Cote, and Yushkevich seemed to understand that he didn't have to do everything by himself any more. He settled into a top defensive role and was paired with Markov to form an effective unit. Yushkevich was outstanding in shutting down Jaromir Jagr in the 1999 playoffs and the Leafs reached the Eastern Conference final. He was given alternate captain status on the team and seemed to prosper in that role.

Yushkevich thrives on taking ice away from the opposition and in delivering a devastating hit at just the right moment. He is a feisty competitor and regained his offence as his confidence rebounded, scoring a career-high six goals in 2001–2. He and Gandler feuded with the Leafs in a contract dispute before the 2000–2001 season, but he came back to play in his usual robust style as soon as everything was settled. He earned his reputation as a real warrior (once playing with two broken toes).

A potentially life-threatening blood clot in his leg cut his 2001–2 season to 55 games, yet Yushkevich was determined to play in the playoffs and it was rumoured that doctors had prepared a plan to allow him to play while still taking blood thinners. But the Leafs were worried about their legal liability and the potential danger to his health and finally decided to keep Yushkevich out of the lineup. They sent the veteran to Florida for Robert Svehla in July of 2002.

Maple Leaf stats:	GP	G	A	P	PIM
regular season	506	25	110	135	409
playoffs	44	2	10	12	38

Dmitry Yushkevich (#36) tries to block a pass to New Jersey's John Madden in front of the Leaf net occupied by Curtis Joseph. Yushkevich is one of the best shot blockers in the NHL. (DM)

THE REBIRTH OF PLAYOFF
MANIA: '78, '93, '99 AND 2002

by John Iaboni

STANLEY CUP PARADES were once a frequent rite of spring in downtown Toronto, but more than three decades have elapsed since the last cavalcade up Bay Street to Old City Hall. Still, the passion for the Leafs spreads from one generation to another. So, too, does that burning desire to unite and celebrate each playoff phase, hoping and praying that this year the drought will end, the Stanley Cup will return and the entire city will shut down for one big party.

In recent years April and May in Toronto have been spellbinding times during which all that matters is the Leafs' Stanley Cup run. GO LEAFS GO signs, blue-and-white jerseys and Maple Leafs flags are everywhere. Victories are celebrated with horn-honking and each advance in a playoff round sparks a mini-parade of enthusiasm. Welcome to the rebirth of playoff mania, even though the Leafs haven't reached the playoff finals since cradling the Stanley Cup at Maple Leaf Gardens on May 2, 1967.

In the years from 1967 to 2002 the Leafs qualified for the playoffs 24 times, more often than not as pretenders to the crown. The zeniths occurred in 1978, 1993, 1994, 1999 and 2002, when reaching the NHL's final four restored pride in the organization and heralded cries of "Wait till next year."

After three playoff misses and seven quarter-final series losses in the decade after 1967, the Leafs of '78 rejuvenated the franchise. Coached by Roger Neilson, the team accumulated 92 points before sweeping the Los Angeles Kings in the best-of-three preliminary round. Then came the New York Islanders, 19 points superior in the standings and heavy favourites in the quarter-finals against the Leafs. What developed was a war on ice and an upset.

A serious eye injury to Leafs defenceman Borje Salming in game 4 had many thinking the magical run would come to an end. But the Leafs were determined, winning the seventh game when Lanny McDonald, battered wrist and all, scored at 4:13 of overtime on Long Island. Thousands of fans hit the streets and crowded Toronto airport in the wee hours of the morning to greet the team's return.

McDonald's goal became a benchmark of Leafs euphoria for a new generation. It was a beacon that grew in intensity as the years

of living in the fog mounted. Oh, sure, hearts flickered in 1986 and '87 when the Leafs lost seven-game divisional finals to the St. Louis Blues and the Detroit Red Wings, respectively. But those events disguised deep-rooted problems within the organization that wouldn't be turned around until the 1990s.

When general manager Cliff Fletcher obtained Doug Gilmour as the centrepiece of a blockbuster trade with the Calgary Flames on January 2, 1992, the club's fortunes changed. Led by the gritty Gilmour and coached by the demanding Pat Burns, the Leafs emerged as serious Stanley Cup contenders in back-to-back years beginning in 1993.

Nikolai Borschevsky's goal at 2:13 of overtime in game 7 at Detroit propelled the Leafs to an exciting conquest of the Red Wings. Amid the sweltering heat at the Gardens, the Leafs needed a seventh-game win to oust the St. Louis Blues in the divisional final. Downtown Toronto was alive with hockey fever that night and it was ready to celebrate again in the Western Conference championship one round later. But Wayne Gretzky and the Kings dashed those Stanley Cup dreams, winning in seven games.

The Vancouver Canucks halted the Leafs' charge in five games during the conference championship in 1994. Then came a series of further setbacks: quarter-final losses in 1995 to Chicago and 1996 to St. Louis gave way to missing the playoffs altogether in 1997 and 1998.

Ken Dryden, tutored in the winning ways of the Montreal Canadiens, joined the Leafs as president on May 30, 1997. He lured Pat Quinn to the organization in June 1998 and in Quinn's first four years as head coach the Leafs registered 97, 100, 90 and 100 points.

Vacating the Gardens for Air Canada Centre in 1999, the Leafs required six games to dispose of the Philadelphia Flyers and Pittsburgh Penguins for a showdown with the Buffalo Sabres in the Eastern Conference championship. The Sabres terminated the Leafs' Stanley Cup quest in five games, but Toronto's competitive spirit ignited another frenzy among its legion of fans.

The New Jersey Devils, en route to the Stanley Cup cham-

A Wayne Gretzky (#99) hat trick in game seven of the 1993 Western Conference final stopped the Leafs from advancing to the finals for the first time since 1967. (HHOF).

pionship in 2000 and the final in 2001, halted the Leafs in their tracks in conference semifinals along the way.

And then came 2002. Never had a team endured so many injuries to key players. Even Quinn would succumb to a heart condition for a time in the third round. However, the patchwork lineup that at times drew one-third of its players from the St.

John's Maple Leafs found a way to win in seven games over the Islanders and the Ottawa Senators before losing in six to the Carolina Hurricanes.

The gas tank, clearly on empty, still had enough fumes in it to fuel playoff hysteria and lift expectations once more. All the Leafs have to do is deliver.

🍁

conclusion

The Future of the Maple Leafs

As the Toronto Maple Leafs head into the future, the organization will be challenged in new and interesting ways. Many of the issues — such as controlling escalating salaries — will involve the National Hockey League head office, but the Toronto club managers will have plenty to consider on their own. Here are some of the key issues.

There has been no Stanley Cup parade in Toronto since the days of captain George Armstrong, shown here holding the fabled trophy for youngsters to see up close. (HHOF)

The Leafs are hoping centre Nik Antropov, drafted tenth overall in 1999, will make a contribution to the team in the near future. (DM)

The Entry Draft

The Leafs recently hired Barry Trapp to head their amateur scouting staff. Respected and experienced, he also had a successful track record in evaluating juniors. Trapp now reports to the Director of Player Personnel, Mike Penny, who moved to the Leafs from the Vancouver Canucks (just like Pat Quinn) in July 2000.

The Leafs need to make more quality selections with their middle draft picks and not just rely on the first-round selection, as they have done so often in the past. They have had some success in taking Europeans in the late rounds but have not done that well since selecting Tomas Kaberle 204th overall in 1996. Unlike teams such as the New Jersey Devils, Toronto has generally stayed away from American college players (the selection of Jeff Farkas 57th overall in 1997 was an exception), preferring to select Europeans. U.S. college players are generally well-trained, in part due to bountiful practice time, and seem better prepared for the NHL than many other amateurs. The Americans are generally not as skilled or flashy as the Europeans, but they are already in North America and often more familiar with what it takes to play in the NHL. Trapp should be a big help in selecting Canadian junior prospects since that is his area of expertise.

However, even with Trapp on board, like many other NHL teams the Maple Leafs are simply not offering contracts to players they consider marginal prospects. That means time and money is spent on scouting but the players selected are not always signed. This strategy is intended to save money over the long term, but it means the team risks losing players to other NHL clubs since draft choices re-enter the draft if they are not signed. Decisions made at the entry draft will become more crucial to Leafs fortunes in the years to come.

Top Prospects

The best junior prospect under contract in the Leafs organization is centre Brad Boyes. He is expected to be an offensive player but will probably have to spend some time with the farm team in St. John's and add a little bulk to his six-foot, 181-pound frame to withstand the rigours of the NHL. Ten junior players whose rights belong to the Leafs played in the 2001 World Junior Championships and the club

hopes defencemen like Jay Harrison (already signed) and Carlo Colaiacovo will be on the Toronto blue line in the near future. Four European-born defencemen were also in the tournament and two forwards and a goaltender give the Leafs more prospects to consider signing.

As for the professional prospects already in the organization, the Leafs truly hope that Luca Cereda, Alexei Ponikarovsky, Karel Pilar, Petr Svoboda, Christian Chartier, Mikael Tellqvist and Sebastian Centomo will all make contributions to the big team in the near future (some already have done so). They also hope big (6'5") and talented Nik Antropov can recover from two serious knee operations and make a contribution to the team or serve as trade bait.

The 2002 playoffs showed that every team needs a strong farm club when injuries strike: for one of the few times in recent history, the Leafs system produced the support needed to get through the season and, more importantly, the postseason. Lou Crawford coached the St. John's club to success in 2001–2 and his work with prospects and veterans such as Paul Healey and Bobby Wren shows that he might be a top candidate for NHL employment as well.

Marketing the Team

In their never-ending search for additional revenues, the Leafs will keep putting their logo on just about any item imaginable. The team has developed a merchandizing catalogue it intends to distribute throughout southern Ontario and especially in Greater Toronto to bring the club closer to people who cannot get to a game at the Air Canada Centre. The Maple Leafs still own the best-selling hockey sweater in Canada (second only to the Detroit Red Wings in North America). A recent survey found that the Leafs logo was the most recognized by Canadians, proof that the blue or white Maple Leaf on the Toronto uniform is as much a national symbol as the red maple leaf on the flag.

Roger Edwards has designed excellent, albeit expensive, clothing for the club and the Leafs have done a great job of marketing their old multi-point logo, so familiar to fans in the '50s and '60s. They have also developed new possibilities by creating merchandise with the

Maple Leafs owner Steve Stavro knows how much the city of Toronto wants to win a Stanley Cup. (GA)

Centre Brad Boyes is the Maple Leafs top prospect in 2002. (GA)

overlapping letters "TML." The club seems to have found a nice compromise between promoting its current team and honouring its illustrious past with a variety of items to appeal to fans of all ages.

Videos, books and other printed materials will only become more plentiful. The Leafs website (www.leafs.com) also offers products and gives fans another avenue for contact and analysis. With four major newspapers, two all-sports radio stations and three sports television networks in the Toronto area all pursuing Maple Leaf stories there is no lack of interest in the team. The media, although justifiably critical of the team at times, in effect serves as another "marketer" and that can only be good news for the team's coffers.

Leafs TV

Leafs TV, the club's official channel, is a digital channel currently only available by special subscription. For the moment, it provides Toronto fans with classic games, pre- and postgame interviews, Leaf games replayed in an hour and features on current and past players. But Leaf fans better get used to regular-season games being broadcast on the team's digital channel, because this is likely to happen in the very near future. The station was to show eight preseason games to start the 2002–3 season, and some of the Leafs schedule (midweek games are the most likely) will inevitably follow.

The only way Leafs TV will not show regular-season games will be if the conventional television networks continue to pay large amounts of money for broadcast rights. Leaf games earn high ratings, especially in the playoffs, but just how much are they worth? The Sports Network (TSN) paid a great deal over the perceived market value for the Leafs regional TV package in 2000 but might not do so again. There are indications that all networks will have to cut back on rights fees and the Leafs could be affected, perhaps to the point of putting their games on their own station.

A game on December 15, 2001 between the Leafs and the Montreal Canadiens broadcast on Leafs TV because of a labour dispute at the CBC attracted 59,000 viewers on a Saturday night, despite the channel's limited distribution. One could imagine those people (and many others if the channel is made more readily available) pay-

ing $5 to $10 for the privilege. Maple Leaf Sports and Entertainment president Richard Peddie has said the Leafs might have to use their own station because they need to make the kind of money required to ice championship teams. He also believes that the season-ticket holder pays too much of the freight and that the Leafs need to "control more of their content" to give subscribers more reasons to buy Leafs TV. Peddie's goal is to see Leafs TV make a profit by its fifth year, but Leafs management would be wise not to touch *Hockey Night in Canada*, which in 2002 is still the best marketing vehicle for the Leafs.

Free Agency

Free agency is here to stay in the NHL and the age of 31 (when a player becomes unrestricted and can sign with any team) may be reduced through the collective bargaining process. The Leafs will always have the resources to keep their own players and entice free agents to Toronto and that should allow the team to be competitive on a yearly basis, but only if management is willing to make funds available to pursue the best free agents on the market. If the Maple Leafs do a better job of drafting and developing players the reliance on free agents will be reduced considerably, while signing players who have always wanted to play for the team (like Gary Roberts and Shayne Corson) will still be an option.

Signing free agents is risky, because if players do not produce as expected their large contracts cannot be moved easily. The Leafs will also be able to pick up players by assuming contracts other teams do not wish to pay, but they have rarely used this method and seem unwilling to do so. The one exception was Robert Reichel, who was signed when Phoenix would not pay him what he wanted, but that did not exactly work out as planned in 2001–2. They only signed one free agent in 2002: goalie Ed Belfour, brought in to replace Curtis Joseph.

Maple Leaf Gardens

The Leafs' old home stands on some very valuable property yet remained closed in June 2002. The sale of the building would help the Leafs pay off the debt incurred in building the Air Canada Centre, but there is no apparent movement in this direction. One redevelopment idea fell through, but the Toronto real estate market in 2002 was described as "white-hot" and the land on which the Gardens sits should bring top dollar if sold. The arena has been declared a historical landmark by the city of Toronto and Leafs owner Steve Stavro has said he will not tear it down. But there is no point in letting the building just sit there.

In 2002 it seemed likely that, eventually, condominiums would be built on the site, either inside the Gardens structure or in a newly erected building. The Leafs would like to have their practice rink at the Gardens, but it is not clear how that would work. If the land sale proves more valuable the whole process might end up in the courts, as the team would have to get permission to knock the building down. Like anyone who buys a new home, the Leafs should be allowed to do what they want with their old house (old hockey buildings in Montreal, Boston and Chicago were torn down or revamped in recent years) even if this leads to the very sad day when the Gardens no longer stand at the corner of Church and Carlton Streets.

Commitment of Ownership

Steve Stavro was still very much in charge of the Maple Leafs as the 2002–3 season approached. In many ways he is the exact opposite of his late friend Harold Ballard — notably in keeping a low profile in the media — but he has as tight a grip on the budget as any past Leafs owner. Stavro paid more for the whole operation than he wanted to, but did not walk away. He knows what the Leafs mean to Toronto and Canada and that he will be remembered more for owning the hockey club than for any of his other business interests. Stavro added partners (including the Ontario Teachers Pension Fund, the Toronto Dominion Bank and construction magnate Larry Tanenbaum) when he purchased the Leafs and went on to found Maple Leaf Sports and Entertainment. But questions about his long-term involvement remain. It has been suggested that the Leafs would be better off in the hands of a multimedia company with more financial resources to deal with their needs.

Under Stavro it has become apparent that the Leafs are willing to spend money up to a point. The ownership is very concerned with turning a profit, as it should be, but this approach risks stopping the team from getting the players needed to win a championship. During the 2001–2 season the Leafs had the eighth-highest payroll (US$48,715,958) in the NHL, and they have promised to be in the top ten every year. But they probably need to be in the top five to win a Stanley Cup title.

Leafs president Ken Dryden says the team's objective is be competitive year after year. That is a worthy sentiment, but is it realistic in a 30-team NHL? Will the Leafs continue to shy away from adding the best players in the game (like Jaromir Jagr or Pavel Bure) because of budget worries? The size of the payroll has always been an issue, but at some point the club will have to decide just how badly it wants the Cup and show the same commitment Dallas, Colorado and Detroit did in winning championships.

Relationship with Fans

Former Leafs coach Pat Burns once remarked how amazing it was that Toronto fans would greet the team at the airport after a playoff *loss!* Fans in Montreal would react a little differently, he added. Leaf fans are a very loyal group who will endure just about anything to see their team win, and they have clearly told the club they will give the Leafs the financial resources to compete in the upper echelons of the NHL. Many in the Toronto media suggest this is a flaw in the populace and that the Leafs would do more to win if fans were not so supportive.

One of the smartest Leaf players in recent years recognized the folly of pointing the finger at supporters: "How can the fans be blamed? Because they stayed loyal and continued to buy tickets?" Leaf centre Alyn McCauley asked in a recent *Toronto Star* interview (May 25, 2002). "Maybe the Leafs should have been better in those years."

The media pressure should be placed squarely on the shoulders of owners who need to show fans they will spend when needed and not be so concerned with profits. What other team could charge full prices for exhibition games and get away with it? How many teams can boast about making a $2-million profit on a playoff game? Do other NHL clubs take in as much as $150,000 (before expenses) per playoff game on food, beverage and merchandizing sales?

These numbers — though they are only estimates — show that the money is clearly there. And dishing out more dough would probably give the Leafs an even greater return. A championship would be a great boon to Leafs TV, for example, and the sale of championship merchandise would be astronomical. The idea that a Stanley Cup title would quench the fans thirst for glory holds no water. In short, there is no reason not to go for it all and the term "budgetary constraints" should be heard less often.

The Leafs 2002 playoff team captured the imagination of the city like few other teams since the Stanley Cup-winning squad of 1967. Bruised, battered and severely injured, the team endured great hardship to advance all the way to the Eastern Conference final. Against tremendous odds they kept battling and winning with an indomitable spirit rarely shown in pro sports today. All Leaf fans were proud of their team and the Toronto newspapers were full of stories describing the lengths devoted followers went to show their enthusiasm for the club, as they always do as soon as the playoffs begin. This most storied franchise has unwavering support from the young and old, men and women. Many fans remember how they grew up idolizing Dave Keon, Darryl Sittler, Lanny McDonald, Borje Salming, Wendel Clark, or Doug Gilmour and today's kids look up to current stars like Gary Roberts and Mats Sundin. Even current Leaf players like Roberts, Corson and Sundin mention former Leafs heroes like McDonald, Sittler and Salming respectively as childhood heroes.

The Maple Leafs are clearly a special team to many people and that passion has been passed from generation to generation since 1927. Becoming a Maple Leaf is still a fantasy for many children and putting on the team sweater for the first time is a precious moment whenever it happens. To be seen on *Hockey Night in Canada* playing for the team in blue and white is a dream that only the Toronto Maple Leafs hockey club can fulfill.

Mats Sundin (smiling) *celebrates a goal with Alex Mogilny* (#89)*, Tomas Kaberle* (#15) *and Bryan McCabe.* (DM)

Index

Page numbers in **bold** refer to illustrations

advertising, 12
Air Canada Centre, 13, 200, 222, 225
Anderson, Glenn, 202–3, **203**
Andreychuk, Dave, **204**, 204–5, **205**
Antropov, Nik, **246**
Apps, Sylvester "Syl," **39**, 46, 48, 50, **52**, 52–55, **53**, **54**, **55**
Armstrong, George, **103**, 104–7, **105**, **106**, **107**, **117**, 245
Art Ross Trophy, 56

Bailey, Irvine "Ace," 19, **20**, 20–21, **21**, 119
Balfour, Earl, 115
Ballard, Harold, 12–13, 20, 91, 146, 151, 164, **184**, 184–85, **185**
Balon, Dave, 109
Barber, Bill
Barilko, Bill, **78**, 78–79, **79**, 96–97, **97**
Bassett, John, 12, 92
Baun, Bob, 108–9, **109**
Bentley, Max, **51**, 56, **56**
Bickell, J. P., 40
Bickell Trophy. *See* J. P. Bickell Memorial Cup
Blair, Andy, 22, **22**
Bodnar, Gus, **49**, 56, 57, **57**
Boesch, Garth, **46**, **85**
Boston Bruins, 29, **55**, **129**
Boudrias, Andre, **122**
Bourque, Ray, **239**
Bower, Johnny, 110–13, **111**, **112**, **113**
Boyes, Brad, 246, **247**
Brewer, Carl, **114**, 114–15, **115**
Brimsek, Frank, 55
Broad Street Bullies, 178

Broda, Walter "Turk," **51**, 58, 58–61, **59**, **60**, **61**, **100**
Burns, Pat, 13, 200

Cahan, Larry, **143**
Calder Trophy, 57, **57**, 86, 87, 119, 130, 135
Canada Cup, 169
Carr, Lorne, 62, **62**
Carson, Bill, **17**
Chabot, Lorne, 23, **23**
Chadwick, Ed, 81
Cherry, Don, 72–73
Chicago Black Hawks (later Blackhawks), 19, 45
Church, Jack, 62
Clancy, Francis Michael "King," 10, **24**, 24–27, **25**, **27**, 41, 196, **197**
Clancy, Terry, 24
Clancy, Tom "King," 24
Clark, Wendel, **15**, 196–97, **206**, 206–9, **208**, **209**
Coffey, Paul, **194**
Conacher, Charlie, 28, 28–29, **29**
Conn Smythe Trophy, 130
Connelly, Wayne, **137**
Corson, Shayne, 228, **228**
Cotton, Harold, 30, **30**, 72

Damphousse, Vincent, 186, **186**, **219**
Davidson, Bob, 53, 63, 63–64, 64
Day, Clarence "Hap," 19, **25**, **31**, 31–32, **32**, 48, **48**, 53, 146
Deacon, Don, 110
Delvecchio, Alex, **115**
Dickens, Ernie, 56
Doraty, Ken, 18
Dorey, Jim, **149**
Dryden, Ken, **156**, 229, **229**
Duff, Dick, 116–17, **117**
Durnan, Bill, **55**

Eagleson, Alan, 114, 139
Eddolls, Frank, 82
Ellett, Dave, **210**, 210–11, **211**
Ellis, Ron, **151**, **175**
Esposito, Phil, **165**
Ezinicki, Bill, **46**, **65**, 65–66, **66**

Favell, Doug, **151**
Ferguson, Elmer, 72
Ferguson, George, **150**
Finnigan, Frank, **25**
Fletcher, Cliff, 13, 200
"Flying Forts," 56
Foster Hewitt Memorial Award, 87
free agents, 201, 247
Fuhr, Grant, **199**

Gadsby, Bill, **133**
Gashouse Gang, **10**, 10–11
Gilbert, Rod, **112**
Gill, Todd, 187, **187**
Gilmour, Doug, 13, **14**, **198**, 212–15, **213**, **214**, **215**
Glennie, Brian, **151**
Godfrey, Warren, **134**
"Gold Dust Twins," 88
Goldham, Bob, **49**, 56, **95**
Green, Ted, **119**
Green, Travis, 226
Gregory, Jim, 150
Gretzky, Wayne, **243**

Hainsworth, George, **41**
Hall, Glenn, **139**
Hammarstrom, Inge, **148**
Hart Trophy, 69, 83
Hay, Bill, **139**
Henderson, Murray, 95
Henderson, Paul, 152–53, **153**
Heron, Red, 62
Hewitson, Bobby, 72
Hewitt, Bill, 12, 80

Hewitt, Foster, **11**, 11–12, 72–73, **73**, 75, 80, 80–81, **81**
Hextall, Ron, 219
Hillman, Larry, **113**
Hillman, Wayne, **105**, 139
Hockey Night in Canada, 12, 72–73, **247**, 249
Hollett, William "Flash," 41
Horner, Reginald "Red," 19, **33**, 33–34, **34**, **41**
Horton, Tim, 120–23, **121**, **122**, **123**
"Hound Line," 189
Howe, Gordie, 90, **145**
"Hue Line," 174
Hull, Brett, **214**

Iafrate, Al, 188, **188**
Imlach, George "Punch," **99**, 114, 124–25, **125**, 135, 146, **197**
Irvin, Dick, 18, 22, 35, **35**

J. P. Bickell Memorial Cup, 63, 89
Jackson, Harvey, 36, **36**, 42
Johnson, Tom, **131**
Johnston, Eddie, **106**, 119, **131**
Joseph, Curtis, 201, 209, **230**, 230–31, **231**

Kaberle, Tomas, 232, **232**, 249
Kelly, Leonard "Red," **111**, 126–29, 127–29
Kennedy, Ted, **53**, 82, 82–85, **83**, **84**, **85**, **100**, 223
Keon, Dave, **130**, 130–33, **131**, **132**, **133**
"Kid Line," 28, 36, 37
Klukay, Joe, **46**
Krushelnyski, Mike, **201**

Lach, Elmer, 67
Lady Byng Trophy, 37, 90, 127, 130
Laparde, Edgar, **59**

Leafs TV, 247
Leeman, Gary, 182, 189, **189, 220**
Lefebvre, Sylvain, 216, **216**
Lindros, Eric, **214**
Liut, Mike, **180**
Lonsberry, Ross, **173**
Lumley, Harry, 54, **90, 94**
Lynn, Vic, **84**

MacCauley, Alyn, **227**
MacDonald, Parker, **123, 141**
MacGregor, Bruce, **163**
MacLaren Advertising, 102
Macoun, Jamie, 217, **217**
Mahovlich, Frank, **134,** 134–37, **136, 137**
Maki, Chico, **111**
Maple Leaf Gardens, 13, **16, 18,** 222–23, 247–48; construction, 10, 39, 40, 42, 222; renovation, 12, 102, 222
Marker, Gus, 62
McCabe, Bryan, 233, **233, 249**
McCool, Frank "Ulcers," 47, **70**
McCormack, Johnny, 42
McDonald, Ab, **113**
McDonald, Lanny, **148,** 154–57, **155, 156, 157**
McDonald, Wilfred, 57
McKenny, Jim, 158, **158**
McKnight, Wes, 72
McNamara, Gerry, 182
McNeil, Gerry, **79**
McSorley, Marty, 209
Meeker, Howie, 76, **85, 86,** 86–87, **87**
Memorial Cup, 93, 108, 118
merchandise, Maple Leafs, 12, 13, 246
Metz, Don, **67,** 67–68, **68**
Metz, Nick, **67,** 67–68, **68, 70**
Migay, Rudy, **74**

Mogilny, Alex, 234, **234, 249**
Molson Cup, 194
Montreal Canadiens, 35, 64, **77, 79**
Morrison, Jim, **81**
Mortson, Gus, 88, **88**
Murphy, Mike, 200

Neely, Bob, **148**
Neilson, Roger, 150, 172
Nesterenko, Eric, **74**
New York Rangers, 23
NHL Players Association, 76, 88, 93, 114, 139
Nieuwendyk, Joe, **220**
Nott, Nick, 62
Nykoluk, Mike, 182

Olczyk, Ed, 190, **190**
Osborne, Mark, 191, **191**
Ottawa Senators, 24

Palmateer, Mike, 159–60, **160**
Pappin, Jim, 138
Parent, Bernie, 161, **161**
Peddie, Richard, 247
Pennington, Bob, **129**
"Pepper Boys Line," 22
Perreault, Robert, **117, 132**
Pilote, Pierre, **143**
Pinder, Herb, **177**
Plante, Jacques, 162–63, **163**
Plante, Pierre, **177**
Players Association, NHL, 76, 88, 93, 114, 139
Poile, Bud, **49,** 56
Potvin, Felix, 211, **218,** 218–19, **219**
Pratt, Walter "Babe," 50, **69,** 69–70, **70**
Primeau, Joe, **37,** 37–38, **38,** 76, 126
Princess Elizabeth, **223**
Pulford, Bob, 107, **138,** 138–39, **139**

Querrie, Charlie, 226
Quinn, Pat, 200, 235, **235**

radio broadcasts, 11, 72
Ramage, Rob, 181
Reise Jr., Leo, **56**
Richard, Maurice "Rocket," 50, **60,** 64, 65
Roberts, Gary, **220,** 236–37, **237**
Rollins, Al, **87**
Ross, Art, 43
Rouse, Bob, 220, **220**

Salming, Borje, **148,** 164–67, **165, 167,** 178–79, **179**
Sawchuk, Terry, **75, 95, 107,** 140–41, **141, 145**
Schriner, David "Sweeney," 71
Schwob, Corey, 225
Selby, Brit, 119
Selke, Frank, 18, 39, **39**
Selke Trophy, 215
Shack, Eddie, **142,** 142–43, **143**
Shore, Eddie, 19, 21
Sittler, Darryl, **168,** 168–71, **170, 171**
Sloan, Aloysius "Tod," 89, **89**
Smith, Billy, **170**
Smith, Floyd, 182
Smith, Mike, 235
Smith, Sid, **54, 90, 90**
Smythe, Constantine "Conn," 9–12, **10,** 17–19, 35, **35,** 39, **40,** 40–45, **41, 43,** 50, 86, **92,** 223
Smythe, Stafford, 12, 44, 91–92, **92**
Sorkin, Richard, 177
Spencer, Brian, **149**
Spencer, Irv, **127**
Stanley Cup, 11, 12, **48,** 50, **68,** 70, **92, 125, 147,** 244–45; winning goal, 48, 77, **79,** 84, 96
Stanley, Allan, **112, 144,** 144–45, **145**

Stanowski, Wally, 18
Stapleton, Pat, **117**
Starr, Harold, 26
Stavro, Steve, 200, **247,** 248
Stellick, Gord, 182
Stemkowski, Peter, 138
Stewart, Gaye, **49,** 56
Stewart, Ron, **90**
Sundin, Mats, **238,** 238–39, **239, 249**

Taylor, Billy, 95
television broadcasts, 11–12, 72–73
Thomas, Cy, 56
Thomas, Wayne, **179**
Thompson, Errol, **179**
Thoms, Bill, 18
Thomson, Jim, 42, **93,** 93–94, **94**
Tobin, Bill, 56
Tucker, Darcy, 240, **240**
Turnbull, Ian, **148,** 172–73, **173**

Ullman, Norm, 174–75, **175**
Unger, Garry, **149**

Vaive, Rick, 180, 192–95, **193, 194, 195**
Vezina Trophy, 60, 110, 112, 140, 162

Watson, Harry, **46, 49,** 95, **95**
Watt, Tom, 200
Weir, Stan, **167**
Williams, Dave "Tiger," 176–77, **177**
World Hockey Association (WHA), 151, 161
Worsley, Gump, **136**

Yushkevich, Dmitry, 241, **241**

Zezel, Peter, 221, **221**

Acknowledgements

THANKS TO: Graig Abel (GA), Dennis Miles (DM), The Harold Barkley Archives (HB), The Hockey Hall of Fame (HHOF) and AP Worldwide Photos (AP) for permission to reproduce their photographs — see credits next to individual photos.

The author would like to thank the following writers for their invaluable books on the Maple Leafs and on hockey in general:

Jack Batten, Dick Beddoes, Howard Berger, Ross Brewitt, Stephen Cole, Charles Coleman, Jim Coleman, David Cruise, Dan Diamond, John Devaney, Bruce Dowbiggin, James Duplacey, David Dupois, Milt Dunnell, Gerald Eskenazi, Trent Frayne, Stan Fischler, Ed Fitkin, Tommy Gaston, Ira Gitler, Burt Goldblatt, Alison Griffiths, Tim Griggs, Peter Gzowski, Foster Hewitt, Zander Hollander, Lance Hornby, William Houston, Jim Hunt, Doug Hunter, John Iaboni, Dick Irvin Jr., Brian Kendall, Bill Libby, Ron MacAllister, Roy MacGregor, Craig MacInnis, Ted Mahovlich, Brian McFarlane, John Melady, Scott Morrison, Andy O'Brien, Jim O'Leary, Stan Obodiac, Frank Orr, Raymond Plante, Andrew Podnieks, Jim Proudfoot, Joseph Romain, Kevin Shea, Al Strachan, Tommy Smythe, Theresa Tedesco, Michael Ulmer, Scott Young.

The author would also like to thank the following former Maple Leaf players, coaches and managers for their memoirs about the team:

Bob Baun, Andy Bathgate, King Clancy, Brian Conacher, Billy Harris, Paul Henderson, Punch Imlach, Frank Mahovlich, Howie Meeker, Bernie Parent, Jacques Plante, Borje Salming, Frank Selke Sr., Eddie Shack, Conn Smythe, Darryl Sittler, Gord Stellick, and Dave Williams.

The following hockey publications were consulted:

The Hockey News, Hockey Illustrated, Hockey Pictorial, NHL Guide and Record Book, The Hockey Encyclopedia, Stanley Cup Playoffs Fact Guide.

The following Maple Leaf publications, videos and broadcasts were consulted:

Maple Leaf game programs, Maple Leaf media guides, the Maple Leafs 75th anniversary video, various Leaf games broadcast on *Hockey Night in Canada*, Foster Hewitt's radio broadcast of May 2, 1967.

The following newspapers and magazines were consulted:

The Toronto Star, The Toronto Telegram, The Globe and Mail, The Toronto Sun, Macleans Magazine, Sports Illustrated.

Previous interviews with the following players were referred to:

Johnny Bower, Brian Conacher, Ted Kennedy, Dave Keon, Frank Mahovlich, Brad Marsh, Lanny McDonald, Rob Ramage, Darryl Sittler, Harry Watson.

The author would also like to thank the following people for their assistance in putting this book together:

Graig Abel, Craig Campbell, Dennis Miles, Paul Patzkou, Phil Pritchard, Tyler Wolosewich.

SPECIAL THANK YOU: *The author would like to thank Maria and David Leonetti for their patience and support while this book was being put together.*

property of
L. E. SHORE
MEMORIAL LIBRARY
THORNBURY, ONTARIO, N0H 2P0